Second Workshop on Multilingual Surface Realisation (MSR 2019)

Hong Kong, China
3 November 2019

ISBN: 978-1-7138-0070-5

EMNLP-IJCNLP 2019

Multilingual Surface Realisation

Proceedings of the Second Workshop

November 3, 2019
Hong Kong, China

Preface

The Second Workshop on Multilingual Surface Realisation (MSR 2019) was held as part of EMNLP 2019 in Hong Kong on 3 November 2019. The MSR workshops aim to bring together researchers interested in surface-oriented Natural Language Generation problems such as word order determination, inflection, functional word determination, etc. A central part of the MSR workshops is an evolving shared task on surface realisation (SR). Following a pilot task in 2011 for English only, the SR shared task went multilingual from 2018, continuing to include both a shallow track (generating from full universal dependency structures) and a deep track (generating from underspecified UD structures). Workshop and shared task are endorsed by the ACL Special Interest Group on Natural Language Generation (SIGGEN).

The 2019 edition of the SR task (SR'19) offered 11 different languages (up from 10 in SR'18) and attracted 33 team registrations from 17 countries (up from 21 registrations for SR'18). 14 teams submitted systems to SR'19 (up from 8 in SR'18), with two teams withdrawing post submission. Nine teams participated in the Shallow Track only, one in the Deep Track only, and two teams took part in both. All submitting teams submitted a system for English, four teams submitted for English only, four teams submitted for all 11 languages, and four teams submitted for between three and 9 languages.

For English, we evaluated 12 Shallow Track systems and four Deep Track systems in human evaluations of readability and meaning similarity (to reference sentences). Not only did we have multiple Deep Track systems (compared to just one in 2018), but the best Deep Track system actually performed equally well or better than most Shallow Track systems for both readability and meaning similarity. Moreover, the best Shallow Track systems are beginning to close the gap to human toplines, in particular for English and Spanish. In terms of progress, the success of the Deep Track systems represents the biggest leap forward from SR'18, while it looks likely that the shallow systems will catch up with human toplines in the near future. The SR tasks have clearly demonstrated that generation from structured meaning representations can be done with impressive success by current neural methods.

MSR 2019 was pleased to host two invited talks, one by Claire Gardent of Nancy University, and one by the artist Maurice Benayoun, also known as MoBen or 莫奔, who is based in Hong Kong. In addition to papers related to the SR'19 shared task, we accepted one paper on wider surface realisation. Given the increased interest and progress we are able to report for SR'19, we plan to continue with a third shared task in 2020, as part of which we plan to investigate ways of linking up to earlier stages of automatic language generation.

We gratefully acknowledge the hard work put in by the SR'19 participating teams, reviewers and local organisers, and more generally, the creativity and enthusiasm generated by participants in the MSR workshops and SR tasks which is of course what keeps them both going.

Organizers:

Simon Mille, Pompeu Fabra University, Spain
Anja Belz, University of Brighton, UK
Bernd Bohnet, Google Research, UK
Yvette Graham, ADAPT Center, Dublin City University, Ireland
Leo Wanner, ICREA and Pompeu Fabra University, Spain

Program Committee:

Jose Maria Alonso, University of Santiago de Compostela, Spain
Miguel Ballesteros, IBM Research, USA
Alberto Bugarín, University of Santiago de Compostela, Spain
Claire Gardent, CNRS, LORIA, France
Kim Gerdes, Sorbonne Nouvelle, France
Yannis Konstas, Heriot Watt University, UK
Emiel Krahmer, Tilburg University, The Netherlands
David McDonald, SIFT, USA
Ryan McDonald, Google Research, USA
Shashi Narayan, University of Edinburgh, UK
Alexis Nasr, University of Aix Marseille, France
Joakim Nivre, Uppsala University, Sweden
Jekaterina Novikova, Heriot Watt University, UK
Stephan Oepen, University of Oslo, Norway
Emily Pitler, Google Research, USA
Ehud Reiter, Aberdeen University, UK
Horacio Saggion, Pompeu Fabra University, Spain
Kees Van Deemter, Utrecht University, The Netherlands
Michael White, Ohio State University, USA
Sina Zarrieß, University of Bielefeld, Germany

Additional Reviewers:

Valerio Basile, Torino University, Italy
Laura Pérez Mayos, Pompeu Fabra University, Spain

Invited Speakers:

Claire Gardent, CNRS-LORIA, France
Maurice Benayoun (a.k.a. MoBen), City University of Hong Kong, China

Table of Contents

Conference Program

Sunday, November 3, 2019

8:45–9:00	*Opening*

Invited talk
9:00–10:00 *Invited Talk by Claire Gardent*

SR'19 Overview and results
10:00–10:30 *The Second Multilingual Surface Realisation Shared Task (SR'19): Overview and Evaluation Results*
Simon Mille, Anja Belz, Bernd Bohnet, Yvette Graham and Leo Wanner

10:30–11:00 *Coffee break*

Oral Presentations
11:00–11:25 *Learning to Order Graph Elements with Application to Multilingual Surface Realization*
Wenchao Du and Alan W Black
11:25–11:50 *DepDist: Surface realization via regex and learned dependency-distance tolerance*
William Dyer
11:50–12:15 *BME-UW at SRST-2019: Surface realization with Interpreted Regular Tree Grammars*
Ádám Kovács, Evelin Ács, Judit Ács, Andras Kornai and Gábor Recski
12:15–12:40 *Realizing Universal Dependencies Structures*
Guy Lapalme

12:40–14:00 *Lunch break*

Invited talk
14:00–15:00 *Invited Talk by Maurice Benayoun (a.k.a. MoBen)*

Oral Presentation
15:00–15:30 *IMSurReal: IMS at the Surface Realization Shared Task 2019*
Xiang Yu, Agnieszka Falenska, Marina Haid, Ngoc Thang Vu and Jonas Kuhn

Poster Session (including break)
15:30–17:00 *Surface Realization Shared Task 2019 (MSR19): The Team 6 Approach*
Thiago Castro Ferreira and Emiel Krahmer
15:30–17:00 *The Concordia NLG Surface Realizer at SRST 2019*
Farhood Farahnak, Laya Rafiee, Leila Kosseim and Thomas Fevens
15:30–17:00 *The OSU/Facebook Realizer for SRST 2019: Seq2Seq Inflection and Serialized Tree2Tree Linearization*
Kartikeya Upasani, David King, Jinfeng Rao, Anusha Balakrishnan and Michael White
15:30–17:00 *Improving Language Generation from Feature-Rich Tree-Structured Data with Relational Graph Convolutional Encoders*
Xudong Hong, Ernie Chang and Vera Demberg

Poster Session (continued)

15:30–17:00 *The DipInfoUniTo Realizer at SRST'19: Learning to Rank and Deep Morphology Prediction for Multilingual Surface Realization*
Alessandro Mazzei and Valerio Basile

15:30–17:00 *LORIA / Lorraine University at Multilingual Surface Realisation 2019*
Anastasia Shimorina and Claire Gardent

15:30–17:00 *Back-Translation as Strategy to Tackle the Lack of Corpus in Natural Language Generation from Semantic Representations*
Marco Antonio Sobrevilla Cabezudo, Simon Mille and Thiago Pardo

17:00–18:00 *Round table*

The Second Multilingual Surface Realisation Shared Task (SR'19): Overview and Evaluation Results

Simon Mille
UPF, Barcelona
simon.mille@upf.edu

Anja Belz
University of Brighton
a.s.belz@brighton.ac.uk

Bernd Bohnet
Google Inc.
bohnetbd@google.com

Yvette Graham
ADAPT Research Centre, DCU
graham.yvette@gmail.com

Leo Wanner
ICREA and UPF, Barcelona
leo.wanner@upf.edu

Abstract

We report results from the SR'19 Shared Task, the second edition of a multilingual surface realisation task organised as part of the EMNLP'19 Workshop on Multilingual Surface Realisation. As in SR'18, the shared task comprised two different tracks: (a) a Shallow Track where the inputs were full UD structures with word order information removed and tokens lemmatised; and (b) a Deep Track where additionally, functional words and morphological information were removed. The Shallow Track was offered in 11, and the Deep Track in three languages. Systems were evaluated (a) automatically, using a range of intrinsic metrics, and (b) by human judges in terms of readability and meaning similarity to a reference. This report presents the evaluation results, along with descriptions of the SR'19 tracks, data and evaluation methods, as well as brief summaries of the participating systems. For full descriptions of the participating systems, please see the separate system reports elsewhere in this volume.

1 Introduction and Task Overview

Following the success of the First Multilingual Surface Realisation Shared Task in 2018 (SR'18), which had the goal to stimulate the exploration of advanced neural models for multilingual sentence generation from Universal Dependency (UD) structures,[1] the second edition of the task (SR'19) aims to build on last year's results and achieve further progress. While Natural Language Generation (NLG) has been gaining increasing attention from NLP researchers, it continues to be a smaller field than e.g. parsing, text classification, sentiment analysis, etc. Universal dependencies are also enjoying increasing attention: the number of UD treebanks is continuously growing, as is their size (and thus the volume of available training material).[2]

The SR tasks require participating systems to generate sentences from structures at the level of abstraction of outputs produced by state-of-the-art parsing. In order to promote linkage with parsing and earlier stages of generation, participants are encouraged to explore the extent to which neural network parsing algorithms can be reversed for generation. As was the case with its predecessor tasks SR'11 (Belz et al., 2011) and SR'18 (Mille et al., 2018), SR'19 comprises two tracks distinguished by the level of specificity of the inputs:

Shallow Track (T1): This track starts from UD structures in which most of the word order information has been removed and tokens have been lemmatised. In other words, it starts from unordered dependency trees with lemmatised nodes that hold PoS tags and morphological information as found in the original treebank annotations. The task in this track therefore amounts to determining the word order and inflecting words.

Deep Track (T2): This track starts from UD structures from which functional words (in particular, auxiliaries, functional prepositions and conjunctions) and surface-oriented morphological and syntactic information have additionally been removed. The task in the Deep Track thus also involves reintroduction of functional words and morphological features, in addition to what is required for the Shallow Track.

The training and development data for both tracks and the evaluation scripts were released on April 5th 2019, the training data on August 3rd 2019 and the outputs were collected two weeks later on August 19th; the teams had up to 4 months to de-

---

[1] http://universaldependencies.org/

[2] UD v2.4 contains 146 treebanks in 83 languages.

1

Proceedings of the 2nd Workshop on Multilingual Surface Realisation (MSR 2019), pages 1–17
Hong Kong, China, November 3rd, 2019. ©2019 Association for Computational Linguistics
https://doi.org/10.18653/v1/P17

velop their systems.[3] Compared to SR'18, SR'19 has a broader variety of languages hence even more emphasis on multilinguality, with 11 languages from 9 language families:[4] Arabic (Afro-Asiatic), Chinese (Sino-Tibetan), English (Germanic), French, Portuguese and Spanish (Italic), Hindi (Indo-Iranian), Indonesian (Austronesian), Japanese (Japonic), Korean (Koreanic) and Russian (Balto-Slavic). This reflects a trend in NLP towards taking into account increasing numbers of languages for the validation of developed models; see e.g., SIGMORPHON 2019, which addressed crosslingual inflection generation in 100 language pairs.[5]

In the remainder of this paper, we describe the Shallow and Deep Track data (Section 2), and the evaluation methods we used to evaluate submitted systems (Sections 3.1 and 3.2). We then introduce the participating systems briefly (Section 4), report and discuss evaluation results (Section 5), and conclude with some discussion and a look to the future (Section 6).

2 Data

2.1 Overview of datasets and additional resources

In order to create the SR'19 training, development and test sets, we used as data sources 20 UD treebanks[6] for which annotations of reasonable quality were available, providing PoS tags and morphologically relevant markup (number, tense, verbal finiteness, etc.). Unlike in SR'18, several treebanks were available for some languages, enabling us to use out-of-domain as well as silver standard datasets as additional test data (for details see Section 2.3). Table 1 gives an overview of the variety and sizes of the datasets.

Teams were allowed to build models trained on any SR'19 dataset(s) of their choice, but not external task-specific data. Other resources were, however, permissible. For example, available parsers such as UUParser (Smith et al., 2018) could be run to create a silver standard versions of provided datasets and use them as additional or alternative training material, and publicly available off-the-

shelf language models such as GPT-2 (Radford et al., 2019), ELMo (Peters et al., 2018), polyglot (Al-Rfou et al., 2013) or BERT (Devlin et al., 2018) could be fine-tuned with publicly available datasets such as WikiText (Merity et al., 2016) or the DeepMind Q&A Dataset (Hermann et al., 2015).

Datasets were created for 11 languages in the Shallow Track, and for three of those languages, namely English, French and Spanish, in the Deep Track. As in 2018, Shallow Track inputs were generated with the aid of Python scripts from the original UD structures, this time using all available input sentences. Deep Track inputs were then generated by automatically processing the Shallow Track structures using a series of graph-transduction grammars covering steps 5–11 in Section 2.2 below. In the training data, there is a node-to-node correspondence between the deep and shallow input structures, and they are both aligned with the original UD structures. We used only information found in the UD syntactic structures to create the deep inputs, and tried to keep their structure simple. Moreover, words were not disambiguated, full prepositions may be missing, and some argument relations may be underspecified or missing.

Structures for both Shallow and Deep Tracks are trees, and are released in a slightly modified CoNLL-U format, comprising the following ten columns: [1] Position, [2] Lemma, [3] Wordform, [4] PoS, [5] Fine-grained PoS (if available), [6] Features (*FEATS*), [7] governor, [8] dependency relation, [9] additional dependency information, and [10] metadata.[7] Figure 1 shows a sample original UD annotation for English; the corresponding shallow and deep input structures derived from it are shown in Figures 2 and 3, respectively (the last two columns are empty for the task).

2.2 Task data creation

To create the data for the Shallow Track, the original UD data was processed as follows:

1. Word order information was removed by randomised scrambling, but in the training data, the alignment with the original position of each word in the sentence was maintained via a feature in the *FEATS* column;

---

[3]In the case of one team, we agreed to move the two week window between test data release and submission to one week earlier.

[4]At SR'18, there were ten languages from five families.

[5]https://www.aclweb.org/portal/content/sigmorphon-shared-task-2019

[6]universaldependencies.org

[7]http://universaldependencies.org/format.html

Data type	Dataset	Track	train	dev	test
In-domain	arabic_padt (ar)	T1	6,075	909	680
	chinese_gsd (zh)	T1	3,997	500	500
	english_ewt (en)	T1, T2	12,543	2,002	2,077
	english_gum (en)	T1, T2	2,914	707	778
	english_lines (en)	T1, T2	2,738	912	914
	english_partut (en)	T1, T2	1,781	156	153
	french_gsd (fr)	T1, T2	14,450	1,476	416
	french_partut (fr)	T1, T2	803	107	110
	french_sequoia (fr)	T1, T2	2,231	412	456
	hindi_hdtb (hi)	T1	13,304	1,659	1,684
	indonesian_gsd (id)	T1	4,477	559	557
	japanese_gsd (ja)	T1	7,133	511	551
	korean_gsd (ko)	T1	4,400	950	989
	korean_kaist (ko)	T1	23,010	2,066	2,287
	portuguese_bosque (pt)	T1	8,328	560	477
	portuguese_gsd (pt)	T1	9,664	1,210	1,204
	russian_gsd (ru)	T1	3,850	579	601
	russian_syntagrus (ru)	T1	48,814	6,584	6,491
	spanish_ancora (es)	T1, T2	14,305	1,654	1,721
	spanish_gsd (es)	T1, T2	14,187	1,400	426
Out-of-domain	english_pud (en)	T1, T2	-	-	1,000
	japanese_pud (ja)	T1	-	-	1,000
	russian_pud (ru)	T1	-	-	1,000
Automatically parsed	english_ewt-HIT (en)	T1, T2	-	-	1,795
	english_pud-LAT (en)	T1, T2	-	-	1,032
	hindi_hdtb-HIT (hi)	T1	-	-	1,675
	korean_kaist-HIT (ko)	T1	-	-	2,287
	portuguese_bosque-Sta (pt)	T1	-	-	471
	spanish_ancora-HIT (es)	T1, T2	-	-	1,723

Table 1: SR'19 dataset sizes for training, development and test sets (number of sentences).

2. Missing lemmas were added in the file, since in some cases the lemma value was empty (e.g. Portuguese-gsd dataset) or generalised (e.g. @card@ or @ord@ for cardinal and ordinal numbers in the English-gum dataset);[8]

3. The lines corresponding to combined lexical units (e.g. Spanish "del" <de+el> lit. *'of.the'*) and the contents of columns [9] and [10] were removed;

4. Information about the relative order of components of named entities, multiple coordinations and punctuation signs was added in the *FEATS* column (dependency relations *compound, compound:prt, compound:svc, flat, flat:foreign, flat:name, fixed, conj, punct*);

For the Deep Track, the following steps were additionally carried out:

5. Edge labels were generalised into predicate/argument labels, in the PropBank/NomBank (Palmer et al., 2005; Meyers et al., 2004) fashion. That is, the syntactic relations were mapped to core (A1, A2, etc.) and non-core (AM) labels, applying the following rules: (i) the first argument is always labeled A1 (i.e. there is no external argument *A0*); (ii) in order to maintain the tree structure and account for some cases of shared arguments, there can be inverted argument relations; (iii) all modifier edges are assigned the same generic label *AM*; (iv) there is a coordinating relation. See also the inventory of relations in Table 2.

6. Functional prepositions and conjunctions in argument position (i.e. prepositions and conjunctions that can be inferred from other lexical units or from the syntactic structure) were removed (e.g. *about* and *that* in Figure 2); prepositions and conjunctions retained in the deep representation can be found under a *A2INV* dependency; a dependency path *Gov AM → Dep A2INV → Prep* is equivalent to a predicate (the conjunction/preposition) with 2 arguments: *Gov ← A1 Prep A2 → Dep*.

7. Definite and indefinite determiners, auxiliaries and modals were converted into at-

Deep label	Description	Example
A1, A2, ..., A6	nth argument of a predicate	fall→ the ball
A1INV, ..., A6INV	nth inverted argument of a predicate	the ball→ fall
AM/AMINV	(i) none of governor or dependent are argument of the other	fall→ last night
	(ii) unknown argument slot	
LIST	List of elements	fall→ [and] bounce
NAME	Part of a name	Tower→ Eiffel
DEP	Undefined dependent	N/A

Table 2: Deep labels.

tribute/value pairs, as were definiteness features, and the universal aspect and mood features[9], see examples in Figure 3.

8. Subject and object relative pronouns directly linked to the main relative verb were removed (instead, the verb was linked to the antecedent of the pronoun); a dummy pronoun node for the subject was added if an originally finite verb had no first argument and no available argument to build a passive; for a pro-drop language such as Spanish, a dummy pronoun was added if the first argument was missing.

9. Surface-level morphologically relevant information as prescribed by syntactic structure or agreement (such as verbal finiteness or verbal number) was removed, whereas semantic-level information such as nominal number and verbal tense was retained.

10. Fine-grained PoS labels found in some treebanks (see e.g. column 5 in Figure 2) were removed, and only coarse-grained ones were retained (column 4 in Figures 2 and 3).

11. In the training data, the alignments with the tokens of the Shallow Track structures were added in the *FEATS* column.

Figure 3 shows an example Deep Track input that corresponds to the original and shallow structures in Figures 1 and 2.

2.3 Additional test data

For additional test data, we used automatically produced UD parses, which we then processed in the same way as the gold-standard structures, using the best parsers from the CoNLL'18 shared task on the dataset in question.[10] We used the UD2.3 version of the dataset, whereas CoNLL'18 used UD2.2; we selected treebanks that had not undergone major updates from one version to the next according to their README files on the UD site, and for which the best available parse reached a Labeled Attachment Score of 85 and over.[11] There were datasets meeting these criteria for English (2), Hindi, Korean, Portuguese and Spanish; the Harbin HIT-SCIR parser (Che et al., 2017) had best scores on four of these datasets; LATTICE (Lim et al., 2018) and Stanford (Qi et al., 2019) had the best scores for the remaining two;[12] see Table 3 for an overview.

As is the case for all test data, in the additional automatically parsed test data alignments with surface tokens and with Shallow Track tokens are not provided; however, in the cases described in 4 above, the relative order is provided.

Treebank	Best system	LAS
english_ewt	HIT-SCIR	84.57
english_pud	LATTICE	87.89
hindi_hdtb	HIT-SCIR	92.41
korean_kaist	HIT-SCIR	86.91
portuguese_bosque	Stanford	87.81
spanish_ancora	HIT-SCIR	90.93

Table 3: The 6 combinations of dataset and parser outputs selected for the automatically parsed test set.

2.4 Data formats for evaluations

Unlike in SR'18, where detokenised outputs only were used, the SR'19 teams were asked to provide tokenised (for automatic evaluations) as well as detokenised (for human evaluations) outputs; if no detokenised outputs were provided, the tokenised files were also used for the human evalu-

---

[9]http://universaldependencies.org/u/feat/index.html

[10]See the rankings per treebanks at https://universaldependencies.org/conll18/results-las.html.

[11]The best score on the English-EWT dataset is slightly below this threshold (84.57), but the dataset was selected anyway because English was expected to be the language most addressed by the participants.

[12]The CoNLL'18 shared task submissions were downloaded from https://lindat.mff.cuni.cz/repository/xmlui/handle/11234/1-2885.

```
# sent_id = weblog-blogspot.com_healingiraq_20040409053012_ENG_20040409_053012-0008
# text = And there is nothing we can do about it really, people who are suggesting that we go out and fight them are living in dream land.
1   And        and      CCONJ  CC    _                                                     3   cc         3:cc                  _
2   there      there    PRON   EX    _                                                     3   expl       3:expl                _
3   is         be       VERB   VBZ   Mood=Ind|Number=Sing|Person=3|Tense=Pres|VerbForm=Fin 0   root       0:root                _
4   nothing    nothing  PRON   NN    Number=Sing                                           3   nsubj      3:nsubj               _
5   we         we       PRON   PRP   Case=Nom|Number=Plur|Person=1|PronType=Prs            7   nsubj      7:nsubj               _
6   can        can      AUX    MD    VerbForm=Fin                                          7   aux        7:aux                 _
7   do         do       VERB   VB    VerbForm=Inf                                          4   acl:relcl  4:acl:relcl           _
8   about      about    ADP    IN    _                                                     9   case       9:case                _
9   it         it       PRON   PRP   Case=Acc|Gender=Neut|Number=Sing|Person=3|PronType=Prs 7   obl        7:obl:about           _
10  really     really   ADV    RB    _                                                     7   advmod     7:advmod              SpaceAfter=No
11  ,          ,        PUNCT  ,     _                                                     3   punct      3:punct               _
12  people     people   NOUN   NNS   Number=Plur                                           24  nsubj      15:nsubj|24:nsubj     _
13  who        who      PRON   WP    PronType=Rel                                          15  nsubj      12:ref                _
14  are        be       AUX    VBP   Mood=Ind|Tense=Pres|VerbForm=Fin                      15  aux        15:aux                _
15  suggesting suggest  VERB   VBG   Tense=Pres|VerbForm=Part                              12  acl:relcl  12:acl:relcl          _
16  that       that     SCONJ  IN    _                                                     18  mark       18:mark               _
17  we         we       PRON   PRP   Case=Nom|Number=Plur|Person=1|PronType=Prs            18  nsubj      18:nsubj|21:nsubj     _
18  go         go       VERB   VBP   Mood=Ind|Tense=Pres|VerbForm=Fin                      15  ccomp      15:ccomp              _
19  out        out      ADV    RB    _                                                     18  advmod     18:advmod             _
20  and        and      CCONJ  CC    _                                                     21  cc         21:cc                 _
21  fight      fight    VERB   VBP   Mood=Ind|Tense=Pres|VerbForm=Fin                      18  conj       15:ccomp|18:conj:and  _
22  them       they     PRON   PRP   Case=Acc|Number=Plur|Person=3|PronType=Prs            21  obj        21:obj                _
23  are        be       AUX    VBP   Mood=Ind|Tense=Pres|VerbForm=Fin                      24  aux        24:aux                _
24  living     live     VERB   VBG   Tense=Pres|VerbForm=Part                              3   parataxis  3:parataxis           _
25  in         in       ADP    IN    _                                                     27  case       27:case               _
26  dream      dream    NOUN   NN    Number=Sing                                           27  compound   27:compound           _
27  land       land     NOUN   NN    Number=Sing                                           24  obl        24:obl:in             SpaceAfter=No
28  .          .        PUNCT  .     _                                                     3   punct      3:punct               _
```

Figure 1: A sample UD structure in English.

```
1   .        _   PUNCT  .    lin=+2                                                27  punct       _  _
2   dream    _   NOUN   NN   lin=-1|Number=Sing                                    21  compound    _  _
3   and      _   CCONJ  CC   _                                                     27  cc          _  _
4   be       _   AUX    VBP  Mood=Ind|Tense=Pres|VerbForm=Fin                      6   aux         _  _
5   they     _   PRON   PRP  Case=Acc|Number=Plur|Person=3|PronType=Prs            19  obj         _  _
6   suggest  _   VERB   VBG  Tense=Pres|VerbForm=Part                              23  acl:relcl   _  _
7   there    _   PRON   EX   _                                                     27  expl        _  _
8   really   _   ADV    RB   _                                                     18  advmod      _  _
9   it       _   PRON   PRP  Case=Acc|Gender=Neut|Number=Sing|Person=3|PronType=Prs 18  obl         _  _
10  we       _   PRON   PRP  Case=Nom|Number=Plur|Person=1|PronType=Prs            18  nsubj       _  _
11  in       _   ADP    IN   _                                                     21  case        _  _
12  who      _   PRON   WP   PronType=Rel                                          6   nsubj       _  _
13  be       _   AUX    VBP  Mood=Ind|Tense=Pres|VerbForm=Fin                      15  aux         _  _
14  can      _   AUX    MD   VerbForm=Fin                                          18  aux         _  _
15  live     _   VERB   VBG  Tense=Pres|VerbForm=Part                              27  parataxis   _  _
16  nothing  _   PRON   NN   Number=Sing                                           27  nsubj       _  _
17  that     _   SCONJ  IN   _                                                     20  mark        _  _
18  do       _   VERB   VB   VerbForm=Inf                                          16  acl:relcl   _  _
19  fight    _   VERB   VBP  Mood=Ind|Tense=Pres|VerbForm=Fin                      20  conj        _  _
20  go       _   VERB   VBP  Mood=Ind|Tense=Pres|VerbForm=Fin                      6   ccomp       _  _
21  land     _   NOUN   NN   Number=Sing                                           15  obl         _  _
22  and      _   CCONJ  CC   _                                                     19  cc          _  _
23  people   _   NOUN   NNS  Number=Plur                                           15  nsubj       _  _
24  about    _   ADP    IN   _                                                     9   case        _  _
25  we       _   PRON   PRP  Case=Nom|Number=Plur|Person=1|PronType=Prs            20  nsubj       _  _
26  ,        _   PUNCT  ,    lin=+1                                                27  punct       _  _
27  be       _   VERB   VBZ  Mood=Ind|Number=Sing|Person=3|Tense=Pres|VerbForm=Fin 0   root        _  _
28  out      _   ADV    RB   _                                                     20  advmod      _  _
```

Figure 2: Shallow input (T1) derived from UD structure in Figure 1

```
1   be       _   VERB   _   Tense=Pres|ClauseType=Dec                     0   ROOT       _  _
2   and      _   CCONJ  _   _                                             1   A2INV      _  _
3   live     _   VERB   _   Tense=Pres|Aspect=Prog                        1   PARATAXIS  _  _
4   nothing  _   PRON   _   Number=Sing                                   1   A1         _  _
5   land     _   NOUN   _   Number=Sing                                   3   AM         _  _
6   people   _   NOUN   _   Number=Plur                                   3   A1         _  _
7   do       _   VERB   _   Tense=Pres|Mood=Pot                           4   A2INV      _  _
8   dream    _   NOUN   _   lin=-1|Number=Sing                            5   NAME       _  _
9   suggest  _   VERB   _   Tense=Pres|Aspect=Prog                        6   A1INV      _  _
10  really   _   ADV    _   _                                             7   A1INV      _  _
11  it       _   PRON   _   Number=Sing|Person=3|PronType=Prs             7   AM         _  _
12  we       _   PRON   _   Number=Plur|Person=1|PronType=Prs             7   A1         _  _
13  go       _   VERB   _   Tense=Pres                                    9   A2         _  _
14  we       _   PRON   _   Number=Plur|Person=1|PronType=Prs             13  A1         _  _
15  out      _   ADV    _   _                                             13  A1INV      _  _
16  fight    _   VERB   _   Tense=Pres                                    13  LIST       _  _
17  and      _   CCONJ  _   _                                             16  A2INV      _  _
18  they     _   PRON   _   Number=Plur|Person=3|PronType=Prs             16  A2         _  _
```

Figure 3: Deep input (T2) derived from UD structure in Figure 1.

ation. The reason for using tokenised outputs for automatic evaluation is the inclusion of languages like Chinese and Japanese where sentences are sequences of characters with no white-space separators. Two of the metrics used in automatic evaluations, BLEU and NIST, compute scores based on matching sequences of characters; if there is no whitespace, the whole sentence is the sequence that is used for matching. As a result, one single different character in a sentence would prevent a match with the reference sentence, and a null score would be assigned to the whole sentence. The following example shows a Spanish sentence in its tokenised and detokenised forms:

- Tokenised sample (Spanish): All tokens are preceded by a white space.
  Elías Jaua , miembro del Congresillo , considera que los nuevos miembros del CNE deben tener experiencia para " dirigir procesos complejos " .
- Detokenised sample (Spanish): White spaces before or after some punctuation signs are removed.
  Elías Jaua, miembro del Congresillo, considera que los nuevos miembros del CNE deben tener experiencia para "dirigir procesos complejos".

In the original UD files, the reference sentences are by default detokenised. In order to carry out the evaluations of the tokenised outputs, we built a tokenised version of the reference sentences by concatenating the words of the second column of the UD structures (see Figure 1) separated by a whitespace.

3 Evaluation Methods

3.1 Automatic methods

We used BLEU, NIST, and inverse normalised character-based string-edit distance (referred to as DIST, for short, below) to assess submitted systems. BLEU (Papineni et al., 2002) is a precision metric that computes the geometric mean of the n-gram precisions between generated text and reference texts and adds a brevity penalty for shorter sentences. We use the smoothed version and report results for $n = 4$.

NIST[13] is a related n-gram similarity metric

weighted in favor of less frequent n-grams which are taken to be more informative.

DIST starts by computing the minimum number of character inserts, deletes and substitutions (all at cost 1) required to turn the system output into the (single) reference text. The resulting number is then divided by the number of characters in the reference text, and finally subtracted from 1, in order to align with the other metrics. Spaces and punctuation marks count as characters; output texts were otherwise normalised as for all metrics (see below).

The figures in the tables below are the system-level scores for BLEU and NIST, and the mean sentence-level scores for DIST.

Text normalisation: Output texts were normalised prior to computing metrics by lowercasing all tokens, removing any extraneous whitespace characters.

Missing outputs: Missing outputs were scored 0. We only report results for all sentences (incorporating the missing-output penalty), rather than also separately reporting scores for just the in-coverage items.

Important note: The SR'19 scores are not directly comparable to the SR'18 ones, since the SR'18 scores were calculated on detokenised outputs, whereas the scores presented in this report were calculated on tokenised outputs (see Section 2.4). In addition, the method for calculating the DIST score in SR'18 was different in that it did not take into account the whole sentence. [14]

3.2 Human-assessed methods

For the human evaluation, we selected a subset of language/track combinations based on number of submissions received and availability of evaluators: four Shallow Track in-domain datasets (Chinese-GSD, English-EWT, Russian-SynTagRus, Spanish-AnCora), one Shallow Track dataset coming from parsed data (Spanish-AnCora$_{HIT}$) and one (in-domain) Deep Track dataset (English-EWT).

As in SR'11 (Belz et al., 2011) and SR'18 (Mille et al., 2018), we assessed two quality criteria in the human evaluations, in separate evaluation experiments, *Readability* and *Meaning Similarity*, and used continuous sliders as rating tools, the evidence being that raters tend to prefer them

---

[13]http://www.itl.nist.gov/iad/mig/tests/mt/doc/ngram-study.pdf; http://www.itl.nist.gov/iad/mig/tests/mt/2009/

[14]Thank you to Yevgeniy Puzikov for pointing this out.

(Belz and Kow, 2011). Slider positions were mapped to values from 0 to 100 (best). Raters were first given brief instructions, including the direction to ignore formatting errors, superfluous whitespace, capitalisation issues, and poor hyphenation. The statement to be assessed in the Readability evaluation was:

> *The text reads well and is free from grammatical errors and awkward constructions.*

The corresponding statement in the Meaning Similarity evaluation, in which system outputs (*'the black text'*) were compared to reference sentences (*'the grey text'*), was as follows:

> *The meaning of the grey text is adequately expressed by the black text.*

Slider design: As in SR'18, and for conformity with what has emerged as an affordable human evaluation standard over the past three years in the main machine translation shared tasks held at WMT (Bojar et al., 2017, 2018; Barrault et al., 2019), we used a slider design as follows, with the pointer starting at 0:

0 %	100 %

Mechanical Turk evaluations: As in SR'18, we ran human evaluation on Mechanical Turk using Direct Assessment (DA) (Graham et al., 2016), the human evaluation used at WMT campaigns to produce official ranking of machine translation systems (Barrault et al., 2019). We ran both meaning similarity and readability evaluations, as separate assessments, but using the same method.

Quality assurance: System outputs are randomly assigned to HITs (following Mechanical Turk terminology) of 100 outputs, of which 20 are used solely for quality assurance (QA) (i.e. do not count towards system scores): (i) some are repeated as-is, (ii) some are repeated in a 'damaged' version and (iii) some are replaced by their corresponding reference texts. In each case, a minimum threshold has to be reached for the HIT to be accepted: for (i), scores must be similar enough, for (ii) the score for the damaged version must be worse, and for (iii) the score for the reference text must be high. For full details of how these additional texts are created and thresholds applied, please refer to Barrault et al. (2019). We report QA figures for the MTurk evaluations below.

Test data sets for human evaluations: Test set sizes out of the box varied for the different languages. For the human test sets we selected either the entire set or a subset of approximately 500, whichever was the smaller number, for a given language, motivated by the power analysis provided by Graham et al. (2019). For subsets, test set items were selected randomly.

Reported scores: In keeping with the WMT approach, we report both average raw scores and average standardised scores per system. In order to produce standardised scores we simply map each individual evaluator's scores to their standard scores (or z-scores) computed on the set of all raw scores by the given evaluator using each evaluator's mean and standard deviation. For both raw and standard scores, we compute the mean of sentence-level scores.

Code: We were able to reuse, with minor adaptations, the code produced for the WMT'17 evaluations.[15]

4 Overview of Submitted Systems

ADAPT is a sequence to sequence model with dependency features attached to word embeddings. A BERT sentence classifier was used as a reranker to choose between different hypotheses. The implementation is very similar to ADAPT's SR'18 submission (Elder and Hokamp, 2018).

The **BME-UW** system (Kovács et al., 2019) learns weighted rules of an Interpreted Regular Tree Grammar (IRTG) to encode the correspondence between word sequences and UD-subgraphs. For the inflection step, a standard sequence-to-sequence model with a biLSTM encoder and an LSTM decoder with attention is used.

CLaC (Farahnak et al., 2019) is a pointer network trained to find the best order of the input. A slightly modified version of the transformer model was used as the encoder and decoder for the pointer network.

The **CMU** (Du and Black, 2019) system uses a graph neural network for end-to-end ordering, and a character RNN for morphology.

DepDist (Dyer, 2019) uses syntactic embeddings and a graph neural network with message passing to learn the tolerances for how far a dependent tends to be from its head. These directed

---

[15] `https://github.com/ygraham/segment-mteval`

dependency distance tolerances form an edge-weighted directed acyclic graph (DAG) (equivalent to a partially ordered set, or *poset*) for each sentence, the topological sort of which generates a surface order. Inflection is addressed with regex patterns and substitutions approximating productive inflectional paradigms.

The **DipInfoUnito** realiser (Mazzei and Basile, 2019) is a supervised statistical system for surface realisation, in which two neural network-based models run in parallel on the same input structure, namely a list-wise learning to rank network for linearisation and a seq2seq network for morphology inflection prediction.

IMS (Yu et al., 2019) uses a pipeline approach for both tracks, consisting of linearisation, completion (for T2 only), inflection, and contraction. All models use the same bidirectional Tree-LSTM encoder architecture. The linearisation model orders each subtree separately with beam search and then combines them into a full projective tree; the completion model generates absent function words in a sequential way given the linearised tree of content words; the inflection model predicts a sequence of edit operations to convert the lemma to word form character by character; the contraction model predicts BIO tags to group the words to be contracted, and then generate the contracted word form of each group with a seq2seq model.

The **LORIA** submission (Shimorina and Gardent, 2019) presents a modular approach to surface realisation with three subsequent steps: word ordering, morphological inflection, and contraction generation (for some languages). For word ordering, the data is delexicalised, the input tree is linearised, and the mapping between an input tree and output lemma sequence is learned using a factored sequence-to-sequence model. Morphological inflection makes use of a neural character-based model, which produces word forms based on lemmas coupled with morphological features; finally, a rule-based contraction generation module is applied for some languages.

The **OSU-FB** pipeline for generation (Upasani et al., 2019) starts by generating inflected word forms in the tree using character seq2seq models. These inflected syntactic trees are then linearised as constituent trees by converting the relations to non-terminals. The linearised constituent trees are fed to seq2seq models (including models with copy and with tree-LSTM encoders) whose outputs also contain tokens marking the tree structure. N-best outputs are obtained for orderings and the highest confidence output sequence with a valid tree is chosen (i.e, one where the input and output trees are isomorphic up to sibling order, ensuring projectivity).

The **RALI** system (Lapalme, 2019) uses a symbolic approach to transform the dependency tree into a tree of constituents that is transformed into an English sentence by an existing English realiser, JSrealB (Molins and Lapalme, 2015). This realiser was then slightly modified for the two tracks.

Surfers (Hong et al., 2019) first performs delexicalisation to obtain a dictionary for proper names and numbers. A GCN is then used to encode the tree inputs, and an LSTM encoder-decoder with copy attention to generate delexicalised outputs. No part-of-speech tags, universal features or pre-trained embeddings / language models are used.

The **Tilburg** approach (Ferreira and Krahmer, 2019), based on Ferreira et al. (2018), realises multilingual texts by first preprocessing an input dependency tree into an ordered linearised string, which is then realised using a rule-based and a statistical machine translation (SMT) model.

Baseline: In order to set a lower boundary for the automatic and human evaluations, a simple English baseline consisting of 7 lines of python code was implemented[16]. It generates from a UD file with an in-order traversal of the tree read by pyconll and outputting the form of each node.

5 Evaluation results

There were 14 submissions to the task, of which two were withdrawn; 9 teams participated in the Shallow Track only, two teams participated in both tracks, and one team in the Deep Track only. For the Shallow Track, four teams (BME, IMS, LORIA and Tilburg) generated outputs for all languages (29 datasets), four teams (ADAPT, CLaC, RALI and OSU-FB) submitted only for the English datasets, and three teams (CMU, DepDist and DipInfo-UniTo) submitted in several but not all languages. For the Deep Track, two of the three teams (IMS, Surfers) addressed all languages (13 datasets), and one team (RALI) addressed English only. IMS is the only team to have submitted results for all 42 datasets.

---

[16]The idea and implementation are from Guy Lapalme, who is also the author of the RALI system.

–T1-BLEU–	ADA	BME	CLa	CMU	Dep	Dip	IMS	LOR	RAL	OSU	Til
ar_padt		26.4			23.01		**64.9**	16.71			21.12
en_ewt	79.69	59.22	22.08	77.47	60.51	43.5	**82.98**	60.37	41.23	62.38	59.57
en_gum	81.39	57.57	15.32	82.39	66.06	44.24	**83.84**	60.7	46.68	49.91	59.39
en_lines	41.62	48.78	15.3	75.49	59.81	32.42	**81**	58.82	41.28	54.56	57.02
en_partut	51	61.37	10.07	78.98	62.68	35.11	**87.25**	53.64	48.43	7.37	64.87
es_ancora		61.09		76.47	59.29		**83.7**	43.02			59.29
es_gsd		53.74		70.15	57.14		**82.98**	53.16			54.48
fr_gsd		43.8		60.15	44.91	27.04	**84**	54.6			52.1
fr_partut		49.17		63.7	55.05	37.69	**83.38**	54.14			66.01
fr_sequoia		46.72		62.79	46.87	28.95	**85.01**	53.71			57.41
hi_hdtb		63.63			64.07		**80.56**	26.51			60.72
id_gsd		54.22			63.71		**85.34**	46.27			53.03
ja_gsd		49.53		63.59	50.19		**87.69**	38.8			43.02
ko_gsd		46.08			41.81		**74.19**	37.85			2.14
ko_kaist		47.23					**73.93**	39.75			1.39
pt_bosque		39.53			39.82		**77.75**	52.69			51.18
pt_gsd		30.39			27.16		**75.93**	33.45			40.48
ru_gsd		54.58			32.04		**71.23**	55.09			6.84
ru_syntagrus		50.91					**76.95**	59.99			30.51
zh_gsd		58.72		68.54	59.64	32.87	**83.85**	48.21			53
en_pud	84.07	60.42	12.36	80.35		45.61	**86.61**	61.43	46.84	67.91	63.29
ja_pud		53.65		66.52			**86.64**	41.72			44.37
ru_pud		10.15					**58.38**	52.37			16.35
en_ewt$_{HIT}$	77.21	58.07	21.21	76.6		43.23	**81.8**	58.5	39.77	60.58	59.08
en_pud$_{LAT}$	80.66	53.46	12.89	76.22		44.06	**82.6**	55.4	41.5	66.18	57.92
es_ancora$_{HIT}$		61.26		77.28			**83.31**	43.2			59.58
hi_hdtb$_{HIT}$		64.27					**80.19**	26.99			61.54
ko_kaist$_{HIT}$		46.72					**74.27**	41.83			1.73
pt_bosque$_{STA}$		40.42					**78.97**	53.64			52.79

Table 4: BLEU-4 scores for the 29 Shallow Track datasets

–T1-NIST–	ADA	BME	CLa	CMU	Dep	Dip	IMS	LOR	RAL	OSU	Til
ar_padt		8.29			7.2		**12.22**	6.25			7.06
en_ewt	13.44	12.62	9.77	13.28	12.5	11.56	**13.61**	11.89	10.69	11.29	12.56
en_gum	12.6	11.99	8.64	**12.73**	12.07	11.15	**12.69**	11.15	10.74	8.5	11.8
en_lines	9.19	11.54	8.23	12.43	11.68	10.05	**12.71**	11.17	10.19	9.89	11.64
en_partut	8.59	10.34	7.14	10.74	10.23	9.08	**11.01**	9.29	9.28	3.21	10.27
es_ancora		13.52		14.27	13.19		**14.69**	11.13			13.44
es_gsd		11.44		11.99	11.43		**12.77**	10.68			11.39
fr_gsd		10.33		10.86	10.32	9.58	**12.45**	10.66			10.89
fr_partut		8.99		9.16	8.94	8.57	**10.36**	8.92			9.29
fr_sequoia		10.55		11.04	10.47	9.72	**12.53**	10.56			10.93
hi_hdtb		12.26			12.09		**13.07**	7.97			12.35
id_gsd		11.82			12.01		**12.83**	9.79			11.41
ja_gsd		9.99		10.62	9.67		**12.42**	8.51			9.36
ko_gsd		11.98			10.54		**12.27**	9.98			3.43
ko_kaist		12.65					**13**	10.62			2.52
pt_bosque		9.77			9.76		**12.15**	10.52			11.01
pt_gsd		8.85			8.57		**13.07**	8.89			10.69
ru_gsd		11.91			9.06		**12.15**	11.43			4.68
ru_syntagrus		13.8					**15.08**	13.98			10.87
zh_gsd		11.85		12.28	11.98	11.16	**12.78**	10.27			11.61
en_pud	13.36	12.6	8.83	13.18		11.81	**13.47**	11.81	11.4	11.74	12.69
ja_pud		10.56		11.35			**13.02**	9.29			9.98
ru_pud		9.64					10.91	**11.16**			7.19
en_ewt$_{HIT}$	13.24	12.49	9.69	13.18		11.44	**13.46**	11.61	10.48	10.96	12.45
en_pud$_{LAT}$	13.17	12.29	8.82	13.02		11.67	**13.26**	11.42	10.93	11.7	12.32
es_ancora$_{HIT}$		13.51		14.3			**14.61**	11.09			13.44
hi_hdtb$_{HIT}$		12.29					**13.05**	8.01			12.46
ko_kaist$_{HIT}$		12.63					**13.02**	10.79			2.81
pt_bosque$_{STA}$		9.73					**12.14**	10.54			11.05

Table 5: NIST scores for the 29 Shallow Track datasets

–T1-DIST–	ADA	BME	CLa	CMU	Dep	Dip	IMS	LOR	RAL	OSU	Til
ar_padt		43.06			55.72		**73.71**	48.96			53.44
en_ewt	83.69	62.69	45.99	80.92	71.99	60.13	**86.72**	73.96	59.78	77.93	73.67
en_gum	83.26	56.07	38.13	**84.41**	68.84	56.04	83.49	72.89	58.6	66.88	69.92
en_lines	63.31	52.77	40.4	79.6	65.93	53.21	**82.21**	71.21	56.68	71.07	67.37
en_partut	70.32	61.22	36.21	78.89	65.9	51.15	**85.68**	66.8	57.64	54.27	66.69
es_ancora		58.15		75.53	62.45		**79.82**	63.2			63.03
es_gsd		59.03		73.69	63.9		**79.45**	66.07			62.55
fr_gsd		59.35		75.18	62.47	47.33	**84.15**	66.55			63.3
fr_partut		56.87		79.83	69.45	54.85	**82.32**	65.76			72.28
fr_sequoia		59.28		76.6	61.96	48.7	**85.13**	67.21			66.24
hi_hdtb		64.04			65.85		**79.07**	60.67			65.63
id_gsd		55.57			71.39		**83.92**	63.41			71.07
ja_gsd		57.03		79.09	69.14		**87.17**	61.03			62.08
ko_gsd		52.1			65.75		**80.95**	62.56			48.54
ko_kaist		50.9					**78.69**	66.17			49.81
pt_bosque		58.72			61.16		**79.8**	65.96			63.37
pt_gsd		54.93			57.93		**79.33**	63.41			59.6
ru_gsd		52.67			55.84		**73.04**	62.98			50.36
ru_syntagrus		55.6					**78.66**	69.06			56.91
zh_gsd		59.29		73.03	65.28	50.57	**83.18**	62.27			65.7
en_pud	85.03	59.84	36.26	81.5		53.26	**87**	72.85	59.45	78.12	71.01
ja_pud		56.72		77.87			**84.04**	61.77			60.2
ru_pud		32.08					**77.12**	68.71			58.68
en_ewt$_{HIT}$	81.57	60.36	43.59	79.41		58.72	**85.35**	71.91	58.67	74.64	72.7
en_pud$_{LAT}$	83.89	56.13	36.67	79.34		54.42	**86.18**	70.49	57.55	76.8	67.54
es_ancora$_{HIT}$		58.38		77.26			**81.14**	64.68			63.24
hi_hdtb$_{HIT}$		64.58					**78.88**	61.58			66.13
ko_kaist$_{HIT}$		50.16					**79.12**	67.33			51.15
pt_bosque$_{STA}$		59.72					**81.56**	68.09			64.32

Table 6: DIST scores for the 29 Shallow Track datasets

5.1 Results from metric evaluations

Tables 4, 5, and 6 show results for the eleven T1 systems in terms of BLEU, NIST and DIST; Table 7 shows results for the three T2 systems in terms of the same three metrics. In general, scores are higher than last year. This is partly due to the fact that the evaluations are performed on tokenised sentences (see Section 2.4). Scores are about 5-10 BLEU points lower when evaluations are run on detokenised sentences; for instance, the BLEU score for ADAPT on English-EWT is 79.69, but using detokenised outputs and references it drops to 70.26, which is very close to the 69.14 score obtained in SR'18 (the SR'18 and SR'19 ADAPT systems are very similar).

IMS obtained the best scores for all metrics on almost all datasets: the only higher scores are the NIST score for the LORIA system on Russian-PUD, and the DIST score for CMU on English-GUM. IMS achieved high macro-average scores on both Shallow and Deep track datasets, with 79.97 BLEU for T1, 51.41 BLEU for T2, 12.79 NIST for T1, 10.94 NIST for T2, 81.62 DIST for T1, and 71.16 DIST for T2.

In the Shallow Track, 8 out of the 11 systems scored 59 BLEU and above on the English-EWT dataset, and three systems achieved a BLEU score of about 80, the highest score being obtained by IMS with 82.98. High scores were also achieved for Spanish, Hindi, Indonesian, French and Chinese (58 BLEU and above on average).

Evaluations of the out-of-domain datasets (PUD) for English and Japanese generally yielded higher scores than those of the in-domain datasets, whereas the opposite is true for Russian. This may be because of the type of language in the different datasets: for instance, the PUD data contains news and Wikipedia texts, i.e. rather cleanly written texts, while the English-EWT corpus contains customer reviews, blog and forum posts, in which a wider variety of language use can be found. Sentences such as *Fun picture websites (:?* or *in n out of the chicago area?* are expected to be generated but are more difficult to predict; for instance, the IMS outputs for these two sentences are *In a out of the chicago area?* and *(: fun picture websites?.* In this case the type of language used seems to have more impact than the fact that the domains are different. On the other hand, the Russian-

–T2–	BLEU			NIST			DIST		
	IMS	RAL	Sur	IMS	RAL	Sur	IMS	RAL	Sur
en_ewt	**54.75**	26.28	23.35	**11.79**	9.42	7.29	**76.3**	55.08	56.88
en_gum	**52.45**	26.17	17.97	**11.04**	9.14	5.88	**73.07**	51.64	49.45
en_lines	**47.29**	24.94	20.96	**10.63**	8.79	6.35	**71.93**	51.2	52.49
en_partut	**45.89**	23.82	17.19	**9.03**	7.67	4.66	**67.45**	48.88	47.2
es_ancora	**53.13**		18.59	**12.38**		5.66	**68.58**		47.19
es_gsd	**51.17**		18.69	**10.82**		5.53	**68.85**		48.06
fr_gsd	**53.62**		15.83	**10.79**		4.53	**68.82**		47.93
fr_partut	**46.95**		14.06	**8.27**		3.61	**68.99**		46.55
fr_sequoia	**57.41**		18.52	**11**		4.8	**72.06**		50.94
en_pud	**51.01**	26.39	18.11	**11.45**	9.63	6.18	**72.31**	49.91	49.88
en_ewt$_{HIT}$	**53.54**	24.54	22.42	**11.55**	9.19	6.9	**74.99**	52.54	54.86
en_pud$_{LAT}$	**47.6**	24.18	17.3	**11.08**	9.21	6.16	**71.65**	50.14	50.17
es_ancora$_{HIT}$	**53.54**		21.1	**12.36**		5.98	**70.02**		48.57

Table 7: BLEU-4, NIST and DIST scores for the 13 Deep Track datasets

SynTagRus and Russian-PUD datasets both contain mostly news texts, so the structures to generate are more similar; in this context, the impact of the change of domain becomes visible.

The results on the automatically parsed datasets are in general very similar to the results on datasets that originate from gold-standard annotations. For English-EWT$_{HIT}$, all scores are slightly lower than the English-EWT scores, with no more than 2 BLEU points, 0.3 NIST points and 2.5 DIST points difference. For the English-PUD$_{LAT}$, the difference is more pronounced, up to 6 BLEU points lower e.g. for BME-UW. However, for the other four datasets, most scores are higher, with improvements up to 2 BLEU points; the exceptions to this trend are IMS on the Hindi data and BME-UW on the Korean-Kaist data, for which the scores according to the three metrics are slightly below scores for gold-standard data.

For the Deep Track datasets, scores are generally substantially lower than for the Shallow Track datasets. The trends observed for the generation from automatically parsed data are confirmed, but the out-of-domain scores for English (the only language with an out of domain dataset in the Deep Track) are lower than the in-domain ones, which could be due in particular to the difficulty of generating punctuation signs.

Finally, the Lower Bound (LB) baseline system results are, as expected, very low (they are not shown in the tables): on the two datasets that are part of the human evaluation, i.e. the T1 and T2 English-EWT, it obtained 7.62 BLEU, 8.26 NIST, 37.99 DIST, and 1.31 BLEU, 4.8 NIST, 35.13 DIST, respectively.

5.2 Results of the human evaluation

Tables 8 and 9 show the results of the human evaluation carried out via Mechanical Turk with Direct Assessment (MTurk DA) for English, Chinese, Russian and Spanish, respectively. See Section 3.2 for details of the evaluation method. 'DA' refers to the specific way in which scores are collected in the WMT approach which follows the evaluation approach of SR'18 but differs from what was done for SR'11.

English: For human evaluation of systems for both the Shallow (T1) and Deep (T2) Tracks, outputs were combined into a single dataset prior to being evaluated and results for all systems are shown in Tables 8 and 9. Average Meaning Similarity DA scores for the Shallow Track for English systems range from 86.6% to 55.3% with ADAPT and IMS achieving highest overall scores in terms of both average raw DA scores and corresponding z-scores. In order to investigate how Readability of system outputs compares to that of human-produced text, we included the original test sentences as a 'system' in the Readability evaluation. Unsurprisingly, human text achieves the highest score in terms of Readability (71.1%) but is closely followed by the best performing systems in terms of Readability, IMS (67.9%) and ADAPT (68.2%), both tied with human readability (and one another) in terms of statistical significance.

In the Deep Track for English, IMS achieved highest results in terms of Meaning Similarity (80.6%), significantly higher than all other systems participating in the Deep Track. In terms of Readability, IMS (61.9%) is tied, in terms of sta-

		English			
Rank	Ave.	Ave. z	n	N	System
1	86.6	0.507	695	810	ADAPT-T1
	85.6	0.503	672	768	IMS-T1
3	82.5	0.407	702	812	CMU-T1
4	80.6	0.324	718	826	IMS-T2
	79.7	0.289	711	816	TILBURG-T1
	79.3	0.276	753	859	DEPDIST-T1
	78.4	0.255	720	836	OSU-FB-T1
	77.0	0.222	702	816	LORIA-T1
	73.5	0.164	695	796	BME-UW-T1
10	72.9	0.110	680	795	RALI-T1
	69.5	−0.006	700	811	DIPINFOUNITO-T1
	67.0	−0.040	692	789	SURFERS-T2
	68.3	−0.052	707	808	RALI-T2
14	60.9	−0.216	752	885	CLAC-T1
15	55.3	−0.390	674	775	LB-BASELINE-T1
	53.0	−0.422	733	853	LB-BASELINE-T2

		Russian			
Rank	Ave.	Ave. z	n	N	System
1	88.3	0.238	481	551	IMS
2	83.7	0.098	477	538	LORIA
	83.0	0.071	447	509	BME-UW
4	77.5	−0.134	503	577	TILBURG

		Chinese			
Rank	Ave.	Ave. z	n	N	System
1	83.0	0.342	481	711	IMS
2	79.5	0.265	471	691	CMU
3	74.8	0.113	479	709	DEPDIST
	73.0	0.043	483	676	BME-UW
	74.7	0.039	479	673	TILBURG
6	66.8	−0.188	477	654	DIPINFOUNITO
	67.0	−0.213	480	699	LORIA

		Pred. Spanish			
Rank	Ave.	Ave. z	n	N	System
1	82.7	0.394	686	799	IMS
2	78.4	0.272	683	804	CMU
3	70.3	−0.042	688	803	TILBURG
	67.8	−0.105	675	789	BME-UW
5	59.2	−0.422	652	754	LORIA

		UD Spanish			
Rank	Ave.	Ave. z	n	N	System
1	81.1	0.378	620	716	IMS
2	75.8	0.168	655	753	CMU
3	72.2	0.006	614	708	TILBURG
4	70.6	−0.080	617	704	DEPDIST
	69.1	−0.111	623	705	BME-UW
6	63.2	−0.302	625	706	LORIA

Table 8: SR'19 human evaluation results for **Meaning Similarity**. Ave. = the average 0-100% received by systems; Ave. z = corresponding average standardized scores; systems are ranked according to Ave. z score; horizontal lines indicate clusters, such that systems in a cluster all significantly outperform all systems in lower ranked clusters; n = total number of distinct test sentences assessed; N = total number of human judgments.

tistical significance, with Surfers (60.9%).[17]

Finally, note that for both Meaning Similarity and Readability, as expected, the Lower Bound Baselines are tied at the last rank with significantly lower scores than the other systems.

Russian: Tables 8 and 9 show average DA scores for systems participating in the Russian task. Meaning Similarity scores for Russian systems range from 88.3% to 77.5% with IMS again achieving highest overall score. In terms of Readability, again IMS achieves the highest average score of 84.1%. Compared to the human results, there is a larger gap than that observed for English outputs, with the best system, IMS, still significantly lower than human performance in terms of Russian readability.

Spanish UD: Tables 8 and 9 show average DA scores for systems participating in Spanish UD. Meaning Similarity scores range from 81.1% to 63.2%, with IMS achieving the highest score, significantly higher than all other participating teams. In terms of Readability, the text produced by the systems ranges from 86.5% to 60.6%, and again IMS achieves the highest score, again significantly higher than all other systems. No system achieves human performance here either, as the human ref-

---

[17]We tested for statistical significance of differences between average DA scores using a Wilcoxon rank sum test.

		English			
Rank	Ave.	Ave. z	n	N	System
–	71.1	0.585	824	1,281	HUMAN
1	67.9	0.507	477	564	IMS-T1
	68.2	0.502	482	573	ADAPT-T1
3	61.9	0.313	512	582	IMS-T2
	62.5	0.285	500	575	LORIA-T1
	62.4	0.260	506	589	CMU-T1
	60.8	0.257	497	572	SURFERS-T2
	60.5	0.211	516	591	DEPDIST-T1
	59.2	0.160	516	594	TILBURG-T1
	58.3	0.156	488	554	BME-UW-T1
	57.4	0.121	507	583	OSU-FB-T1
	57.5	0.096	497	569	RALI-T1
12	50.3	−0.117	494	549	RALI-T2
	49.6	−0.195	515	598	DIPINFOUNITO-T1
	48.1	−0.202	524	610	CLAC-T1
15	37.8	−0.594	492	569	LB-Baseline-T2
	36.5	−0.677	468	534	LB-Baseline-T1

		Russian			
Rank	Ave.	Ave. z	n	N	System
–	87.5	0.430	404	432	HUMAN
1	84.1	0.238	736	838	IMS
2	80.9	0.110	747	861	LORIA
3	77.7	0.022	739	846	BME-UW
4	72.7	−0.214	792	902	TILBURG

		Chinese			
Rank	Ave.	Ave. z	n	N	System
–	72.8	0.730	323	646	HUMAN
1	68.2	0.541	500	780	IMS
2	61.4	0.319	500	735	CMU
3	54.1	0.056	500	727	LORIA
	53.6	0.019	500	737	DEPDIST
	53.2	−0.016	500	709	TILBURG
6	50.0	−0.122	500	746	BME-UW
7	39.1	−0.524	500	705	DIPINFOUNITO

		Pred. Spanish			
Rank	Ave.	Ave. z	n	N	System
–	89.2	0.736	405	442	HUMAN
1	82.8	0.519	613	713	IMS
2	74.7	0.147	609	686	CMU
3	66.0	−0.103	642	737	TILBURG
	64.7	−0.169	640	734	BME-UW
5	53.8	−0.531	594	670	LORIA

		UD Spanish			
Rank	Ave.	Ave. z	n	N	System
–	89.0	0.582	389	438	HUMAN
1	86.5	0.517	511	584	IMS
2	78.9	0.236	523	601	CMU
3	72.1	−0.009	513	596	BME-UW
	71.5	−0.037	498	562	TILBURG
5	67.7	−0.181	498	562	DEPDIST
6	60.6	−0.458	506	577	LORIA

Table 9: SR'19 human evaluation results for **Readability**. Ave. = the average 0-100% received by systems; Ave. z = corresponding average standardized scores; HUMAN denotes scores attributed to the original reference texts; systems are ranked according to Ave. z score; horizontal lines indicate clusters, such that systems in a cluster all significantly outperform all systems in lower ranked clusters; n = total number of distinct test sentences assessed; N = total number of human judgments.

erences achieve a significantly higher score than all systems in terms of readability.

Spanish Automatically Parsed ('Pred. Spanish' in the tables): Tables 8 and 9 show average DA scores for system outputs for the Spanish automatically parsed data. Meaning Similarity scores range from 82.7% to 59.2%, with IMS achieving the highest score, significantly higher than all other participating teams. IMS and CMU achieve better scores than on the regular Spanish UD dataset, while the other systems score lower.

In terms of Readability, the text produced by the systems ranges from 82.8% to 53.8%, and again IMS achieves the highest score, again significantly higher than all other systems. But for the automatically parsed data, all systems score lower than on the Spanish UD dataset, showing that whereas there was no clear difference between the two datasets according to the automatic metrics, the human evaluation shows that the systems do not manage to generate texts with the same quality.

Chinese: Tables 8 and 9 show average DA

scores for all participating systems. Meaning Similarity scores range from 83% to 67%, with IMS achieving the highest score, significantly higher than all other participating teams. In terms of Readability, the produced text ranges from 68.2% to 39.1%, and again IMS achieves the highest score, again significantly higher than all other systems. As for the other non-English languages, no system achieves human performance.

Results from MTurk DA quality control: Similar to SR'18, only 31% of workers passed quality control (being able to replicate scores for same sentences and scoring damaged sentences lower), again highlighting the danger of crowd-sourcing without good quality control measures. The remaining 69%, who did not meet this criterion, were omitted from computation of the official DA results above. Such levels of low quality workers are consistent with what we have seen in DA used for Machine Translation (Graham et al., 2016) and Video Captioning evaluation (Graham et al., 2017).

5.3 Correlation of metrics with human assessment

Table 10 shows the Pearson correlation of BLEU, NIST and DIST scores with human assessment for systems in tasks for which we ran human evaluations this year. These were computed on the average z scores. While BLEU is the metric that correlates best with the human judgements in general, NIST and DIST are more erratic.

None of the automatic metrics correlate well with human judgements of Readability on the English Deep Track data ('English T2' in the tables), in particular NIST with only 0.15. This contrasts with corresponding correlations for Meaning Similarity which do not appear to be affected. Combined with the fact that human assessment scores the deep systems higher for Readability than the metrics, this indicates that some deep systems are producing fluent text that is however dissimilar to the reference texts. The correlations for T2 should be interpreted cautiously since only four T2 systems are being evaluated, which possibly distorts the numbers.

6 Conclusion

The 2019 edition of the SR task (SR'19) saw increased language coverage (11 languages from 9 language families, up from 10 languages in 5 families), as well as increased participation (33 team registrations from 17 countries, up from 21 registrations for SR'18), with 14 teams submitting systems to SR'19 (up from 8 in SR'18). Datasets, evaluation scripts, system outputs and more about the task can be found on the GenChal repository.[18]

Among the notable trends we can observe in evaluations are the following: (i) the best Shallow Track English systems are closing the gap to human-written texts in terms of human evaluation of Readability; (ii) there is a notable gap between human assessment (higher) and metric assessment (lower) of deep track systems, in particular for the best deep track systems; and (iii) the correlation between BLEU and human evaluations of both Readability and Meaning Similarity is consistently above 0.9 for outputs for the gold-standard shallow track datasets, but substantially lower for deep track systems (NIST and DIST are both more erratic).

The biggest progress has been made in SR'19 for deep track systems: not only did we have multiple Deep Track systems to evaluate (compared to just one in 2018), but the best Deep Track system performed equally well or better than most Shallow Track systems for both Readability and Meaning similarity.

Another notable development has been the introduction of silver-standard data. Even though the quality of the texts obtained when generating from automatically parsed data is lower than when using gold-standard data, the high scores according to human evaluations suggest that the shallow inputs could be used as pivot representations in text-to-text systems such as paraphrasing, simplification or summarisation applications.

Overall, the SR tasks have clearly demonstrated that generation from structured meaning representations can be done with impressive success by current neural methods. Given the increased interest and progress we have been able to report for SR'19, we plan to continue with a third shared task in 2020, as part of which we plan to investigate ways of linking up to earlier stages of automatic language generation.

---

[18] `https://sites.google.com/site/genchalrepository/surface-realisation/sr-19-multilingual`

Correlation of Metrics with **Readability**					Correlation of Metrics with **Meaning Similarity**			
	BLEU	NIST	DIST	Mean. Sim.		BLEU	NIST	DIST	Read.
English T1	0.899	0.813	0.874	0.959	English T1	0.975	0.896	0.966	0.959
English T2	*0.53*	*0.15*	*0.66*	0.892	English T2	0.994	0.867	0.999	0.892
Russian	0.994	0.981	0.836	0.992	Russian	0.990	0.985	0.806	0.992
Chinese	0.932	0.587	0.976	0.801	Chinese	0.926	0.948	0.866	0.801
Spanish UD	0.983	0.938	0.794	0.974	Spanish UD	0.971	0.906	0.863	0.974
Spanish Pred	0.973	0.911	0.801	0.978	Spanish Pred	0.994	0.943	0.81	0.978

Table 10: Pearson correlation of BLEU, NIST and DIST scores with human assessment of Readability (left) and Meaning Similarity (right).

Acknowledgments

SR'19 is endorsed by SIGGEN. The work on its organisation, realisation, and evaluation was supported in part by (1) Science Foundation Ireland (sfi.ie) under the SFI Research Centres Programme co-funded under the European Regional Development Fund, grant number 13/RC/2106 (ADAPT Centre for Digital Content Technology, www.adaptcentre.ie) at Dublin City University; (2) the Applied Data Analytics Research & Enterprise Group, University of Brighton, UK; and (3) the European Commission under the H2020 via contracts to UPF, with the numbers 779962-RIA, 700475-IA, 7000024-RIA, and 645012RIA.

References

Rami Al-Rfou, Bryan Perozzi, and Steven Skiena. 2013. Polyglot: Distributed word representations for multilingual NLP. In *Proceedings of the Seventeenth Conference on Computational Natural Language Learning*, pages 183–192, Sofia, Bulgaria. Association for Computational Linguistics.

Loc Barrault, Ondej Bojar, Marta R. Costa-juss, Christian Federmann, Mark Fishel, Yvette Graham, Barry Haddow, Matthias Huck, Philipp Koehn, Shervin Malmasi, Christof Monz, Mathias Mller, Santanu Pal, Matt Post, and Marcos Zampieri. 2019. Findings of the 2019 conference on machine translation (wmt19). In *Proceedings of the Fourth Conference on Machine Translation (Volume 2: Shared Task Papers, Day 1)*, pages 1–61, Florence, Italy. Association for Computational Linguistics.

Anja Belz and Eric Kow. 2011. Discrete vs. continuous rating scales for language evaluation in NLP. In *Proceedings of the 49th Annual Meeting of the Association for Computational Linguistics (ACL-HLT'11)*.

Anja Belz, Michael White, Dominic Espinosa, Eric Kow, Deirdre Hogan, and Amanda Stent. 2011. The first surface realisation shared task: Overview and evaluation results. In *Proceedings of the 13th European Workshop on Natural Language Generation*, ENLG '11, pages 217–226, Stroudsburg, PA, USA. Association for Computational Linguistics.

Ondřej Bojar, Rajen Chatterjee, Christian Federmann, Yvette Graham, Barry Haddow, Shujian Huang, Matthias Huck, Philipp Koehn, Qun Liu, Varvara Logacheva, Christof Monz, Matteo Negri, Matt Post, Raphael Rubino, Lucia Specia, and Marco Turchi. 2017. Findings of the 2017 conference on machine translation (WMT'17). In *Proceedings of the Second Conference on Machine Translation, Volume 2: Shared Task Papers*, pages 169–214, Copenhagen, Denmark. Association for Computational Linguistics.

Ondej Bojar, Christian Federmann, Mark Fishel, Yvette Graham, Barry Haddow, Matthias Huck, Philipp Koehn, and Christof Monz. 2018. Findings of the 2018 conference on machine translation (wmt18). In *Proceedings of the Third Conference on Machine Translation, Volume 2: Shared Task Papers*, pages 272–307, Belgium, Brussels. Association for Computational Linguistics.

Wanxiang Che, Jiang Guo, Yuxuan Wang, Bo Zheng, Huaipeng Zhao, Yang Liu, Dechuan Teng, and Ting Liu. 2017. The hit-scir system for end-to-end parsing of universal dependencies. In *Proceedings of the CoNLL 2017 Shared Task: Multilingual Parsing from Raw Text to Universal Dependencies*, pages 52–62.

Jacob Devlin, Ming-Wei Chang, Kenton Lee, and Kristina Toutanova. 2018. Bert: Pre-training of deep bidirectional transformers for language understanding. *arXiv preprint arXiv:1810.04805*.

Wenchao Du and Alan W Black. 2019. Learning to Order Graph Elements with Application to Multilingual Surface Realization. In *Proceedings of the 2nd Workshop on Multilingual Surface Realisation*, Hong Kong, China.

William Dyer. 2019. DepDist: Surface Realization via Regex and Dependency Distance Tolerance. In *Proceedings of the 2nd Workshop on Multilingual Surface Realisation*, Hong Kong, China.

Henry Elder and Chris Hokamp. 2018. Generating High-Quality Surface Realizations Using Data Augmentation and Factored Sequence Models. In *Pro-

ceedings of the First Workshop on Multilingual Surface Realisation, Melbourne, Australia.

Farhood Farahnak, Laya Rafiee, Leila Kosseim, and Thomas Fevens. 2019. The Concordia NLG Surface Realizer at SR19. In *Proceedings of the 2nd Workshop on Multilingual Surface Realisation*, Hong Kong, China.

Thiago Castro Ferreira and Emiel Krahmer. 2019. Surface Realization Shared Task 2019 (SR'19): The Tilburg University Approach. In *Proceedings of the 2nd Workshop on Multilingual Surface Realisation*, Hong Kong, China.

Thiago Castro Ferreira, Sander Wubben, and Emiel Krahmer. 2018. Surface realization shared task 2018 (sr18): The tilburg university approach. In *Proceedings of the First Workshop on Multilingual Surface Realisation*, pages 35–38.

Yvette Graham, George Awad, and Alan Smeaton. 2017. Evaluation of Automatic Video Captioning Using Direct Assessment. *ArXiv e-prints*.

Yvette Graham, Timothy Baldwin, Alistair Moffat, and Justin Zobel. 2016. Can machine translation systems be evaluated by the crowd alone. *Natural Language Engineering*, FirstView:1–28.

Yvette Graham, Barry Haddow, and Philipp Koehn. 2019. Translationese in machine translation evaluation. *CoRR*, abs/1906.09833.

Karl Moritz Hermann, Tomas Kocisky, Edward Grefenstette, Lasse Espeholt, Will Kay, Mustafa Suleyman, and Phil Blunsom. 2015. Teaching machines to read and comprehend. In *Advances in neural information processing systems*, pages 1693–1701.

Xudong Hong, Ernie Chang, and Vera Demberg. 2019. Improving Language Generation from Feature-Rich Tree-Structured Data with Relational Graph Convolutional Encoders. In *Proceedings of the 2nd Workshop on Multilingual Surface Realisation*, Hong Kong, China.

Adám Kovács, Evelin Ács, Judit Ács, András Kornai, and Gábor Recski. 2019. BME-UW at SR19: Surface Realization with Interpreted Regular Tree Grammars. In *Proceedings of the 2nd Workshop on Multilingual Surface Realisation*, Hong Kong, China.

Guy Lapalme. 2019. Realizing Universal Dependencies Structures Using a Symbolic Approach. In *Proceedings of the 2nd Workshop on Multilingual Surface Realisation*, Hong Kong, China.

KyungTae Lim, Cheoneum Park, Changki Lee, and Thierry Poibeau. 2018. Sex bist: A multi-source trainable parser with deep contextualized lexical representations. In *Proceedings of the CoNLL 2018 Shared Task: Multilingual Parsing from Raw Text to Universal Dependencies*, pages 143–152.

Alessandro Mazzei and Valerio Basile. 2019. The DipInfoUniTo Realizer at SR19: Learning to Rank and Deep Morphology Prediction for Multilingual Surface Realization. In *Proceedings of the 2nd Workshop on Multilingual Surface Realisation*, Hong Kong, China.

Stephen Merity, Caiming Xiong, James Bradbury, and Richard Socher. 2016. Pointer sentinel mixture models. *arXiv preprint arXiv:1609.07843*.

Adam Meyers, R. Reeves, C. Macleod, R. Szekely, V. Zielinska, B. Young, and R. Grishman. 2004. The NomBank project: An interim report. In *HLT-NAACL 2004 Workshop: Frontiers in Corpus Annotation, Boston, MA, May 2004*, pages 24–31.

Simon Mille, Anja Belz, Bernd Bohnet, Yvette Graham, Emily Pitler, and Leo Wanner. 2018. The First Multilingual Surface Realisation Shared Task (SR'18): Overview and Evaluation Results. In *Proceedings of the 1st Workshop on Multilingual Surface Realisation (MSR), 56th Annual Meeting of the Association for Computational Linguistics (ACL)*, pages 1–12, Melbourne, Australia.

Paul Molins and Guy Lapalme. 2015. Jsrealb: A bilingual text realizer for web programming. In *Proceedings of the 15th European Workshop on Natural Language Generation (ENLG)*, pages 109–111.

Martha Palmer, Daniel Gildea, and Paul Kingsbury. 2005. The proposition bank: An annotated corpus of semantic roles. *Computational Linguistics*, 31(1):71–105.

K. Papineni, S. Roukos, T. Ward, and W. j. Zhu. 2002. BLEU: A method for automatic evaluation of machine translation. In *Proc. 40th Annual Meeting on Association for Computational Linguistics*, pages 311–318, Philadelphia, Pennsylvania.

Matthew E Peters, Mark Neumann, Mohit Iyyer, Matt Gardner, Christopher Clark, Kenton Lee, and Luke Zettlemoyer. 2018. Deep contextualized word representations. *arXiv preprint arXiv:1802.05365*.

Peng Qi, Timothy Dozat, Yuhao Zhang, and Christopher D Manning. 2019. Universal dependency parsing from scratch. *arXiv preprint arXiv:1901.10457*.

Alec Radford, Jeff Wu, Rewon Child, David Luan, Dario Amodei, and Ilya Sutskever. 2019. Language models are unsupervised multitask learners. *OpenAI Blog*, 1(8).

Anastasia Shimorina and Claire Gardent. 2019. LORIA / Lorraine University at Multilingual Surface Realisation 2019. In *Proceedings of the 2nd Workshop on Multilingual Surface Realisation*, Hong Kong, China.

Aaron Smith, Bernd Bohnet, Miryam de Lhoneux, Joakim Nivre, Yan Shao, and Sara Stymne. 2018. 82 treebanks, 34 models: Universal dependency parsing with cross-treebank models. In *Proceedings of the CoNLL 2018 Shared Task: Multilingual Parsing from Raw Text to Universal Dependencies*. Association for Computational Linguistics.

Kartikeya Upasani, David L. King, Jinfeng Rao, Anusha Balakrishnan, and Michael White. 2019. The OSU-Facebook Realizer for SR19: Seq2seq Inflection and Serialized Tree2Tree Linearization. In *Proceedings of the 2nd Workshop on Multilingual Surface Realisation*, Hong Kong, China.

Xiang Yu, Agnieszka Falenska, Marina Haid, Ngoc Thang Vu, and Jonas Kuhn. 2019. IM-SurReal: IMS at the Surface Realization Shared Task 2019. In *Proceedings of the 2nd Workshop on Multilingual Surface Realisation*, Hong Kong, China.

Learning to Order Graph Elements with Application to Multilingual Surface Realization

Wenchao Du
Language Technologies Institute
Carnegie Mellon University
Pittsburgh, PA 15213
wenchaod@cs.cmu.edu

Alan W Black
Language Technologies Institute
Carnegie Mellon University
Pittsburgh, PA 15213
awb@cs.cmu.edu

Abstract

Recent advances in deep learning have shown promises in solving complex combinatorial optimization problems, such as sorting variable-sized sequences. In this work, we take a step further and tackle the problem of ordering the elements of sequences that come with graph structures. Our solution adopts an encoder-decoder framework, in which the encoder is a graph neural network that learns the representation for each element, and the decoder predicts the ordering of each local neighborhood of the graph in turn. We apply our framework to multilingual surface realization, which is the task of ordering and completing sentences with their dependency parses given but without the ordering of words. Experiments show that our approach is much better for this task than prior works that do not consider graph structures. We participated in 2019 Surface Realization Shared Task (SR'19) , and we ranked second out of 14 teams while outperforming those teams below by a large margin.

1 Introduction

Sorting and ordering a sequence of items is a fundamental problem to computer science and artificial intelligence. When under the problem setting where a pairwise comparison function is not clear, one may wish to adopt a learning approach to rank any two elements in the sequence, and heuristically find the ordering that optimally agrees with the ranking function (Cohen et al., 1998). However, in many real world problems, the ordering of two elements may largely depend on the other items in the sequence (e.g. word order in natural languages), which makes learning a good pairwise ranking function very hard.

Recent advances in deep learning have opened many doors in solving sequence prediction problems. These neural-network-based frameworks typically involve an encoder that learns a context-sensitive representation for each element, and a decoder that predicts a probability distribution over possible outputs at each time step in an auto-regressive manner (Sutskever et al., 2014). This framework has been adapted to performing the task of sorting by using an encoder that is "orderless" and a decoder that predicts the indices of elements in the sequence (Vinyals et al., 2016).

Many important machine learning problems involves graph-structured data, such as social networks, citation networks, or parse trees in natural language processing (NLP). There has been a surging interest in modelling graphs with deep neural networks in the last few years. Unlike traditional spectral approaches that work with the spectral representations of graphs (Belkin and Niyogi, 2002), deep learning has the flexibility that it provides end-to-end solutions to much more complex problems such as graph generation and transduction.

Surface realization is a natural language generation task in which sentences are generated given input meanings. In particular, the Multilingual Surface Realization Task (Mille et al., 2019) derived inputs from universal dependency (UD) treebank (De Marneffe et al., 2014), a framework that aims to facilitate cross-lingually consistent grammatical annotations. The task consists of two tracks. The shallow track starts from UDs with word order information removed and words are lemmatized. The task consists in determining the word order and inflecting the words. The deep track further removes function words that are leaves in the dependency structures, and the task additionally consists in introducing removed function words.

In this paper, we are interested in the scenario where the sequences to be sorted have graph structures embedded. Our main contribution is a novel

Proceedings of the 2nd Workshop on Multilingual Surface Realisation (MSR 2019), pages 18–24
Hong Kong, China, November 3rd, 2019. ©2019 Association for Computational Linguistics
https://doi.org/10.18653/v1/P17

graph-to-graph learning framework for ordering graph elements. Furthermore, we evaluated our framework on a downstream task – surface realization – that has many impactful applications. We believe our approach is applicable to other problem domains.

2   Related Work

We survey the work related to our approach from the following three aspects: deep learning for combinatorial optimization, deep learning for graphs, and structured language generation.

2.1   Neural Combinatorial Optimization

Most sequence-to-sequence models only handles outputs of fixed vocabulary. Pointer Network (Vinyals et al., 2015) was first proposed for predicting the indices of elements of any given output set, and was applied to solving combinatorial problems suchs as Travelling Salesman Problem (TSP). A set-to-sequence (Vinyals et al., 2016) model was developed for investigation on the importance of order in various machine learning problems. This framework learns a holistic representation of the input set by repeatedly applying attention on the entire set. Last but not least, deep reinforcement learning has also been investigated for solving more complex combinatorial problems such as TSP (Bello et al., 2016).

2.2   Graph Neural Networks

Learning representations of graphs with deep neural networks has attracted a lot of attention in the recent years, and deep learning has achieved success in graph-related tasks such as classification (Kipf and Welling, 2017) and generation (You et al., 2018). Graph neural networks generally follow a recursive neighborhood aggregation scheme, where the embedding of each node is computed with the embeddings of its neighbors and itself. After k iterations, the embedding contains the information of its k-hop neighborhood in the graph. Besides graph representation learning, extensive research has been conducted on the transduction between sequences and graphs, including sequence-to-graph (Aharoni and Goldberg, 2017), graph-to-sequence (Beck et al., 2018), and graph-to-graph (Sun and Li, 2019) learning problems.

2.3   Structured Language Generation

Graph structures are ubiquitous in representations of natural language. Despite the success of sequence-to-sequence learning for language generation (especially machine translation), NLP researchers have started to pay a substantial amount of efforts into incorporating tree structures into neural language generation in the recent years. Application domains include machine translation (Wang et al., 2018), dialog response generation (Du and Black, 2019), and document summarization (Liu et al., 2019). Tree-based language generation models typically sequentialize the parse tree of sentences by some pre-defined traversal order, and generate the tree node in an autoregressive manner. The most common traversal orders are depth-first, left-to-right (pre-order) and breadth-first, left-to-right (level-order).

3   Methods

3.1   Problem Definition

We first give the mathematical formulation of the problem. Given graph $G = (V, E)$ where V is the vertices and E is the edges, we try to learn an ordering function $\pi : V \longrightarrow \{n \in \mathbb{N} \mid 1 \leq n \leq |V|\}$. Each vertex has multiple attributes of discrete type. Denote the attribute a of v_i by $a(v_i)$.

3.2   Encoder Architecture

Our encoder uses a Graph Attention Network (GAT) (Veličković et al., 2018). Attention mechanism has been widely used for handling orderless inputs, such as sets (Vinyals et al., 2016) and memory (Sukhbaatar et al., 2015). GAT learns representations for each graph node through a stack of graph attention layers. At each layer, the information of local neighborhood of each node is aggregated through attention and integrated to the embedding of the node. More specifically, let $\mathbf{g}_{il}$ be the embedding of node i at layer l. Embeddings of layer 0 are input features, which are the sum of embeddings of each node attributes:

$$\mathbf{h}_{i0} = \sum_{a} \mathbf{E}_{a(v_i)}$$

where $\mathbf{E}$ is the embedding matrix of attributes.

For each node i, the importance of neighbor j is computed with the scaled inner product of projected features of i and j and normalized by soft-

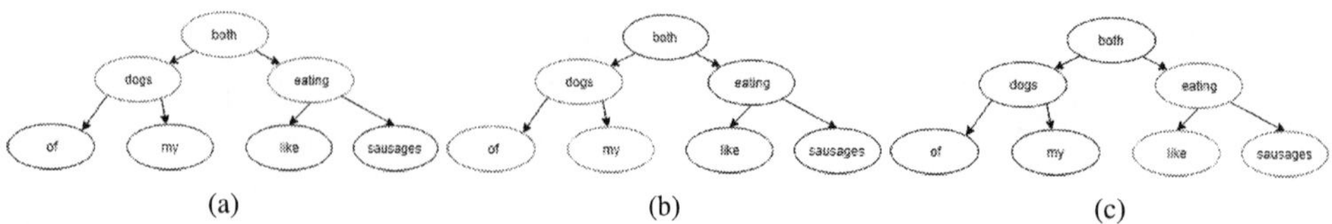

(a)   (b)   (c)

Figure 1: The order of visits for sentence "Both of my dogs like eating sausages." in our decoding algorithm. The nodes being considered for ordering are highlighted with red.

max:

$$e_{ijl} = \frac{1}{\sqrt{d}} \langle \mathbf{W}_l^k \mathbf{g}_{i,l-1}, \mathbf{W}_l^k \mathbf{g}_{j,l-1} \rangle$$

$$\alpha_{ijl} = \frac{\exp(e_{ijl})}{\sum\limits_{j,(i,j)\in E} \exp(e_{ijl})}$$

and the local neighborhood is aggregated through the weighted sum of the embeddings. Similar to Transformer (Vaswani et al., 2017), we employ multi-head attention

$$\mathbf{g}_{il}^k = \sum_{j,(i,j)\in E} \alpha_{ijl}^k \mathbf{g}_{j,l-1}^k$$

$$\mathbf{g}_{il}' = Concat(\mathbf{g}_{il}^k)$$

where k is the index of attention heads. The attention values are transformed by a one-layered feed-forward network with residual connection.

$$\mathbf{g}_{il} = \mathbf{g}_{il}' + FFN_l(\mathbf{g}_{il}')$$

It is clear that these graph embeddings are invariant to permutation through attention mechanism. When modelling graphs with GAT, all vertices are considered adjacent to itself. Consequently, the embeddings of each node at all graph attention layers include the embedding of itself. Since the inner product between oneself is always maximal, the embeddings of the node itself will always dominate the embeddings of its neighbors when aggregating its local neighborhood. It is also clear that the embeddings at layer k represent the information of k-hop neighborhood of each node. We use the summation of embeddings from all layers as the final representation of graph nodes:

$$\mathbf{g}_i = \sum_l \mathbf{g}_{il}$$

We also tried concatenation followed by linear transform for aggregating all layers, but this approach is no better than simple summation.

Since dependency graphs are directed, it might be natural to perform *unilateral* attention (i.e. the parent uses the information of its children but not the other way around). However, we found from experiments that ignoring the directed-ness of graphs and using *bilateral* attention (i.e. the children also use the information of their parent) would perform much better than the first approach.

3.3 Decoder Architecture

At decoding stage, we order the graph elements by selecting the next element one by one. At each step of selection, we have the sequence of past elements that are already ordered available. A natural choice would be using a recurrent neural network (RNN) to encode the ordered elements. The hidden state from RNN decoder at each step would be used for selecting the next element. This idea is developed as Pointer Network (Vinyals et al., 2015). Let $\mathbf{h}_t$ be the hidden state of RNN decoder at time t, Pointer Network predicts the distribution over the next element through attention:

$$u_{it} = v^T tanh(W_1 \mathbf{e}_i + W_2 \mathbf{h}_t)$$

$$P(i \mid v_{\pi(1)} \ldots v_{\pi(t)}) = softmax_i(u_{it})$$

where $\mathbf{e}_i$ is the embedding of element i. In our architecture, we propose two modifications. First, we use dot product for computing attention. Second, we add *candidate component* when computing attention.

$$u_{it} = \langle \mathbf{g}_i, W_1 \mathbf{h}_t \rangle + \langle \mathbf{g}_i, \sum_{j \in C_t} \mathbf{g}_j \rangle$$

where $C_t = \{j \mid j \notin \{\pi(1) \ldots \pi(t-1)\}\}$ is the set of candidate indices that are not selected in previous steps. It is intuitive to add the embedding of candidates to bias the model towards selecting from the remaining nodes. We found this modification significantly improves the performance.

The model described above is not inherently designed to handle graphs. To incorporate graph structures in decoding, we predict the order of nodes of each neighborhood in turn. We start with the root of the graph, and order the set consisting of the root and its neighbors. Then we recursively repeat the process for each of the children of the parent from left to right based their predicted order. An example is provided in the figure above. We also provide pseudocode for our decoding algorithm. *TreeSort* is used for arranging the order of each local neighborhood, and *TreeLinearize* is for converting the sorted tree into a sentence. The *sort* function sorts the input elements using the decoder architecture described above. It takes two arguments: the first one is the set to be sorted, and the second one is the initial state of the RNN decoder. It returns the sorted set and the last hidden state from the RNN decoder. *TreeLinearize* simply merges subtrees by interpolating spaces.

One limitation of using *TreeLinearize* is that it cannot generate non-projective trees, i.e. when nodes are put in linear order, there are edges crossing over each other. There are about 2.5% parses are non-projective in the English dataset, so the degradation in performance is negligible. In order to generate non-projective trees, one may want to use a linearization algorithm alternative to *TreeLinearize* that generates the whole sequence based on the topological order of nodes returned by *TreeSort*. At each step, the choices of nodes should be limited to those that are not preceded by any unselected nodes with higher topological order.

To see why tree decoding is advantageous over ordering the whole sequence at a time, consider the size of the search space of both approaches. The hypothesis space of sequence decoding is factorial in the number of vertices (i.e. $|V|!$). In graph decoding, at each node v, the number of nodes to be ordered is the degree of v, $d(v)$ (since the nodes to be ordered include v but not parent of v). In the example shown above, the total number of permutations of the sentence is $7! = 5040$, while with tree decoding, the number of ordering to be considered reduced to $(3!)^3 = 216$. The difference is even larger when there are more words in the sentence. So tree decoding gains performance by reducing the size of search space.

The full model is trained by maximizing the likelihood of choices of indices. We apply candidate masking, i.e. the candidates that are already selected in previous steps are assigned zero probability.

Algorithm 1 Pseudocode for tree decoding procedures.

---

    procedure TREESORT(node, h)
        if $node$ is a leaf **then**
            return
        else
            $n \leftarrow node$
            $n.children \leftarrow []$
            $l \leftarrow n \cup node.children$
            $l, h \leftarrow sort(l, h)$
            $node.sorted \leftarrow l$
            for ch in l **do**
                TreeSort(ch, h)

    procedure TREELINEARIZE(node)
        if node is a leaf **then**
            return node.word
        else
            $s \leftarrow$ empty string
            for ch in $node.sorted$ **do**
                $s \leftarrow s +' \ '+ TreeLinearize(ch)$
        return s

3.4 Morphology

The MSR challenge requires realizaton of lemmatized words. Since this is not the main focus of our paper, we briefly describe our approach here. After the words are ordered into sentences in the first stage described above, we obtain BERT embeddings (Devlin et al., 2019) of each word. We train a character-level sequence-to-sequence model with attention for morphological inflection, where the source is the lemmatized word and the target is the realization. The BERT embedding is used for constructing the initial state of the decoder, so that the morphology model may use contextual information. The concatenation of decoder hidden states and embeddings of syntactic information such as tense and number is used for predicting characters.

4 Experiments

4.1 Data and Preprocessing

We use SR'19 challenge dataset (Mille et al., 2018). The data is obtained from the universal dependency treebank (Zeman et al., 2018). The dataset includes many major languages, such as English, Spanish, and Chinese. Word orders are hidden and words are randomly shuffled. Our model uses the following attributes for graph at-

Table 1: Average performance on English dataset (dev) of shallow track with different hyperparameters. All results are evaluated without morphological inflections.

	BLEU	DIST	NIST
$L = 0$	76.4	85.3	14.4
$L = 1, H = 8$	79.9	90.6	14.5
$L = 2, H = 8$	82.8	91.5	14.7
$L = 3, H = 8$	83.2	91.4	14.7
$L = 4, H = 8$	83.5	91.1	14.7
$L = 5, H = 8$	83.6	92.1	14.7
$L = 6, H = 8$	83.3	91.0	14.7
$L = 5, H = 4$	82.3	91.3	14.6
$L = 5, H = 16$	83.9	92.0	14.7

Table 2: Comparison between different learning paradigms on English dev sets. All results are evaluated without morphological inflections.

	BLEU	DIST	NIST
set-to-graph (no attention)	76.4	85.3	14.4
set-to-graph (global attention)	79.9	90.6	14.5
graph-to-sequence	63.6	88.9	13.7
graph-to-graph	83.2	91.4	14.7

tention networks: lexicons, part-of-speech tags, types of the dependency relation with the governor, depths in the dependency graph, and relative positions to the parent. All relative positions farther than 2 are considered as one type.

4.2 Metrics

Three quantitative measure are used for evaluating performance. BLEU measures the average precisions of n-gram overlap with references. NIST is similar to BLEU but gives more weights to less frequent n-grams. DIST measures the edit distance between hypotheses and references, in which either insertion, deletion, or substitution of a word is considered an edit.

4.3 Model and Training Details

All models are implemented in PyTorch [1]. The Graph Attention Networks has output size of 512 for each attention layer, and the feedforward networks' middle layers have 1024 dimension. RNN decoders have hidden size of 512. Dropout is applied with rate 0.5. We use Adam optimizer with learning rate 0.001. We did not use learning rate warm-up as we did not find much improvement.

4.4 Main Results

We show the effects of hyperparameters of GAT on performance. We vary the number of attention layers and the number of heads in GAT. The results are summarized in Table 1. Note that these results are for hypotheses without morphological inflections, which are measured against lemmatized references. We first examine the impact of number of graph attention layers on performance. With only

one layer of graph attention, performances are significantly worse than multiple layers. On the other hand, the improvement beyond using 3 layers is marginal. Without any graph attention layer, the model is essentially taking inputs as mathematical sets, in which case its performance is the worst. We are also interested in the effect of number of attention heads. It appears that the best performance is achieved with 8 heads, while attentions with 4 heads and 16 heads are slightly worse off.

Table 1 shows that given local neighborhood information, the model learns more useful graph embeddings than without. We are interested in the other end of the spectrum: what if each node has global information of the set from the beginning? We apply attention over the whole input graph for each node without masking. This ignores the local structures in graphs and is essentially treating the inputs as sets. Results are listed in Table 2. It seems that learning the embeddings of set elements holistically is better than learning for each element in isolation, but still not as good as learning with graph structures.

We are also interested in the advantage of graph-to-graph decoding over graph-to-sequence. Graph-to-sequence baseline uses the graph embeddings from graph encoder, and follows the normal sequence decoding procedure. The results are shown in Table 2. The difference between graph-to-sequence and graph-to-graph is huge. Even if graph-to-sequence decoding is capable of producing non-projective trees, learning is much more difficult due to much larger hypothesis space. On the other hand, graph-to-graph decoding deals with smaller search space and exploits the hierarchical structure of sentences.

We also include the results with morphological inflections in Table 3. It seems that the morphology of English and Spanish are relatively easy,

[1] https://github.com/wenchaodudu/MSR

Table 3: Final performance on dev sets after word inflections. Results without considering inflections are parenthesized. We did not perform word inflection for Chinese datasets.

	BLEU	DIST	NIST
English	80.0 (83.6)	87.4 (92.1)	14.4 (14.7)
Chinese	66.5	63.4	12.3
Spanish	81.1 (83.2)	84.3 (85.2)	15.2 (15.4)
French	75.4 (85.5)	86.0 (88.6)	13.8 (14.8)
Japanese	67.1 (84.3)	72.5 (72.9)	10.8 (12.2)

hence the differences between the final numbers and the results without inflections are smallest. Solving morphological inflections for French is harder than English and Spanish, and Japanese is the hardest. Our approach achieved worst results on Chinese dataset. We hypothesize this is because 1) the Chinese dataset contains more non-projective trees and 2), the Chinese dataset is the smallest one comparing to other languages.

5 Conclusion

In this work, we proposed a novel graph-to-graph framework for ordering graph elements and generating sentences with projective dependency structure. Empirical results show competitive performance on surface realization task. Furthermore, exploiting graph structures is indeed helpful for such task. One future direction would be finding an end-to-end approach for jointly finishing and ordering graphs, as required in the deep track of surface realization challenge. Another direction would be finding an end-to-end approach for generating both projective and non-projective trees.

References

Roee Aharoni and Yoav Goldberg. 2017. Towards string-to-tree neural machine translation. In *Proceedings of the 55th Annual Meeting of the Association for Computational Linguistics (Volume 2: Short Papers)*, pages 132–140.

Daniel Beck, Gholamreza Haffari, and Trevor Cohn. 2018. Graph-to-sequence learning using gated graph neural networks. In *Proceedings of the 56th Annual Meeting of the Association for Computational Linguistics (Volume 1: Long Papers)*, pages 273–283.

Mikhail Belkin and Partha Niyogi. 2002. Laplacian eigenmaps and spectral techniques for embedding and clustering. In *Advances in neural information processing systems*, pages 585–591.

Irwan Bello, Hieu Pham, Quoc V Le, Mohammad Norouzi, and Samy Bengio. 2016. Neural combinatorial optimization with reinforcement learning. *arXiv preprint arXiv:1611.09940*.

William W Cohen, Robert E Schapire, and Yoram Singer. 1998. Learning to order things. In *Advances in Neural Information Processing Systems*, pages 451–457.

Marie-Catherine De Marneffe, Timothy Dozat, Natalia Silveira, Katri Haverinen, Filip Ginter, Joakim Nivre, and Christopher D Manning. 2014. Universal stanford dependencies: A cross-linguistic typology. In *LREC*, volume 14, pages 4585–4592.

Jacob Devlin, Ming-Wei Chang, Kenton Lee, and Kristina Toutanova. 2019. Bert: Pre-training of deep bidirectional transformers for language understanding. In *Proceedings of the 2019 Conference of the North American Chapter of the Association for Computational Linguistics: Human Language Technologies, Volume 1 (Long and Short Papers)*, pages 4171–4186.

Wenchao Du and Alan W Black. 2019. Top-down structurally-constrained neural response generation with lexicalized probabilistic context-free grammar. In *Proceedings of the 2019 Conference of the North American Chapter of the Association for Computational Linguistics: Human Language Technologies, Volume 1 (Long and Short Papers)*, pages 3762–3771.

Thomas N Kipf and Max Welling. 2017. Semi-supervised classification with graph convolutional networks. *ICLR*.

Yang Liu, Ivan Titov, and Mirella Lapata. 2019. Single document summarization as tree induction. In *Proceedings of the 2019 Conference of the North American Chapter of the Association for Computational Linguistics: Human Language Technologies, Volume 1 (Long and Short Papers)*, pages 1745–1755.

Simon Mille, Anja Belz, Bernd Bohnet, Yvette Graham, and Leo Wanner. 2019. The Second Multilingual Surface Realisation Shared Task (SR'19): Overview and Evaluation Results. In *Proceedings of the 2nd Workshop on Multilingual Surface Realisation (MSR), 2019 Conference on Empirical Methods in Natural Language Processing (EMNLP)*, Hong Kong, China.

Simon Mille, Anja Belz, Bernd Bohnet, and Leo Wanner. 2018. Underspecified universal dependency structures as inputs for multilingual surface realisation. In *Proceedings of the 11th International Conference on Natural Language Generation*, pages 199–209.

Sainbayar Sukhbaatar, Jason Weston, Rob Fergus, et al. 2015. End-to-end memory networks. In *Advances in neural information processing systems*, pages 2440–2448.

Mingming Sun and Ping Li. 2019. Graph to graph: a topology aware approach for graph structures learning and generation. In *The 22nd International Conference on Artificial Intelligence and Statistics*, pages 2946–2955.

Ilya Sutskever, Oriol Vinyals, and Quoc V Le. 2014. Sequence to sequence learning with neural networks. In *Advances in neural information processing systems*, pages 3104–3112.

Ashish Vaswani, Noam Shazeer, Niki Parmar, Jakob Uszkoreit, Llion Jones, Aidan N Gomez, Łukasz Kaiser, and Illia Polosukhin. 2017. Attention is all you need. In *Advances in neural information processing systems*, pages 5998–6008.

Petar Veličković, Guillem Cucurull, Arantxa Casanova, Adriana Romero, Pietro Lio, and Yoshua Bengio. 2018. Graph attention networks. *ICLR*.

Oriol Vinyals, Samy Bengio, and Manjunath Kudlur. 2016. Order matters: Sequence to sequence for sets. *ICLR*.

Oriol Vinyals, Meire Fortunato, and Navdeep Jaitly. 2015. Pointer networks. In *Advances in Neural Information Processing Systems*, pages 2692–2700.

Xinyi Wang, Hieu Pham, Pengcheng Yin, and Graham Neubig. 2018. A tree-based decoder for neural machine translation. In *Proceedings of the 2018 Conference on Empirical Methods in Natural Language Processing*, pages 4772–4777.

Jiaxuan You, Rex Ying, Xiang Ren, William Hamilton, and Jure Leskovec. 2018. Graphrnn: Generating realistic graphs with deep auto-regressive models. In *International Conference on Machine Learning*, pages 5694–5703.

Daniel Zeman, Jan Hajič, Martin Popel, Martin Potthast, Milan Straka, Filip Ginter, Joakim Nivre, and Slav Petrov. 2018. Conll 2018 shared task: multilingual parsing from raw text to universal dependencies. In *Proceedings of the CoNLL 2018 Shared Task: Multilingual Parsing from Raw Text to Universal Dependencies*, pages 1–21.

DepDist: Surface realization via regex and dependency distance tolerance

William Dyer
Oracle Corp
`william.dyer@oracle.com`

Abstract

This paper describes a method of inflecting and linearizing a lemmatized dependency tree by: (1) determining a regular expression and substitution to describe each productive word-form rule; (2) learning the dependency distance tolerance for each head-dependent pair, resulting in an edge-weighted directed acyclic graph (DAG); and (3) topologically sorting the DAG into a surface realization based on edge weight. The method's output for 11 languages across 18 treebanks is competitive with the other submissions to the Second Multilingual Surface Realization Shared Task (SR'19).

1   Introduction

The goal of the Second Multilingual Surface Realization Shared Task (SR'19) is to generate a morphologically inflected surface order from a lemmatized and unordered dependency tree (Mille et al., 2019). In track 1, all lemmas in the dependency tree are given, and the task is closed in the sense that only the provided training data may be used; outside data is not allowed.

Though conceptually straightforward, linearizing a dependency tree in an automated way is a relatively difficult task given issues such as projectivity, flexibility or variation in word-order preferences among humans, polysemy and homography, among others. Determining surface inflections is similarly difficult given the sometimes opaque relationship between spoken and written language, diversity among language varieties, usage preferences changing over time, and vestigial inflectional forms which may or may not be productive.

The approach outlined in this paper tackles the inflection part of the task by attempting to determine the productive rules for word forms, implemented as a series of regular expressions and substitutions. Given the closed nature of the task, these regular expressions are based on orthographic forms, rather than what would likely be more accurate phonological representations.

To linearize a dependency tree, the current study's approach is two-fold: first, learn the tolerance for how far apart a dependent and its head can be within the context of a given sentence; second, use this dependency distance tolerance to sort the tree into a surface order. The sorting can be accomplished such that only projective surface orders are generated, or without any baked-in notion of projectivity. Algorithms for both are presented here, but given the nature of the task—and based on empirical testing—only projective linearizations were submitted as part of the shared task.

2   Inflecting

The current model's approach to inflecting lemmas to arrive at wordforms is to first look up the lemma and target morphological form in the training data—if the form exists in the training data for the lemma, it is used in the test data. For example, the past participle of the lemma *do* is most likely present in the training data, so when the testing data prompts for it, *done* is simply supplied from the training set. More interestingly, lemmas unseen during training are handled with a series of regular expressions (regex) built up from the training data in an attempt to define a natural language's productive inflectional rules.

From a linguistic perspective, inflecting unseen test-set words is analogous to inflecting nonce words, a rather long-studied area. For example, the 'wug' test (Berko, 1958) shows that children possess knowledge about morphological rules. It is intuitive to conceive of these rules as regular or irregular—*box* → *boxes* illustrates the regular plural in English, *ox* → *oxen* an irregular form—and

Proceedings of the 2nd Workshop on Multilingual Surface Realisation (MSR 2019), pages 25–34
Hong Kong, China, November 3rd, 2019. ©2019 Association for Computational Linguistics
https://doi.org/10.18653/v1/P17

lemma / wordform	regex / substitution	nonce lemma / nonce wordform
like- / liked	`^(.*)(e)$` / `\1\2d`	chortle / chortled
attach-- / attached	`^(.*)(h)$` / `\1\2ed`	gallumph / gallumphed
presentar / presentó	`^(.*)(t)ar$` / `\1\2ó`	risotar / risotó
triunfar / triunfó	`^(.*)(f)ar$` / `\1\2ó`	galonfar / galonfó

Table 1: Regular expressions and substitutions for simple past with nonces from *Jabberwocky* (Carroll, 1872) and Spanish translation *El Fablistanón* (Pascual, 1977).

to subsequently equate productive rules with regular forms only. However, a more accurate model is that speakers seem to inflect nonce words according to categories which span what we tend to think of as both regular and irregular classes. The college students studied by Bybee and Moder (1983) produce simple past forms for nonces such as *spling* ← *splung*, akin to 'strong' verbs such as *cling* ← *clung* and *string* ← *strung* (Wiese, 1996). Prasada and Pinker (1993) find that the production and acceptance of inflected nonces correlates with phonological distance from irregular clusters, with a bias towards regular forms (p. 48).

The current model approximates the phonological environment of word stems with regular expressions and morphological inflections with substitutions. There is no notion of regular or irregular classes; regexes and substitutions are built for all classes and sorted according to frequency. If a nonce word's lemma matches the regex of a morphological class from the training data, the associated substitution will provide an inflected form. Importantly, given the closed nature of SR '19—no outside data is allowed—the generated regexes and substitutions are defined and employed orthographically rather than phonetically or phonologically. As such, depending on the opacity of a language's orthographic system, information about allophones, syllables, and other phonetically important structures is lost. Interestingly, this loss does not seem to impact neural-network models of inflection (Wiemerslage et al., 2018), though the current model's rule-based approach likely suffers.

Defining the orthographic environment such that known lemma-to-wordform exemplars can be used to create a prototypical regex for a given class can be accomplished by (1) aligning the lemma and wordform; (2) recording the characters surrounding a replacement as atoms; (3) generalizing atoms not surrounding substitutions; and (4) determining the substitution(s).

Table 1 shows this process for a sample of simple past forms. For example, the English lemma *like* is aligned with the target wordform *liked*, the regex defining the environment is `^(.*)(e)$`, and the substitution with back-references is `\1\2d`. When applied to the nonce lemma *chortle*, the correct wordform *chortled* is produced. That is, the regex matches the lemma *chortle* ending in the character *e*, and the substitution maintains the atomic root *chortl*, maintains the final character *e*, and appends the character *d*.

Alignment of lemmas and wordforms is accomplished with the `pairwise2` module from Biopython (Cock et al., 2009). Regex and substitution generation is done with a deterministic algorithm which generalizes uninvolved atoms (`.*`), records adjacent atoms in the lemma, and produces back-references and inflectional morphemes for the substitution. Morphological features are treated as full strings rather than as discrete features—something like `Mood=Ind|Person=3|Tense=Past|-VerbForm=Fin|VERB`, depending on the corpus. Each of these feature sets is generally associated with multiple patterns, as in Table 1.

There are at least two intuitive approaches for choosing a regex pattern for an unknown lemma: the most detailed or the most frequent. The first approach relies on a principle going back to Pāṇini in which inflections obey specific conditions before general ones (cf. Embick and Marantz, 2005). However, during testing, this approach resulted in archaisms or typos in the generated text. Thus the most frequent pattern was chosen instead.

3 Linearizing

The task of linearizing a dependency tree can be informed by long-standing linguistic principles describing the placement of words in general—"what belongs together semantically is also placed close together" (Behaghel, 1932, p. 4), for example—as well as more recent work on dependency trees specifically, such as Dependency Distance minimization (DDM) (Hudson, 1995; Futrell et al., 2015; Liu et al., 2017). DDM is a general principle of tree ordering based on Head

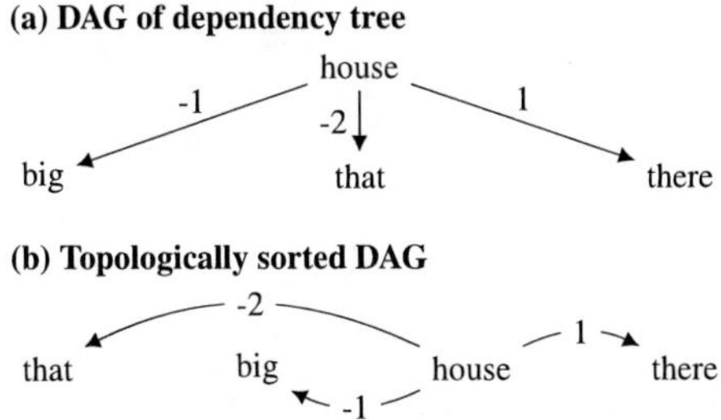

Figure 1: Target dependency distance tolerances for *that big house there*, represented as **(a)** a DAG showing dependency relations and **(b)** the topological sort.

Proximity (Rijkhoff, 1986), Early Immediate Constituents (Hawkins, 1994), Dependency Locality Theory (Gibson, 2000), and Minimize Domains (Hawkins, 2004), among others.

Submissions to SR '18, the first multilingual shared task, are generally based on sequence-to-sequence machine translation (Elder and Hokamp, 2018; Sobrevilla Cabezudo and Pardo, 2018), binary classification (Castro Ferreira et al., 2018; Puzikov and Gurevych, 2018; King and White, 2018; Madsack et al., 2018), or probabilistic n-gram language models (Singh et al., 2018).

3.1 Dependency distance tolerance

The DepDist approach to linearization relies on dependency distance tolerance, the idea that a dependent and head tolerate a certain contextual distance, measured as the number of intervening words, relative to other words in a sentence (Dyer, 2019). This dependency distance tolerance is learned from training data via a graph neural network (GNN) implemented within the Graph Nets framework (Battaglia et al., 2018) based on `word2vecf` syntactic embeddings (Levy and Goldberg, 2014). GNNs take advantage of message-passing neural networks (MPNN), in which nodes pass information and spatial-based convolutions and pooling are implemented (Gilmer et al., 2017; Wu et al., 2019).

Specifically, each word's 300-element syntactic embedding is included as a node attribute for a `networkx` graph constructed for each sentence in the training, dev, and testing sets. Input edge attributes are the average dependency distance between words from the training set. For example, if the determiner *the* precedes the noun *cat* by an average of 1.3 words in the training data, the input edge attribute for *the* $\leftarrow$ *cat* will be 1.3. After 5 training epochs of 100 iterations on a GNN with 64 neurons and 8 MPNN layers using an Adam optimizer in TensorFlow, output edge attributes reflect the learned dependency distance tolerances for each dependent-head pair in a given sentence.

For example, given a simple tree of one head, *houses*, three dependents—*big*, *that*, and *there*—and a target linearization of *that big house there*, the learned directed dependency distances would be *that* $\xleftarrow{-2}$ *house*, *big* $\xleftarrow{-1}$ *house*, and *house* $\xrightarrow{1}$ *there*. In other words, the dependent *that* precedes its head *house* by two words, *big* precedes *house* by one word, and *there* follows *house* by one word. This example is shown in Figure 1(a).

The GNN framework allows for non-Euclidean data representations, such as graphs, to be explored from a deep learning perspective (Bronstein et al., 2017). Further, GNNs are invariant to permutations in the graph elements—ideal for this surface realization shared task—and can operate on inputs of varying sizes (Battaglia et al., 2018).

3.2 Topological sorting

A dependency tree can be represented by a directed acyclic graph (DAG) based on the [head $\rightarrow$ dependent] relation. Adding edge weights representing directed dependency distances—the number of words a dependent precedes or follows its head—allows the DAG to also represent the precedence relation. Thus an edge-weighted DAG is equivalent to a partially ordered set (poset).

The topological sort of a non-weighted DAG or poset is not guaranteed to be unique, but adding edge weights allows a single linear order to be generated. For example, Figure 1(b) shows the unique topological sort for *that big house there*, based on the precedence relations *house* $\xrightarrow{-2}$ *that*, *house* $\xrightarrow{-1}$ *big*, and *house* $\xrightarrow{1}$ *there*[1].

The linearization of a dependency tree can be projective (Marcus, 1965), in which there are no crossing arcs, or non-projective. More formally, a projective order is one in which every word w occurring between a dependent d and head h is dominated by h (Nivre, 2006), and as such is only defined for dependency-based DAGs[2].

---

[1] The notation of *house* $\xrightarrow{-2}$ *that* indicates the dependency relation by the direction of the edge and distance by edge weight. An equivalent notation would be *that* $\stackrel{2}{\prec}$ *house*.

[2] Posets can be classified according to their planarity, and while half-planarity corresponds to the 'no-crossing-arcs' sense of projectivity (Pitler et al., 2013), it does not capture the dominance definition.

Algorithm 1: Topologically sort DAG (non-projective)

```
1:  function NonProjTopoSort(dag)
2:      tuples ← ∅
3:      tuples.add(0, dag.root)
4:      CalcI(root, dag, tuples)
5:      return tuples.sort()
6:  end function
7:  function CalcI(node, dag, tuples)
8:      if node.hasHead then
9:          head ← head(dag, node)
10:         edge = dag[node][node.head]
11:         tuples.add(head.i + edge, node)
12:     end if
13:     for child ∈ node.children do
14:         CalcI(child, dag, tuples)
15:     end for
16: end function
```

Algorithm 2: Topologically sort DAG (projective)

```
1:  function ProjTopoSort(dag)
2:      tuples ← ∅
3:      tuples.add(0, dag.root)
4:      CalcI(root, dag, tuples)
5:      return tuples.sort()
6:  end function
7:  function CalcI(node, dag, tuples)
8:      head ← head(dag, node)
9:      edge = dag[node][node.head]
10:     children ← 0
11:     for desc ∈ node.descendents do
12:         children+ ← abs(dag[desc][desc.head])
13:     end for
14:     if edge < 0 then
15:         children ← −children
16:     end if
17:     tuples.add(head.i + edge + children, node)
18:     for child ∈ node.children do
19:         CalcI(child, dag, tuples)
20:     end for
21: end function
```

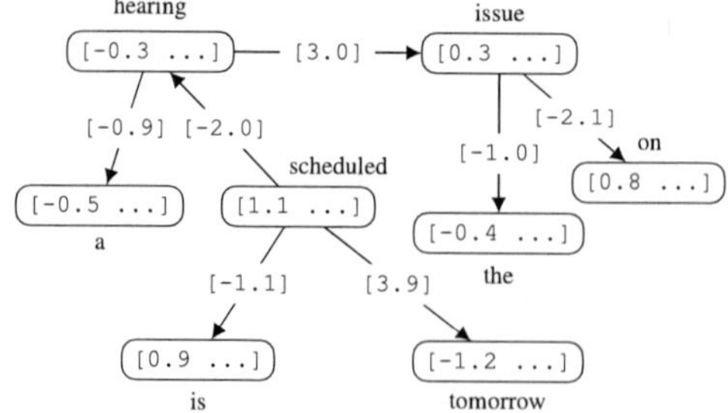

(b) non-projective linearization

a	hearing	is	scheduled	on	the	issue	tomorrow
-2.9	-2.0	-1.1	0.0	0.9	2.0	3.0	3.9

(c) projective linearization

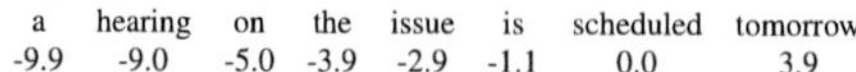

a	hearing	on	the	issue	is	scheduled	tomorrow
-9.9	-9.0	-5.0	-3.9	-2.9	-1.1	0.0	3.9

Figure 2: Linearizing a DAG. **(a)** A `networkx` graph provides the input and output of the GNN. Input node attributes are each word's syntactic embedding, and input edge attributes are the average directed dependency distances between connected words in the training data. Target edge attributes are the actual dependency distances between the words in the sentence. The GNN learns edge attributes for the test sentences. In practice, edge directions may be reversed to better take advantage of MPNN. **(b)** Non-projective linearization in which each word's index reflects its distance from the root. **(c)** Projective linearization, in which each word's index is set such that all descendents will be adjacent.

Algorithm 1 sorts an edge-weighted DAG without regard to projectivity. Each node's distance from the root is calculated by adding the weight of the node's edge with its head to its head's index (lines 9-11). This distance becomes an index i for each word; sorting these indexes from smallest to largest (line 5) creates a linearization for the dependency tree which may or may not be projective. The calculation of root distance in Algorithm 1 runs in $\mathcal{O}(n)$ time, since each node is only visited once and is able to calculate its distance based on the index of its parent node. The sorting algorithm is not specified, but assuming something like merge sort (Knuth, 1998) with a time complexity of $\mathcal{O}(n \log n)$, the overall complexity of Algorithm 1 would be $\mathcal{O}(n \log n)$.

Algorithm 2 sorts an edge-weighted DAG into a projective linearization based on the idea that each dependent d should be placed *vis-à-vis* its head h such that all descendents of d could be placed between d and h. The index i in a linearization for dependent d is the sum of (1) the index of its head h (line 8); (2) the edge weight between d and h (line 9); and (3) the summed absolute value of the edges of all descendents of d whose polarity matches that of d (lines 10-16). The calculation of i in Algorithm 2 runs in $\mathcal{O}(n \log n)$ time, since each node is visited once by CalcI, and then in lines 11-13 each descendent node is visited. Coupled with merge sort, Algorithm 2 overall runs in $\mathcal{O}(n \log n)$ time.

Algorithms 1 and 2 are exemplified in Figure 2, in which a dependency tree (a), is sorted into a valid non-projective linearization (b) and a projective linearization (c). Due to the nature of GNNs, the size of the graph need not be standardized—the graph is simply a series of connected nodes and edges. Input node attributes are passed along directed edges, and output edges reflect learned distance tolerances. These tolerances are then used to topologically sort the DAG.

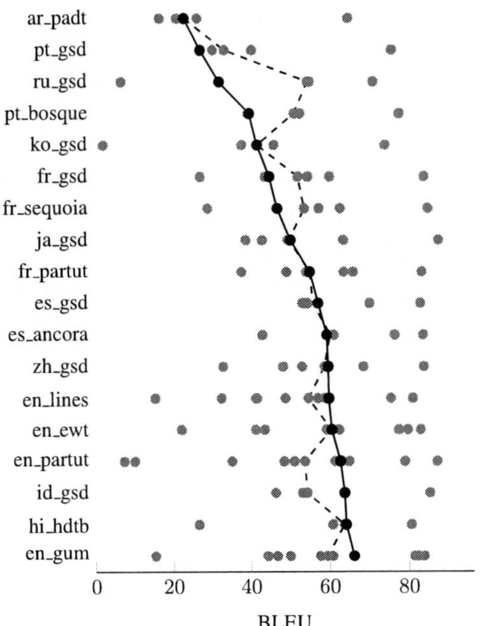
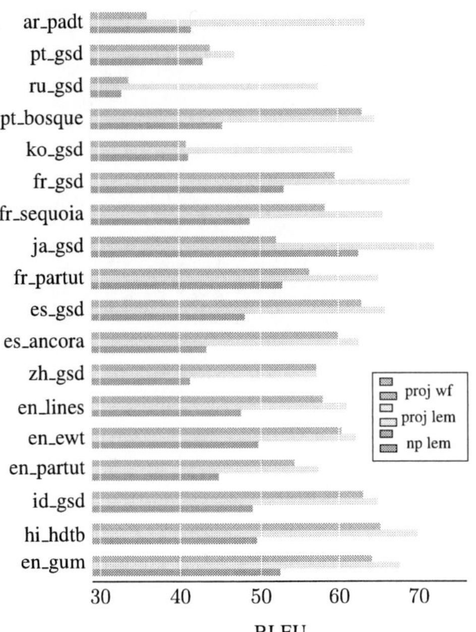

Figure 3: BLEU scores per corpus for all track-1 submissions. DepDist shown by black connected points. Median indicated by dashed line.

Figure 4: BLEU scores from dev sets realized as projective wordforms (red), projective lemmas (green), and non-projective lemmas (blue).

3.3 Projective linearizations

Imposing a projective limitation on generated outputs is a theoretically dubious action when describing natural language (Ferrer-i Cancho and Gómez-Rodríguez, 2016; Yadav et al., 2019). However, given the strong tendency towards projectivity (Mambrini and Passarotti, 2013; Gómez-Rodríguez, 2016), the nature of SR'19 as a fundamentally Natural Language Generation (NLG) rather than descriptive task, as well as empirical observation of the projective and non-projective outputs of the current model (§4.1), it was decided to submit only projective linearizations.

4 Results

DepDist was run on 18 corpora across 11 languages provided by the organizers of SR'19, based on Universal Dependencies corpora. Due to time constraints, only the largest corpus for each language was used for training, though linearizations were generated for nearly all test corpora[3].

Results for the DepDist submission measured by BLEU score (Papineni et al., 2002) compared

to other track-1 submissions for the 18 corpora are shown in Figure 3. DepDist performed below the median for six corpora: Portuguese (GSD & Bosque), Russian (GSD), French (GSD & Sequoia), and Spanish (Ancora). DepDist was the median for three corpora: Arabic (GSD), Korean (GSD), and French (ParTUT). DepDist performed better than the median for nine corpora: Japanese, (GSD), Spanish (GSD), Chinese (GSD), English (LinES, EWT, ParTUT, & GUM), Indonesian (GSD), and Hindi (HDTB).

While the performance on some corpora was significantly below the median—especially Russian and both Portuguese—DepDist generally performed close to or slightly better than the median. Thus DepDist seems to be fairly average in terms of BLEU score compared to the other submissions, suggesting that it is a competitive solution.

4.1 Error analysis

Figure 4 plots BLEU scores for the dev set of each corpus differentiated based on projectivity and inflections. The first, red bar shows the projective linearization of wordforms. The second, green bars show the scores based on linearization only, without inflecting. The third, blue bars show non-projective linearizations of lemmas.

---

[3]Though ko_kaist was the largest supplied Korean corpus, parsing errors prevented training and generation of output; thus only ko_gsd was used. Similarly, the large size of ru_syntagrus inhibited training, so only ru_gsd was used.

corpus	lemmas	morph features		wordforms	
		given	%	generated	%
ar_padt	28264	21901	77.5	2138	9.8
en_ewt	25096	16653	66.4	2324	14.0
en_gum	13326	8880	66.6	1691	19.0
en_lines	15623	9796	62.7	1007	10.3
en_partut	3408	2179	63.9	179	8.2
es_ancora	52617	43676	83.0	8196	18.8
es_gsd	12000	6854	57.1	646	9.4
fr_gsd	10021	5770	57.6	400	6.9
fr_partut	2604	1752	67.3	147	8.4
fr_sequoia	10050	6306	62.7	384	6.1
hi_hdtb	35430	30137	85.1	2605	8.6
id_gsd	11780	6036	51.2	661	11.0
ja_gsd	12438	219	1.8	21	9.6
ko_gsd	11677	82	0.7	35	42.7
pt_bosque	10199	6553	64.3	1062	16.2
pt_gsd	31496	3065	9.7	294	9.6
ru_gsd	11548	7268	62.9	3236	44.5
zh_gsd	12012	1349	11.2	112	8.3

Table 2: The number of lemmas in each test corpus showing (1) the number and percentage for which morphological features were given and (2) the number and percentage of wordforms generated via regex.

Across all corpora, projective linearizations of lemmas in the dev set generate the highest BLEU scores. The difference between the first two bars for each corpus indicates how well the inflection subtask performed, and the difference between the second and third bars indicates the performance of the linearization subtask.

In all languages other than Chinese, poor inflections hurt the scores, and in Arabic, Japanese, Korean, and Russian, the inflections were quite detrimental. The regex methodology used in the current study depends on a set of morphological features to use as a key for finding an appropriate pattern, but corpora vary as to what proportion of lemmas have this morphological listing. Table 2 shows the number and rate of lemmas at which morphological features are listed, as well as how many of those were generated by the regex pattern-substitution methodology. For example, of the 28,264 lemmas in the Arabic (PADT) test corpus, 21,901 (77.5%) had associated morphological information; of those 21,901, only 2,138 (9.8%) were generated via regex substitution—the other 90.2% were found in the training data.

Both Japanese (GSD) and Korean (GSD) provide exceedingly low rates of morphological data—1.8% and 0.7%, respectively. Thus the differential between the BLEU scores of projective wordforms (first, red bars) and projective lemmas (second, green bars) in Figure 4 for these two lan-

guages is likely due to lack of morphological feature sets in the corpora.

Corpora with especially high rates of wordforms being generated via regex rather than found in the training data include Portuguese (Bosque) at 16.2%, Spanish (Ancora) at 18.8%, English (GUM) at 19%, Korean (GSD) at 42.7%[4], and Russian (GSD) at 44.5%. While the performance of the inflection systems for the first three of those corpora is relatively good, the very poor performance of Russian is surprising. The cause of the exceedingly poor performance of Arabic inflection is also unclear, given the high rate of provided morphological features (77.5%) and fairly normal rate of wordform generation (9.8%); perhaps the methodology is poorly suited to Arabic and/or Russian inflectional patterns.

One possible source of error is the use of the most frequent regex pattern when generating wordforms, rather than the most detailed or specific. This likely creates a bias towards overly 'regular' forms whereby the phonetic environment is not able to properly trigger substitutions. This effect may be more strongly felt by languages with richer morphologies, such as Arabic and Russian.

In general, the reliance on orthography for defining phonetic environments for regexes and substitutions almost certainly contributes to error. This could probably be improved by using IPA transcriptions or distinctive phonetic features rather than standard orthography, as well as a more flexible regex patterning which could better handle allophones. A relatively straightforward way to implement a bit of phonetic flexibility would be to utilize substitution matrices when aligning lemmas to their target wordforms (Smith and Waterman, 1981). This approach would allow, for example, a [b] and [v] to be seen as more similar than other phones, and could therefore be combined into a single regex atom for a given language.

The second and third bars in Figure 4 for each corpus differentiate based on projectivity: in all cases the non-projective linearizations (third, blue bars) have lower scores than the projective ones (second, red bars). This is not too surprising, since a single misplaced word can drastically reduce BLEU scores. However, if the GNN were able to better learn dependency distance tolerances, the non-projective sorting algorithm should produce

---

[4]The exceedingly low rate of provided morphological features for Korean (GSD) renders the percentage of generated wordforms a rather uninformative number for this corpus.

results similar to the projective algorithm, if not better, given the existence of non-projective sentences in possibly all natural languages (Ferrer-i Cancho and Gómez-Rodríguez, 2016) and preference for certain linearizations such as Figure 2(b).

Because the same GNN is used to learn distances, and projectivity is only realized during linearization, the difference in performance between projective and non-projective linearizations suggests that the GNN is learning tendencies for dependents to precede or follow their heads, as well as the relative tolerances among sibling dependents, to a certain degree. However, the accuracy of those tolerances with respect to all other words in a sentence leaves room for improvement, probably via an enhanced GNN architecture.

5 Discussion

The regex-based approach to inflection employed in the current study is linguistically motivated. Regex patterns would seem to be an adequate method for modeling exemplars and grouping them into templates, and substitutions allow for productive inflectional patterns to be applied to uninflected lemmas. The choice of which regex pattern to employ for a given lemma may be more complex than outlined here—a choice between the most frequent or the most detailed, and given the error rates around inflections in Figure 4, perhaps the most detailed would perform better. Still, the notion is plausible. A trade-off between frequency and level of regex detail might go some way towards modeling the loss of increasingly obscure inflectional patterns in favor of those which are more frequent.

DepDist tackles the problem of linearization entirely within a dependency framework. Words are represented by their syntactic embeddings, and the neural network is a graph built from a dependency tree. The learning of dependency distance tolerances is accomplished via these embeddings and graphs. The only point at which the notion of linearity comes into play is after all learning has completed, when distance tolerances are fed into a deterministic algorithm for topological sorting.

This approach is quite different from an n-gram language model or one based on machine translation. With DepDist, if adjacent words are not connected by a dependency relation, their linear adjacency is in a sense emergent, a necessary by-product of converting a two-dimensional tree into a one-dimensional linearization. Thus the order of sibling dependents is not directly modeled, but is instead implicitly reflected in the relative distance tolerances. However, due to message passing, siblings can be made indirectly aware of each other—since dependents pass their embedding node attributes to the head, the calculation of edge attributes between the head and each dependent reflects the presence of other siblings.

Further, DepDist is not an end-to-end machine-learning model. The actual linearized strings are not the target; rather, individual dependency distance tolerances are the target of learning. The data structure which results from weighting the edges of a directed graph and its subsequent topological sort generate a linearization based on dependency distance tolerance.

Although a projectivity constraint was artificially employed in the implementation of DepDist outlined here, if the GNN were to better learn dependency distance tolerances, that constraint would not be needed. Instead, observed rates of projectivity among languages should arise as a result of topologically sorting based on distance tolerance. Crucially, the rate of projectivity is not directly learned. A GNN—or human—is exposed to language in which head-dependent pairs have certain distance tolerances, tolerances which can be learned. Assembling the pairs such that these tolerances are obeyed results in largely projective linearizations, though not exclusively so, thereby reflecting a tendency towards projectivity.

Dependency distance tolerance seems to be a psychologically real measure. In the current study, the tolerances are learned via GNN, but they might be operationalized in other ways, especially by psycholinguistic or information-theoretic measures (cf. Scontras et al., 2017; Dyer, 2018; Hahn et al., 2018). That is, a dependent which tolerates a large linear distance from its head, such as the adverb *tomorrow* in the example in Figure 2, may have a lower pointwise mutual information (Church and Hanks, 1989) or surprisal (Futrell and Levy, 2017) with its head, or may have higher or lower subjectivity than the auxiliary *is*. As such, because *tomorrow* and *scheduled* belong together semantically less than *is* and *scheduled*, or they depend on each other less, the adverb is allowed to be placed farther away. This is a sort of conceptual inversion of Behaghel (1932)—what does not necessarily belong together can be placed far apart.

5.1 Future directions

Given that the performance of DepDist is competitive with many of the other submissions to SR '19, the approach seems promising. The error analysis indicates deficiencies in the rule-based approach to inflections, possibly due to reliance on orthography to approximate phonetic environments, as well as a reliance on morphological-feature listings which may not always be present in Universal Dependencies corpora. The GNN's ability to learn accurate dependency distance tolerances at the sentence level is promising, but leaves significant room for improvement. For example, the GNN's architecture may be too small, the syntactic embedding framework may be too old to properly generalize from training data, the training data may be too limited, and the training of only 5 epochs may be too few to properly learn distance tolerances. All of these areas can be explored in future study.

Finally, training was confined to a single training corpus per language—future study should at least take advantage of all available corpora for a given language. More promisingly, transfer learning could be employed to take advantage of cross-linguistic tendencies regarding dependency distance tolerance.

6 Summary

This paper describes the DepDist submission to SR '19. The approach to inflecting uses regular expressions and substitutions to learn morphological prototypes from training exemplars, which can be applied to words unseen during training. Linearizing a tree is accomplished by first learning dependency distance tolerances via syntactic word embeddings and a graph neural network (GNN), then sorting the resulting edge-weighted directed acyclic graph (DAG) according to either projective or non-projective algorithms, only the former of which were submitted. The results of DepDist are competitive, the approach is linguistically grounded, and there is ample room for improvement to both the inflectional module and GNN architecture.

Acknowledgments

Special thanks to Ariel Gutman for insight into tree-sorting algorithms and to the anonymous reviewers for their comments and suggestions.

References

Peter W. Battaglia, Jessica B. Hamrick, Victor Bapst, Alvaro Sanchez-Gonzalez, Vinicius Zambaldi, Mateusz Malinowski, Andrea Tacchetti, David Raposo, Adam Santoro, Ryan Faulkner, Caglar Gulcehre, Francis Song, Andrew Ballard, Justin Gilmer, George Dahl, Ashish Vaswani, Kelsey Allen, Charles Nash, Victoria Langston, Chris Dyer, Nicolas Heess, Daan Wierstra, Pushmeet Kohli, Matt Botvinick, Oriol Vinyals, Yujia Li, and Razvan Pascanu. 2018. Relational inductive biases, deep learning, and graph networks. *arXiv:1806.01261 [cs, stat]*.

Otto Behaghel. 1932. *Deutsche Syntax eine geschichtliche Darstellung*. Carl Winters Unversitätsbuchhandlung, Heidelberg.

Jean Berko. 1958. The Child's Learning of English Morphology. *WORD*, 14(2-3):150–177.

Michael M. Bronstein, Joan Bruna, Yann LeCun, Arthur Szlam, and Pierre Vandergheynst. 2017. Geometric deep learning: going beyond Euclidean data. *IEEE Signal Processing Magazine*, 34(4):18–42. ArXiv: 1611.08097.

Joan L. Bybee and Carol Lynn Moder. 1983. Morphological Classes as Natural Categories. *Language*, 59(2):251–270.

Ramon Ferrer-i Cancho and Carlos Gómez-Rodríguez. 2016. Crossings as a side effect of dependency lengths. *Complexity*, 21(S2):320–328.

Lewis Carroll. 1872. *Through the Looking-Glass, and What Alice Found There*. MacMillan and Co, London.

Thiago Castro Ferreira, Sander Wubben, and Emiel Krahmer. 2018. Surface Realization Shared Task 2018 (SR18): The Tilburg University Approach. In *Proceedings of the First Workshop on Multilingual Surface Realisation*, pages 35–38, Melbourne, Australia. Association for Computational Linguistics.

Kenneth Ward Church and Patrick Hanks. 1989. Word association norms, mutual information, and lexicography. In *Proceedings of the 27th annual meeting on Association for Computational Linguistics -*, pages 76–83, Vancouver, British Columbia, Canada. Association for Computational Linguistics.

Peter J. A. Cock, Tiago Antao, Jeffrey T. Chang, Brad A. Chapman, Cymon J. Cox, Andrew Dalke, Iddo Friedberg, Thomas Hamelryck, Frank Kauff, Bartek Wilczynski, and Michiel J. L. de Hoon. 2009. Biopython: freely available Python tools for computational molecular biology and bioinformatics. *Bioinformatics*, 25(11):1422–1423.

William Dyer. 2018. Integration complexity and the order of cosisters. In *Proceedings of the Second Workshop on Universal Dependencies (UDW 2018)*, pages 55–65, Brussels, Belgium. Association for Computational Linguistics.

William Dyer. 2019. Weighted posets: Learning surface order from dependency trees. In *Proceedings of the 18th International Workshop on Treebanks and Linguistic Theories*, Paris, France. Association for Computational Linguistics.

Henry Elder and Chris Hokamp. 2018. Generating High-Quality Surface Realizations Using Data Augmentation and Factored Sequence Models. In *Proceedings of the First Workshop on Multilingual Surface Realisation*, pages 49–53, Melbourne, Australia. Association for Computational Linguistics.

David Embick and Alec Marantz. 2005. Cognitive neuroscience and the English past tense: Comments on the paper by Ullman et al.*. *Brain and Language*, 93(2):243–247.

Richard Futrell and Roger Levy. 2017. Noisy-context surprisal as a human sentence processing cost model. In *Proceedings of the 15th Conference of the European Chapter of the Association for Computational Linguistics*, pages 688–698.

Richard Futrell, Kyle Mahowald, and Edward Gibson. 2015. Large-scale evidence of dependency length minimization in 37 languages. *Proceedings of the National Academy of Sciences*, 112(33):10336–10341.

Edward Gibson. 2000. The dependency locality theory: A distance-based theory of linguistic complexity. *Image, language, brain*, pages 95–126.

Justin Gilmer, Samuel S. Schoenholz, Patrick F. Riley, Oriol Vinyals, and George E. Dahl. 2017. Neural Message Passing for Quantum Chemistry. *arXiv:1704.01212 [cs]*.

Carlos Gómez-Rodríguez. 2016. Restricted Non-Projectivity: Coverage vs. Efficiency. *Computational Linguistics*, 42(4):809–817.

Michael Hahn, Judith Degen, Noah Goodman, Dan Jurafsky, and Richard Futrell. 2018. An Information-Theoretic Explanation of Adjective Ordering Preferences. In *Proceedings of the 40th annual conference of the Cognitive Science Society.*, London. Cognitive Science Society.

John A. Hawkins. 1994. *A Performance Theory of Order and Constituency*. Cambridge University Press, Cambridge.

John A. Hawkins. 2004. *Efficiency and Complexity in Grammars*. Oxford University Press, Oxford.

Richard Hudson. 1995. Measuring syntactic difficulty.

David King and Michael White. 2018. The OSU Realizer for SRST '18: Neural Sequence-to-Sequence Inflection and Incremental Locality-Based Linearization. In *Proceedings of the First Workshop on Multilingual Surface Realisation*, pages 39–48, Melbourne, Australia. Association for Computational Linguistics.

Donald Knuth. 1998. *The Art of Computer Programming*, volume 3: Sorting and Searching. Addison-Wesley, Boston.

Omer Levy and Yoav Goldberg. 2014. Dependency-Based Word Embeddings. In *ACL (2)*, pages 302–208. Citeseer.

Haitao Liu, Chunshan Xu, and Junying Liang. 2017. Dependency distance: A new perspective on syntactic patterns in natural languages. *Physics of Life Reviews*, 21:171–193.

Andreas Madsack, Johanna Heininger, Nyamsuren Davaasambuu, Vitaliia Voronik, Michael Käufl, and Robert Weißgraeber. 2018. AX Semantics' Submission to the Surface Realization Shared Task 2018. In *Proceedings of the First Workshop on Multilingual Surface Realisation*, pages 54–57, Melbourne, Australia. Association for Computational Linguistics.

Francesco Mambrini and Marco Passarotti. 2013. Non-Projectivity in the Ancient Greek Dependency Treebank. In *DepLing*, pages 177–186.

Solomon Marcus. 1965. Sur la notion de projectivité. *Mathematical Logic Quarterly*, 11(2):181–192.

Simon Mille, Anja Belz, Bernd Bohnet, Yvette Graham, and Leo Wanner. 2019. The Second Multilingual Surface Realisation Shared Task (SR'19): Overview and Evaluation Results. In *Proceedings of the 2nd Workshop on Multilingual Surface Realisation (MSR), 2019 Conference on Empirical Methods in Natural Language Processing (EMNLP)*. Hong Kong, China.

Joakim Nivre. 2006. *Inductive Dependency Parsing*. Springer, Dordrecht, The Netherlands.

Kishore Papineni, Salim Roukos, Todd Ward, and Wei-Jing Zhu. 2002. Bleu: a Method for Automatic Evaluation of Machine Translation. In *Proceedings of 40th Annual Meeting of the Association for Computational Linguistics*, pages 311–318, Philadelphia, Pennsylvania, USA. Association for Computational Linguistics.

Emilio Pascual. 1977. *El Fablistanón*. Edival-Ortells.

Emily Pitler, Sampath Kannan, and Mitchell Marcus. 2013. Finding Optimal 1-Endpoint-Crossing Trees. *Transactions of the Association for Computational Linguistics*, 1:13–24.

Prasada and S. Pinker. 1993. Generalizations of regular and irregular morphology. *Language and Cognitive Processes*, 8(1):1–56.

Yevgeniy Puzikov and Iryna Gurevych. 2018. BinLin: A Simple Method of Dependency Tree Linearization. In *Proceedings of the First Workshop on Multilingual Surface Realisation*, pages 13–28, Melbourne, Australia. Association for Computational Linguistics.

Jan Rijkhoff. 1986. Word Order Universals Revisited: The Principle of Head Proximity. *Belgian Journal of Linguistics*, 1:95–125.

Gregory Scontras, Judith Degen, and Noah D. Goodman. 2017. Subjectivity Predicts Adjective Ordering Preferences. *Open Mind*, pages 1–14.

Shreyansh Singh, Ayush Sharma, Avi Chawla, and A.K. Singh. 2018. IIT (BHU) Varanasi at MSR-SRST 2018: A Language Model Based Approach for Natural Language Generation. In *Proceedings of the First Workshop on Multilingual Surface Realisation*, pages 29–34, Melbourne, Australia. Association for Computational Linguistics.

T.F. Smith and M.S. Waterman. 1981. Identification of common molecular subsequences. *Journal of Molecular Biology*, 147(1):195–197.

Marco Antonio Sobrevilla Cabezudo and Thiago Pardo. 2018. NILC-SWORNEMO at the Surface Realization Shared Task: Exploring Syntax-Based Word Ordering using Neural Models. In *Proceedings of the First Workshop on Multilingual Surface Realisation*, pages 58–64, Melbourne, Australia. Association for Computational Linguistics.

Adam Wiemerslage, Miikka Silfverberg, and Mans Hulden. 2018. Phonological Features for Morphological Inflection. In *Proceedings of the Fifteenth Workshop on Computational Research in Phonetics, Phonology, and Morphology*, pages 161–166, Brussels, Belgium. Association for Computational Linguistics.

Richard Wiese. 1996. Phonological versus morphological rules: on German Umlaut and Ablaut. *Journal of Linguistics*, 32(1):113–135.

Zonghan Wu, Shirui Pan, Fengwen Chen, Guodong Long, Chengqi Zhang, and Philip S. Yu. 2019. A Comprehensive Survey on Graph Neural Networks. *arXiv:1901.00596 [cs, stat]*.

Himanshu Yadav, Samar Husain, and Richard Futrell. 2019. Are formal restrictions on crossing dependencies epiphenomenal? In *Proceedings of the 18th International Workshop on Treebanks and Linguistic Theories*, Paris, France. Association for Computational Linguistics.

BME-UW at SR'19: Surface realization with Interpreted Regular Tree Grammars

Ádám Kovács[1,2], Evelin Ács[1], Judit Ács[1,2,3], András Kornai[2], Gábor Recski[1,4]
[1]Dept. of Automation and Applied Informatics, Budapest U of Technology
`lastname.firstname@aut.bme.hu`

[2]SZTAKI Insititute of Computer Science
`andras@kornai.com`

[3]University of Washington

[4]Sclable

Abstract

The Surface Realization Shared Task involves mapping Universal Dependency graphs to raw text, i.e. restoring word order and inflection from a graph of typed, directed dependencies between lemmas. Interpreted Regular Tree Grammars (IRTGs) encode the correspondence between generations in multiple algebras, and have previously been used for semantic parsing from raw text. Our system induces an IRTG for simultaneously building pairs of surface forms and UD graphs in the SR'19 training data, then prunes this grammar for each UD graph in the test data for efficient parsing and generation of the surface ordering of lemmas. For the inflection step we use a standard sequence-to-sequence model with a biLSTM encoder and an LSTM decoder with attention. Both components of our system are available on GitHub under an MIT license.

1 Introduction

The 'shallow' (T1) track of the Surface Realization task (Mille et al., 2019) involves mapping Universal Dependencies (UD) graphs (De Marneffe et al., 2014) to surface forms, i.e. restoring word order and inflection based on the typed grammatical dependencies among a set of lemmas. We used a hybrid method that restores word order by IRTG rules, see Section 2, induced from the training data, see Section 3, and performs inflection using a standard sequence-to-sequence model with a biLSTM encoder and an LSTM decoder with attention, see Section 4. This architecture fits well with the recent trend toward eXplainable AI (Gunning, 2017), and is not as data-hungry as end-to-end neural systems. Only 8 of the 12 teams participated on the non-English portion of the track, with BME-UW ranked second in automated, and generally in the top three in human evaluation. The IRTG based system is available under `https://github.com/adaamko/surface_realization`, the inflection system was trained using the framework under `https://github.com/juditacs/deep-morphology`

2 Rule format: IRTGs and s-graphs

Several common tasks in natural language processing involve graph transformations, in particular those that handle syntactic trees, dependency structures such as UD, or semantic graphs such as AMR (Banarescu et al., 2013) and 4lang (Kornai et al., 2015). Interpreted Regular Tree Grammars (IRTGs) (Koller, 2015) encode the correspondence between sets of such structures and have in recent years been used to perform syntactic parsing (Koller and Kuhlmann, 2012), generation (Koller and Engonopoulos, 2017), and semantic parsing (Groschwitz et al., 2015, 2018). In previous work (Ács et al., 2019) we encoded transformations between raw text, phrase structure (PS) trees, UD and 4lang semantic graphs to build a single IRTG that allows for mapping between any pair of such structures.

IRTGs are Regular Tree Grammars in which each rule is mapped to operations in an arbitrary number of algebras. Hence, derivations of an IRTG correspond to synchronous generation of objects in each of these algebras, and an IRTG

35

Proceedings of the 2nd Workshop on Multilingual Surface Realisation (MSR 2019), pages 35–40
Hong Kong, China, November 3rd, 2019. ©2019 Association for Computational Linguistics
https://doi.org/10.18653/v1/P17

parser such as `alto` (Gontrum et al., 2017) can be used to map from one set of objects to all others. For the word order restoration task our system constructs an IRTG operating on strings and UD graphs, simultaneously constructing sentences from words and UD graphs from nodes. Operations of the simple string algebra $(S, \cdot)$ are mapped to those of an S-graph algebra (Courcelle, 1993), a formalism also used by (Groschwitz et al., 2015) to perform semantic parsing via IRTGs. Here we give only an informal overview of s-graph algebras, see (Koller and Kuhlmann, 2011; Courcelle and Engelfriet, 2012) for a more formal explanation. S-graphs are graphs whose vertices may be labeled by one of a countable set of *sources*. The central operation of an s-graph algebra is the binary `merge`, which unifies pairs of s-graphs in a way that vertices with matching sources are merged, i.e. when two s-graphs G_1 and G_2 are `merged`, the resulting s-graph G' will contain all nodes of G_1 and G_2, and when a pair of nodes $(v_1, v_2) \in E(G_1) \times E(G_2)$ have the same source name, they will be mapped to a single node v' in G' that has all adjacent edges of v_1 and v_2. Sources can also be *renamed* or *forgotten* using the operations $ren_{a\leftrightarrow b}$ and fg_a, where a and b are sources from the set $\mathcal{A}$. Next we shall provide a small example with string and s-graph interpretations.

The Algebraic Language Toolkit, or `alto`[1] (Gontrum et al., 2017), is an open-source parser for IRTGs that implements a variety of algebras to use as intepretations of IRTGs, including the string algebra and s-graph algebra. An `alto` grammar file must declare all interpretation algebras and for each RTG rule provide mappings to operations in each of these algebras. Figure 1 shows a minimal example of an IRTG with two interpretations. The abstract RTG rule `_nsubj`, so named after the corresponding UD relation, has two abstract arguments, designated `VERB` and `NOUN`. The `string` interpretation establishes that the surface form of the second argument (`NOUN`) is to precede the first argument (`VERB`). The `ud` interpretation adds a directed `nsubj` edge between the subgraphs corresponding to each argument, by a series of `rename`, `merge`, and `forget` operations. Angle brackets after nodes indicate source names. In our s-graph grammars, every subgraph at every point of the derivation

---

[1] `https://github.com/coli-saar/alto`

```
interpretation string:
de.up.ling.irtg.algebra.StringAlgebra

interpretation ud:
de.up.ling.irtg.algebra.GraphAlgebra

VERB -> _nsubj(VERB, NOUN)
[string] *(?2, ?1)
[ud] f_dep1(merge(
    merge(?1, "(r<root> :nsubj d1<dep1>)
        ↪ "),
    r_dep1(?2)))

PROPN -> John
[string] John
[ud] "(John<root> / John)"

VERB -> sleeps
[string] sleeps
[ud] "(sleeps<root> / sleeps)"
```

Figure 1: Toy IRTG grammar

has exactly one node labeled with the `<root>` source, indicating the head of the phrase, which could be connected to a `ROOT` node to create a well-formed UD-graph. The intepretation in our example contains a graph literal, describing the graph $r\texttt{<root>} \xrightarrow{nsubj} \texttt{d1<dep1>}$. This graph is first merged with the graph corresponding to the first argument, then the result is merged with the graph obtained by renaming the root source of the second argument's graph to `dep`. `r_dep` and `f_dep` are `Alto`'s shorthands for renaming the root source to `dep` and forgetting the `dep` source. Terminal rules create string and UD literals. This toy grammar is therefore a representation of the parallel derivations of the sentence *John sleeps* and the UD graph $\texttt{sleeps} \xrightarrow{nsubj} \texttt{John}$. The next section will describe our method for building such grammars automatically from UD datasets and using them for the word order restoration step of the Surface Realization task.

3 Rule induction

As seen already in the example IRTG in the previous section, we represent the correspondence between strings and UD graphs as synchronized generations in two algebras. Since our goal is to learn rules of such a grammar using UD datasets containing sentences and corresponding UD graphs, we need a method to assign derivations to UD graphs in the s-graph algebra, i.e. a series of steps that build the UD graph from its nodes, through subgraphs. We choose to represent the construc-

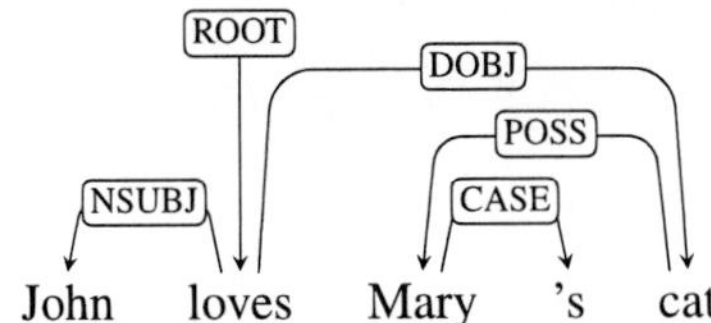

Figure 2: Sample UD analysis

```
S! -> start_VERB(VERB)
PROPN -> rule_1(PROPN,PART)
NOUN -> rule_2(NOUN,PROPN)
VERB -> rule_3(VERB,PROPN,NOUN)
```

Figure 3: sample RTG rules (interpretations omitted)

tion of UD graphs as follows: for each node in the graph we establish one generation step, which is responsible for attaching all its dependents to it. The UD graph depicted in Figure 2 would hence correspond to the RTG rules in Figure 3 (interpretations are omitted for better readability). Note that we create rules that operate at the part-of-speech level, lemmas can then be inserted by terminal rules generated separately for each sentence.

The simplest approach to constructing a (weighted) IRTG would be to simply include all rules "observed" in the training data, along with a probablity calculated from the relative frequency of a given configuration among all occurences of a head of a particular POS-tag. In practice we prune this grammar to include only those rules that are applicable to a given sentence and that are compatible with the value of the `lin` feature (see below), and parse each UD graph using a much smaller grammar. We may also add new rules to the pruned grammar to ensure a successful parsing process (that may or may not yield the correct results).

After generating a static list of IRTG rules from the training data, we dynamically generate a reduced IRTG grammar for each sentence. In a preprocessing step we read all UD graphs that are to be parsed, and for each node and its set of dependents we check if there's a rule in our grammar covering this subgraph. If there's more than one matching rule, we check if the `lin` feature is present in the input, which allows us to identify the single matching rule. If we identify a unique rule matching the subgraph, we add one to its frequency to increase the rule's probability. In other words, sufficiently specific patterns of the

test data are used as additional training data. If no rules matching a subgraph are present in our static grammar, we add binary rules for each dependent, some of which rules may already be present in the grammar, in which case we increase their frequencies. This ensures that the grammar will cover the new subgraph but will prefer to build it from subgraphs we have already seen in the training data. If the `lin` feature is not present in the input, we add two rules per dependent, corresponding to each possible word order.

When parsing individual UD graphs, we prune the grammar by deleting all rules that generate POS tags that are not present in the graph (or generate more instances of a POS tag than the tag's total frequency in the graph). We further delete all rules that contradict any `lin` features present in the input (only the $+/-$ sign of feature values is considered). This step must be skipped if it would mean deleting both of a pair of rules, e.g. because a word has punctuation both before and after it. We can then use this pruned grammar to obtain the most probable parse of the UD-graph and the corresponding string interpretation. The average parsing time of `alto` is around 2 seconds per sentence. In a few cases, sentence length would slow down parsing considerably; for all graphs that would take more than one minute to parse (less than 1.5% of the data) we fall back to a grammar that uses binary rules only, i.e. connects all edges of the graph one-by-one.

We illustrate the kind of decisions the parser must make through a simple example. Consider the sentence in Figure 4. Our system correctly predicted the word order based on the UD graph, the top parse involves attaching all dependencies of the predicate *enjoy* using the two rules in Figure 5 (s-graph interpretations are omitted for readability). The second most probable derivation applies the three rules in Figure 6 and would yield the incorrect surface realization *I enjoyed really reading it.*

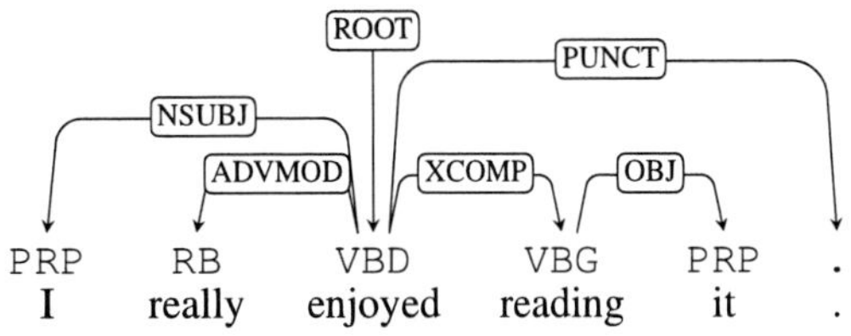

Figure 4: Example from the UD dataset

```
VBD -> rule_22276(VBD,PRP,RB,VBG,PERIOD) [8.14e-06]
[string] *(*(*(?2,?3),*(?1,?4)),?5)

VBG -> rule_615(VBG,PRP) [4.88e-05]
[string] *(?1,?2)
```

Figure 5: Most likely parse of the graph in Fig. 4

```
VBD -> rule_2004(VBD,PRP,VBG,PERIOD) [1.62e-05]
[string] *(*(?2,?1),*(?3,?4))

VBD -> rule_2698(VBD,RB) [1.22e-05]
[string] *(?1,?2)

VBG -> rule_615(VBG,PRP) [4.88e-05]
[string] *(?1,?2)
```

Figure 6: Second most likely parse

These parses illustrate a more general phenomenon: since the probabilities of individual rules are roughly similar, the system prefers derivations with fewer rules, which attach more nodes at the same time. Counterexamples with radically different rule probabilities are in principle possible, but on average the system prefers specific (more detailed) rules over generic (less detailed) ones, which makes the Elsewhere Principle (Kiparsky, 1973) an emergent, rather than an externally enforced, property of the grammar as a whole.

4   Reinflection

In order to map sequences of lemmas to surface forms, we train a standard seq2seq (Sutskever et al., 2014) system with a bidirectional LSTM (Hochreiter and Schmidhuber, 1997) encoder and an LSTM decoder with Luong's attention (Luong et al., 2015). We include all CoNLL-U fields in the input, namely the lemma, the UPOS, the XPOS and the list of morphological tags. We also experimented with adding the position of the token in the sentence (`original_id=N`) during training time. For inference, we use the order generated by the IRTG component. This improves the performance in most, but not all languages (see Table 1). Figure 7 shows an English example of our input and output format.

We split the sentences from the train data into 80% train and 20% development sets for the inflection module. A full-scale hyperparameter search being prohibitively expensive, we only tried a few hyperparameter combinations and use the ones performing best on the dev set for the final submission. Table 1 lists the best configuration

```
Input: <L> f a m i l y </L> <P> UPOS=
   ↪ NOUN XPOS=NNS </P> <T> Number=
   ↪ Plur original_id=2 </T>
Output: f a m i l i e s
```

Figure 7: Example input and output of the inflection component.

and the word accuracy on the dev set by language. We use the Adam optimizer ($lr = 0.001, \beta_1 = 0.9, \beta_2 = 0.999$) with early stopping based on dev accuracy and loss. Dropout is set to 0.4. Including the position of a token in the sentence (`use position`) is also a hyperparameter.

5   Evaluation

5.1   The Surface Realization Task

We participate in the 'shallow' track of the 2019 Surface Realization Shared Task (SR'19). The task involves mapping UD graphs of lemmas to surface forms in 11 languages. Training data for the task was created from the Universal Dependencies treebanks (Nivre et al., 2018) using methods described in (Mille et al., 2018) and contains UD treebanks with word forms replaced by lemmas word order information removed via scrambling. Two additional features have been added to the dataset, the `lin` feature encoding the relative order of a word and its governor and the `originalId` for reconstructing word order (in the training data only).

5.2   Results

The primary method of evaluation at SR'19 is human evaluation of two aspects of each output sentence: readability and semantic similarity to the original sentence. The detailed results are presented in (Mille et al., 2019). On 4 of the 5 datasets involved in the human evaluation scheme, our system was outperformed significantly by only two other systems in terms of readability. In terms of semantic similarity we are outperformed by only 1 or 2 systems on three of the five datasets. Automatic evaluation was performed using three metrics, described also in (Mille et al., 2019). Table 2 presents macro-average values for the top four teams, those that submitted outputs for all datasets. Our system ranks second among these four teams on two out of three metrics. On individual datasets, our system mostly performs below or around the average of all systems, with the ex-

	use position	batch size	hidden size	layers	embedding size	dev acc
ar	True	128	512	2	100	93.68
en	True	128	512	2	100	96.09
es	True	128	512	2	100	98.70
fr	True	128	512	2	100	94.59
hi	True	128	512	2	100	98.26
id	True	256	128	1	100	93.77
ja	False	32	1024	2	100	91.61
ko	True	128	512	2	100	98.43
pt	True	128	512	2	100	91.43
ru	True	128	512	2	100	97.46
zh	False	32	128	1	100	98.81

Table 1: Highest performing configurations for each language. Dev acc refers to a randomly selected subsection of the train data as the dev sets did not have gold standard inflection.

	BLEU	NIST	DIST
IMS	79.97	12.79	81.62
BME-UW	50.04	11.39	56.11
LORIA	47.67	10.32	65.78
Tilburg	45.18	10.05	56.11

Table 2: Macro-average of the top four systems across all datasets

ception of one Russian and two Korean datasets where we are outperformed by only one system (IMS).

6 Conclusions, further work

The weighting scheme described in Section 3 is in many ways similar to the way psycholinguists think about grammatical rules. Those rules that are based on fewer examples are used more rarely. In the limiting case, singleton examples are rarely abstracted into rules, they are memorized as is, and the key mechanism for such examples to override the general rules, e.g. that *mice* overrides *mouses*, is the same Elsewhere Principle (Giegerich, 2001) that we see as a derived, emergent property of the system.

Perhaps one modification that would bring the system even closer to psychological reality would be to use morphological features when restoring the id-s. While this remains future work, we consider it a strong point in favor of XAI that such questions can be raised: explainability makes it possible to leverage decades of psycholinguistic work, currently almost entirely ignored in the deep neural net paradigm which, in its laboratory pure form, pays no attention to biological or psychological evidence.

References

Laura Banarescu, Claire Bonial, Shu Cai, Madalina Georgescu, Kira Griffitt, Ulf Hermjakob, Kevin Knight, Philipp Koehn, Martha Palmer, and Nathan Schneider. 2013. Abstract meaning representation for sembanking. In *Proceedings of the 7th Linguistic Annotation Workshop and Interoperability with Discourse*, pages 178–186, Sofia, Bulgaria. Association for Computational Linguistics.

Bruno Courcelle. 1993. Graph grammars, monadic second-order logic and the theory of graph minors. *Contemporary Mathematics*, 147:565–565.

Bruno Courcelle and Joost Engelfriet. 2012. *Graph structure and monadic second-order logic*. Cambridge University Press.

Marie-Catherine De Marneffe, Timothy Dozat, Natalia Silveira, Katri Haverinen, Filip Ginter, Joakim Nivre, and Christopher D Manning. 2014. Universal Stanford dependencies: A cross-linguistic typology. In *LREC*, volume 14, pages 4585–92.

Heinz J. Giegerich. 2001. Synonymy blocking and the elsewhere condition: lexical morphology and the speaker. *Transactions of the Philological Society*, 99(1):65–98.

Johannes Gontrum, Jonas Groschwitz, Alexander Koller, and Christoph Teichmann. 2017. Alto: Rapid prototyping for parsing and translation. In *Proceedings of the Software Demonstrations of the 15th Conference of the European Chapter of the Association for Computational Linguistics*, pages 29–32.

Jonas Groschwitz, Alexander Koller, and Christoph Teichmann. 2015. Graph parsing with s-graph grammars. In *Proceedings of the 53rd ACL and 7th IJC-
NLP*, Beijing.

Jonas Groschwitz, Matthias Lindemann, Meaghan
Fowlie, Mark Johnson, and Alexander Koller. 2018.
AMR dependency parsing with a typed semantic algebra. In *Proceedings of the 56th Annual Meeting of
the Association for Computational Linguistics (Volume 1: Long Papers)*, pages 1831–1841, Melbourne,
Australia. Association for Computational Linguistics.

David Gunning. 2017. Explainable Artificial Intelligence (XAI). Defense Advanced
Research Projects Agency, DARPA/I20.
https://www.darpa.mil/attachments/
XAIProgramUpdate.pdf.

Sepp Hochreiter and Jürgen Schmidhuber. 1997.
Long short-term memory. *Neural Computation*,
9(8):1735–1780.

Paul Kiparsky. 1973. 'elsewhere' in phonology. In
Stephen R. Anderson and Paul Kiparsky, editors, *A
Festschrift for Morris Halle*, pages 93–106. Holt,
Rinehart, and Winston, New York.

Alexander Koller. 2015. Semantic construction with
graph grammars. In *Proceedings of the 14th International Conference on Computational Semantics
(IWCS)*, London.

Alexander Koller and Nikos Engonopoulos. 2017. Integrated sentence generation using charts. In *Proceedings of the 10th International Conference on
Natural Language Generation*, pages 139–143.

Alexander Koller and Marco Kuhlmann. 2011. A generalized view on parsing and translation. In *Proceedings of the 12th International Conference on
Parsing Technologies (IWPT)*, Dublin.

Alexander Koller and Marco Kuhlmann. 2012. Decomposing tag algorithms using simple algebraiza-
tions. In *Proceedings of the 11th International
Workshop on Tree Adjoining Grammars and Related
Formalisms (TAG+ 11)*, pages 135–143.

András Kornai, Judit Ács, Márton Makrai, Dávid Márk
Nemeskey, Katalin Pajkossy, and Gábor Recski.
2015. Competence in lexical semantics. In *Proceedings of the Fourth Joint Conference on Lexical
and Computational Semantics (*SEM 2015)*, pages
165–175, Denver, Colorado. Association for Computational Linguistics.

Thang Luong, Hieu Pham, and Christopher D. Manning. 2015. Effective approaches to attention-based
neural machine translation. In *Proceedings of the
2015 Conference on Empirical Methods in Natural
Language Processing*, pages 1412–1421. Association for Computational Linguistics.

Simon Mille, Anja Belz, Bernd Bohnet, Yvette Graham, and Leo Wanner. 2019. The Second Multilingual Surface Realisation Shared Task (SR'19):
Overview and Evaluation Results. In *Proceedings of
the 2nd Workshop on Multilingual Surface Realisation (MSR), 2019 Conference on Empirical Methods
in Natural Language Processing (EMNLP)*, Hong
Kong, China.

Simon Mille, Anja Belz, Bernd Bohnet, and Leo Wanner. 2018. Underspecified universal dependency
structures as inputs for multilingual surface realisation. In *Proceedings of the 11th International
Conference on Natural Language Generation*, pages
199–209, Tilburg University, The Netherlands. Association for Computational Linguistics.

Joakim Nivre, Mitchell Abrams, Željko Agić, et al.
2018. Universal dependencies 2.3. LIN-
DAT/CLARIN digital library at the Institute of Formal and Applied Linguistics (ÚFAL), Faculty of
Mathematics and Physics, Charles University.

Ilya Sutskever, Oriol Vinyals, and Quoc V. Le. 2014.
Sequence to sequence learning with neural net-
works. In *Proc. NIPS*, pages 3104–3112, Montreal,
CA.

Evelin Ács, Ákos Holló-Szabó, and Gábor Recski.
2019. Parsing noun phrases with Interpreted Regular Tree Grammars. In *XV. Magyar Számítógépes
Nyelvészeti Konferencia*, pages 301–313.

Realizing **Universal Dependencies** Structures using a symbolic approach

Guy Lapalme
RALI-DIRO, Université de Montréal
`lapalme@iro.umontreal.ca`

Abstract

We first describe a surface realizer for Universal Dependencies (UD) structures. The system uses a symbolic approach to transform the dependency tree into a tree of constituents that is transformed into an English sentence by an existing realizer. This approach was then adapted for the two shared tasks of SR'19. The system is quite fast and showed competitive results for English sentences using automatic and manual evaluation measures.

1   Introduction

This paper describe the system that we submitted to the Surface Realization Shared Task 2019 (SR'19)[1] in conjunction with Second Workshop on Multilingual Surface Realization (Mille et al., 2019). The data used by this shared task was created by modifying original Universal Dependencies structures (Nivre et al., 2016) (UD) to create two tracks:

Shallow Track (T1) in which word order is permuted and tokens have been lemmatized and some information about linear order about the governor has been added. The task consists in determining the word order and inflecting the words.

Deep Track (T2) in which functional and surface-oriented morphological information has been removed from the T1 structures. The goal is to reintroduce the missing functional words and morphological features.

The creation of the data set is described in (Mille et al., 2018). The output of the systems have been evaluated using automated metrics and a subset of those, evaluated manually.

The organizers of SR'19 have taken for granted that this task would be solved using statistical and machine learning approaches, which seems to be an *obvious* way of going given the recent trends in NLP. They provide a list of *authorized* resources such as language models and distributed representations of words.

We decided to try an alternative approach by first building UD-SURFR (Universal Dependency Surface Realizer), a symbolic system for the original UD structures and then adapting it for the two tasks of SR'19. We thought it would be interesting to see how this *classical* approach compares with machine learning systems.

Written in Prolog, UD-SURFR parses the original UD structure and builds the corresponding dependency tree which is then converted to a tree of constituents realized using JSREALB,[2] a web-based English and French realizer written in JavaScript; only the English realizer is used here because we worked only on the English corpora of UD. The UD structures are provided in tab separated files in a well-defined format (see row 1 of Table 1 for a small example). Given the fact that the input and output representations are trees, Prolog seemed a natural symbolic of choice for a tree to tree transformation engine.

We are aware that *we are not following the rules* of SR'19 as we use JSREALB, a system that is not *authorized* by the competition, but we think this experiment is still interesting. It does not require any specialized hardware and huge amount of memory as is often the case by modern machine learning approaches. It has been developed using only a few hand selected examples. These results could be used as a baseline on which statistical systems could build. We have deliberately shirked from adding any statistical techniques on

---

[1] `http://taln.upf.edu/pages/msr2019-ws/SRST.html`

[2] `http://rali.iro.umontreal.ca/rali/?q=en/jsrealb-bilingual-text-realiser`

Proceedings of the 2nd Workshop on Multilingual Surface Realisation (MSR 2019), pages 41–49
Hong Kong, China, November 3rd, 2019. ©2019 Association for Computational Linguistics
https://doi.org/10.18653/v1/P17

the output of UD-SURFR just to determine how far a symbolic approach can go. In a production setting, it would surely be better to combine statistical and symbolic systems.

We did not find any text realizer that takes UD annotations as input except for Ranta and Kolachina (2017) who present an algorithm to transform many UDs into Grammatical Framework structures from with English sentences can be generated.

A UD realizer might seem pointless, because UD annotations are created from realized sentences. As UDs contains all the tokens in their original form (except for elision in some cases), the realization can be obtained trivially by listing the FORM in the second column of each line.

What we propose in this paper is a *full* realizer that uses only the lemmas and the syntactic information contained in the UD to create the final sentence from scratch which can be compared to the original. The linear ordering of the tokens is extracted from the tree structure given by the HEAD links (column 7) of the UD. We can imagine two interesting uses for such a realizer:

- Should a *What to say* module of an NLG system produce UD structures, then UD-SURFR could be used as the *How to say* module.

- Providing help to annotators to check if the information they entered is correct by regenerating the sentence from the dependencies. This enables to catch more types of errors in the annotation; this is not foolproof, but it is easier to detect a *strange* sentence than a bad link buried in lines of dependencies. During our development, we encountered a concrete example where the automatic realization revealed an error in the original annotation; the error was later confirmed by the maintainer of the corpus.

The next section shows the tree representations used by our system using a simple example from the training test. Section 3 describes the development of UD-SURFR for the original UD structures and how it was adapted for SR'19. As T1 structures are a permutation of the lines of the original structure, but we conjectured that, once the tree structure would be retrieved, the differences would be minor after *sorting* the leaves at each level of the tree. For T2, we took the realizer for T1 and *abstracted* the name of the dependencies by

reversing the transformations described in (Mille et al., 2018). Section 4 gives the results of the evaluation obtained using the evaluation scripts provided with the task. We also compare our results with the automatic and manual scores obtained by other systems that participated in the task. We conclude with some lessons learned from this development.

2 Representations

Table 1 illustrates the transformation steps between an input UD (row 1) and an English sentence using a short example from the *train* set (en_ewt-ud-train.conllu). Row 1 shows the CONLLU format,[3] a series of tab separated lines into fields giving information for each token of the sentence. Row 2 shows the dependencies either as a set of links between words (on the left part) or as a tree (on the right) Row 3 shows the Prolog structure corresponding to the tree which is transformed into the **Deep Syntactic Representation** shown in Row 4. Row 5 shows the **Surface Syntactic Representation** which is used by JSREALB to realize the sentence shown in Row 6.

2.1 UD in Prolog

The first step is to parse a group of lines in CONLLU format corresponding to UD structure and to build the corresponding tree. The root is easily identified: its HEAD (field 7) is 0. Its children are found by looking for lines that have the root as HEAD. Each child is then taken as the root of the subtree and recursively parsed and transformed in the following format, using the official CONLLU field names:

```
[DEPREL>LR, [UPOS:LEMMA | FEATS]
  | children]
```

LR is either l or r depending on whether the relation is to the left or the right of the HEAD. In Prolog, "|" separates the start of a list within brackets from the rest of the list which can be empty.

This representation keeps intact the parent-child relations and the relative ordering between the children, it also keeps track of the fact that some children occur to the left or to the right of the parent. This is easily inferred from the ID of each token compared with the value of its HEAD. This

---

[3]https://universaldependencies.org/
format.html

1	Universal Dependencies in CONLLU	``` # sent_id = weblog-juancole.com_juancole_20051126063000_ENG_20051126_063000-0020 # text = His mother was also killed in the attack. 1 His he PRON PRP Gender=Masc|... 2 nmod:poss 2 mother mother NOUN NN Number=Sing 5 nsubj:pass 3 was be AUX VBD Mood=Ind|... 5 aux:pass 4 also also ADV RB _ 5 advmod 5 killed kill VERB VBN Tense=Past|... 0 root 6 in in ADP IN _ 8 case 7 the the DET DT Definite=Def|... 8 det 8 attack attack NOUN NN Number=Sing 5 obl 9 . . PUNCT . _ 5 punct ```
2	Linked and tree representations	*(dependency link and tree diagrams for "His mother was also killed in the attack .")*

3	Universal Dependencies in Prolog	```
		[root>r, [verb:"kill",tense:past,verbform:part,voice:pass],
		        [aux:pass>l, [aux:"be",mood:ind,number:sing,person:3,
		                      tense:past,verbform:fin]],
		        [obl>l, [noun:"attack",number:sing],
		            [det>r, [det:"the",definite:def,prontype:art]],
		            [case>r, [adp:"in"]]],
		        [nsubj:pass>l, [noun:"mother",number:sing],
		            [nmod:poss>r, [pron:"he",gender:masc,
		                           number:sing,person:3,
		                           poss:yes,prontype:prs]]],
		        [punct>l, [punct:".",lin:1]],
		        [advmod>l, [adv:"also"]]]
		``

4	Deep Syntactic Representation	```
		s(vp(ls(v("kill")*t("ps"),
		        adv("also")),
		     np(d("my")*pe(3)*ow("s")*n("s")*g("m")*g("m"),
		        n("mother")*n("s")),
		     pp(p("in"),
		        np(d("the"),
		           n("attack")*n("s")))))*typ({pas:true})*a(".")
		``

5	Surface Syntactic Representation	```
		S(VP(V("kill").t("ps"),
		     Adv("also"),
		     NP(D("my").pe(3).ow("s").n("s").g("m").g("m"),
		        N("mother").n("s")),
		     PP(P("in"),
		        NP(D("the"),
		           N("attack").n("s"))))).typ({pas:true}).a(".")
		``

6	English	`His mother was killed also in the attack.`

Table 1: Representations used in the transformation of the Universal Dependencies in CONLLU format in row 1 to the sentence shown in row 6.

is useful in some cases for putting compounds and complements before or after the head. But for the T1 and T2, this information is not reliable because the nodes have been permuted and it is the job of the realizer to get the compound and complements in the right order.

2.2 Deep Syntactic Representation (DSR)

The DSR is an intermediary Prolog structure that corresponds to the constituency tree of the realized sentence. A Definite Clause Grammar (DCG) transforms this structure into the Surface Syntactic Representation (SSR) described in the next subsection. In principle, it would have been possible to create the SSR directly, but, for technical reasons, it proved more convenient to use this intermediary step.

The creation of the DSR from the UD in Prolog, which is the core part of the system, is described in Section 3.

2.3 Surface Syntactic Representation (SSR)

The SSR is the input form for JSREALB(Molins and Lapalme, 2015), a surface realizer written in JavaScript similar in principle to SIMPLENLG (Gatt and Reiter, 2009) in which programming language instructions create data structures corresponding to the constituents of the sentence to be produced. Once the data structure (a tree) is built in memory, it is traversed to produce the list of tokens of the sentence.

This data structure is built by function calls whose names are the same as the symbols usually used for classical syntax trees: for example, N to create a *noun* structure, NP for a *noun phrase*, V for a *verb*, D for a *determiner*, S for a *sentence* and so on. Options added to the structures using the dot notation can modify the values according to what is intended.

The JSREALB syntactic representation is patterned after classical constituent grammar notations. For example:

```
S(NP(D("a"),N("woman"))).n("p"),
  VP(V("eat"),
     NP(D("the"),
        A("red"),
        N("apple"))).t("ps"))
```

is the JSREALB specification for `Women ate the red apple`. Plural is indicated with the option `n("p")` where `n` indicates the number and `"p"` plural; this explains why the determiner `"a"` does not appear in the output. The verb is conjugated to past tense indicated by the option tense `t` with value `"ps"`. Agreement within the NP and between NP and VP is performed automatically.

JSREALB is aimed at web developers that want to produce web pages from data.[4] It takes care of morphology, declension and conjugation to create well-formed texts. Some options allow adding HTML tags to the realized text.

An interesting feature of JSREALB, inspired by a similar mechanism in SIMPLENLG, is

the fact that once the sentence structure has been built, many variations can be obtained by adding a set of options to the sentences, to get negative, progressive, passive, modality and some type of questions. For example, adding `.typ({neg:true,pas:true,mod:"poss"})` to the previous JSREALB structure will be realized as `The red apple cannot be eaten by women.`, a negative passive sentence with a modal verb for possibility.

Row 5 of Table 1 is the JSREALB structure that is realized as the bottom part of the table. The structure of constituents written as an active sentence has been realized as a passive one, the original complement becoming the subject. The verb was also conjugated to the past tense. This was made possible by the options given to JSREALB.

3 Deep Syntactic Representation

We now describe how a UD in Prolog is transformed into a DSR. The main idea is to *reverse engineer* the universal dependencies annotation guidelines[5].

3.1 Morphology

Word forms in UD are lists without children that are mapped to terminal symbols in JSREALB. So we transform the UD notation to the DSR one by mapping lemma and feature names, see Table 2.

As shown in the last example, we had to *normalize* pronouns to what JSREALB considers as its base form. In the morphology principles of UD[6], it is specified that

> *treebanks have considerable leeway in interpreting what "canonical or base form" means*

In the English UD corpora, it seems that the LEMMA of pronoun is always the same as its FORM. We decided to *lemmatize further* instead of merely copying the lemma as a string input to JSREALB so that verb agreement can be performed.

What should be a LEMMA is a hotly discussed subject on the UD GitHub, but there are still too many debatable lemmas such as *an*, *n't*, plural nouns etc. In one corpus, lowercasing has been applied to some proper nouns, but not all. We think

---

[4]Tutorial and demos are available at `http://rali.iro.umontreal.ca/JSrealB/current/documentation/in_action/README.html`

[5]`https://universaldependencies.org/guidelines.html`

[6]`https://universaldependencies.org/u/overview/morphology.html`

UD	JSREALB
`[noun:"mother",number:sing]`	`n("mother")*n("s")`
`[verb:"be",mood:ind,number:sing,person:3,` `    tense:pres,verbform:fin]`	`v("be")*t("p")*pe(3)`
`[pron:"we",case:nom,number:plur,person:1,` `    prontype:prs]`	`pro("I")*n("p")*pe(1)`

Table 2: Some examples of mapping between UD features and JSREALB options

it would be preferable to do a more `aggressive` lemmatization to lower the number of base forms in order to help further NLP processing that is often dependent on the number of different types.

3.2 UD to Deep Syntactic Representation

The essential idea is to transform recursively each child to produce a list of DSRs labeled with the name of the relation. The head of the relation is used as the constituent to which are added the dependents.

According to the annotation guidelines, there are two main types of dependents: nominals and clauses[7] which themselves can be simple or complex.

Nominals are triggered when the head is either a noun, an adjective, a proper noun, a pronoun or a number. When it is a noun, most often a `NP` is created using information gathered from the dependents depending on their part of speech tags such as `det`, `nummod`, `amod`, `compound` or `nmod:poss`. Special cases are needed for proper nouns, possessives with `'s`, prepositional phrases and appositions. Nouns and adjectives can be transformed to a sentence when its dependent is a `nsubj` with a possible `cop`; if the copula is not given, then `be` is used.

Clauses (both simple and complex) are triggered when a verb is encountered as the head. In this case, a `S` is created taking as subject a `expl` or `nsubj`; the `V` of the `VP` is the lemma of the head and the complements are all other dependencies in order of appearance which corresponds to the order of the original sentence.

Prepositional phrases are dealt specially by removing the preposition and dealing with the other dependents like an *ordinary* clause that is then nested into the prepositional phrase. Proper nouns with `flat` dependents are built beforehand.

This mechanism (25 rules in 100 lines of commented and indented Prolog) was first developed by reading the annotation guidelines and then refined by experience on the UD corpus.

---

[7]not to be confused with the Prolog clauses...

This exercise in transforming UD structures to JSREALB revealed an important difference in their level of representation. By design UD stays at the level of the form in the sentence, while JSREALB works at the constituent level. For example, in UD, negation is indicated by annotating `not` and the auxiliary elsewhere in the sentence, while in JSREALB the negation is given as an *option* for the whole sentence. So before starting the transformation previously described, the structure is checked for the occurrence of `part:"not"` and an auxiliary to generate the `.typ({neg:true})` option for JSREALB; these dependents are then removed for the rest of the processing. Similar checks must also be performed for passive constructs, modal verbs, progressive, perfect and even future tense in order to *abstract* the UD annotations into the corresponding structure for JSREALB.

3.3 T1 to Deep Syntactic Representation

The algorithm given in the previous section cannot be used directly on the input of the Shallow Track because the word order has been permuted while keeping the intact the relations between the words.

Proper lemmatization is performed by JSREALB. Unfortunately, lemmatization for T1 is not always systematic, there are a few cases such as *grounds* or *rights* where the plural was left in the lemma; no pronoun is lemmatized, so we find *he, them, she, it* while a canonical pronoun should be used, JSREALB uses *I*. Not having to find the appropriate pronoun simplifies realization because this is one of the difficulties of English generation whose morphology is otherwise relatively simple at least compared to other languages.

Given the fact that the permutation left intact the links between the words, we used a very simple approach: we first build the tree and then sort the dependents at each level. The sorting first takes into account the information about the linear order added to make sure proper nouns and punctuation can be added at the appropriate place. Then a fixed

```
# sent_id = weblog-juancole.com_juancole_20051126063000_ENG_20051126_063000-0020
# text = His mother was also killed in the attack.
1   kill     _   VERB   _   Tense=Past|id2=1|id1=9|original_id=5|...     0   ROOT
2   mother   _   NOUN   _   Number=Sing|id1=3|original_id=2         ...  1   A2
3   also     _   ADV    _   id1=7|original_id=4                     ...  1   A1INV
4   attack   _   NOUN   _   Number=Sing|id2=5|id1=2|id3=8|origina...    1   AM
5   he       _   PRON   _   Number=Sing|id1=4|Poss=Yes|original_i...    2   AM
```

```
['ROOT'>r,[verb:"kill",tense:past,clausetype:dec],
        ['A2'>r,[noun:"mother",number:sing],
                ['AM'>r,[pron:"he",number:sing,poss:yes,person:3,prontype:prs]]],
        ['A1INV'>r,[adv:"also"]],
        ['AM'>r,[noun:"attack",number:sing,definite:def]]]
```

```
s(vp(v("kill")*t("ps"),
    adv("also"),
    np(d("my")*pe(3)*ow("s")*n("s")*g("m"),
      n("mother")*n("s")),
    pp(p("in"),
      np(d("the"),
        n("attack"))*n("s")))))*typ({pas:true})
```

```
His mother was killed also in the attack.
```

Table 3: The T2 dependency given at the top is parsed into the nested list structure shown in the second line; the id and original_id features are ignored as they are given for easing the training of learning algorithms. It is then transformed into a Deep Syntactic Representation shown in the third line and then into a Surface Syntactic Representation (not shown here) which is given to JSREALB to realize the sentence shown at the bottom which is the same as the original sentence given at the top of Table 1.

order of relation name is chosen so that a subject appears before the verb or its complements, a determiner will be placed before an adjective and a noun, etc.

Once the T1 structure has been sorted, it is processed like a UD structure using the algorithm described above. In this case, the algorithm does not use the fact the left or right position of the children in relation to the head; this relation being lost by the permutation applied in creating T1. For the two previous examples, the sorting process recreates almost exactly the structure of the original UD and the output sentence is the same. This happens because small differences in the placement of aux, mark or prep do not change the realization.

3.4 T2 to Deep Syntactic Representation

The SR'19 documentation dataset[8] provides a mapping between the universal dependencies and the ones used for T2. So we adapted the algorithm given for the UD by changing the names of the relations.

The tree is built by reading the T2 dependencies and the dependents are sorted at each level

according to the relation names. Then the NAME dependents are processed using the linear order information.

Using a similar process as described for UD, we deal with nominals and clauses. For nominals, all A1 and AM dependents are used for building a NP. A sentence is built when a verb is encountered as a head, the subject being the value of the A1 relation, the verb phrase comprises the head verb and all other dependents. Some care has to be given to the A*i*INV relations that are used as relative sentences for verbs and noun complements. Given the fact that important information has been removed in the T2 structures, the results *leave much room for improvement*. It would surely be interesting to improve this output using a statistical spell or style checker.

Table 3 shows the T2 structure for the example shown in Table 1. That this sentence should be written in passive mode is not specified in the input, but the transformation rules indicate that a passive subject is indicated by a A2 relation without any A1. Prepositions being absent from T2 structures, we computed the most frequent preposition used with each word as head in the original UD corpora; this is the only statistical pro-

---

[8]http://taln.upf.edu/pages/msr2019-ws/srst_dataset_doc.txt

cess used in our system, but there should be more. This preposition is added for all dependents having relation AM and Ai (i>= 3). For the verb *kill*, the most frequent preposition being *in*, it is added (correctly in this case) before *the attack*. The original sentence was thus reproduced *verbatim* but, of course, this is not always the case...

4 Results and Evaluation

We ran the program on all training ($\approx$ 20 000 sentences) and development ($\approx$ 4 000 sentences) sets provided by the organizers of SR'19 for English. We also ran them on the test sets of the 2018 and 2019 competitions. Using SWI-Prolog V8.1, the whole set is processed in about 5 minutes of real time (half of which is CPU) on a 2.2 GHz Mac-Book Pro, including the production of evaluation files, a good example of *Green AI* (Schwartz et al., 2019).

4.1 Automatic Evaluation

4.1.1 Training and development sets

Table 4 shows the BLEU, NIST and DIST scores on the 2019 training and development sets for the four English corpora. The scores for T1 and UD are quite similar and their value are within the scores obtained by systems on a similar task in 2018. Comparing the automatic results on the train and development sets, we see that the results for T1 are only slightly worse than the ones for UD (especially for BLEU), so we consider that this approach is valuable for this special task.

It seems to us that the permutation of the lines in the dependency file does not change the input so much to warrant a special task. In fact, from an NLG point of view, T1 seems artificial, as we cannot imagine a generation system that determines all the tokens but in a random order.

4.1.2 Test sets

Table 5 gives these scores for the test set used in the 2018 competition. These scores are competitive for T1 and only slightly less in BLEU than the unique participant for this task in 2018. A cursory manual evaluation of the output for T2 shows the need for improvement for long sentences even though the automatic scores are quite similar except for BLEU. This can be explained by the fact that a lot of information is not given in the output, but is expected to be inferred by the NLG system. For the moment, the only *real* information added

by the system is the most frequent preposition encountered in the test and development set for complements of nouns or of verbs.

The 2019 test set was much more comprehensive with more languages and different types of corpora. Evaluation was done on both tokenized and *detokenized* input. In the case of UD-SURFR, as JSREALB was already realizing a *detokenized* output, we had to write a tokenizer to separate the tokens in order to make the output comparable with the one of other systems working at the token level and then applying some postprocessing to produce a more readable output with proper casing and appropriate spacing around punctuation. In terms of automatic scores, UD-SURFR is competitive: it is more or less the average between the best and worst scores obtained by other systems. And this seems consistent across all types of corpora. Figure 1 shows a graph of the BLEU scores for the tokenized sentences which seem to be typical of the comparison across the scores for all participants to the tasks. For T1 (left part of the figure), the score for UD-SURFR (the black stripped bar on the left) is approximately in the middle of the score of other systems. For T2, except for the very best system, UD-SURFR does surprisingly well compared with other participants.

4.2 Manual Evaluation

The SR'19 organizers evaluated the output of 16 systems on two aspects:

- *The text adequately expresses the meaning of the sentence* for which our T1 system obtained 73% (ranked 11th) and T2 obtained 68% (ranked 14th) after scoring about 700 sentences; in fact these scores are not statistically different from each other.

- *the text reads well and is free from grammatical errors and awkward constructions* for with our T1 system obtained 58% which corresponds to the second group of system over 4. Note that the human reference only obtained 71% on this evaluation. These scores were based on about 550 sentences. We were quite surprised to see that the T2 system managed to get 50% even though no effort was put in adding any language model.

Given the relative simplicity of our approach, we are quite satisfied with these scores.

	ewt			gum			lines			partut		
	BLEU	DIST	NIST	BLEU	DIST	NIST	BLEU	DIST	NIST	BLEU	DIST	NIST
train	12 543 sent.			2 914 sent.			2 738 sent.			1 781 sent.		
UD	0.49	0.64	12.26	0.48	0.58	10.93	0.46	0.56	10.53	0.44	0.48	10.37
T1	0.38	0.62	10.88	0.40	0.55	10.17	0.36	0.53	9.42	0.38	0.48	9.73
T2	0.25	0.56	9.24	0.26	0.47	8.63	0.24	0.49	8.11	0.24	0.42	8.03
dev	2002 sent.			707 sent.			912 sent			156 sent.		
UD	0.48	0.69	10.39	0.49	0.60	9.87	0.48	0.60	9.96	0.39	0.61	7.76
T1	0.37	0.66	9.33	0.41	0.57	9.23	0.38	0.56	9.00	0.33	0.60	7.31
T2	0.25	0.64	8.21	0.25	0.49	7.83	0.24	0.54	7.66	0.23	0.54	6.46

Table 4: Automatic evaluation scores produced by the evaluation scripts of the SR'19 organizers on the train and dev sets. For UD and T1, the scores seem competitive with the ones obtained by the participants at the 2018 competition shown in Table 5.

	BLEU	DIST	NIST
T1	0.38	0.69	9.38
2018-best	0.69	0.80	12.02
2018-worst	0.08	0.47	7.71
T2	0.19	0.60	7.87
2018	0.22	0.49	6.95

Table 5: Automatic evaluation on the 2061 sentences of the 2018 test set compared with the scores obtained by systems participating in the 2018 shared task. Only one system provided output for the T2 task.

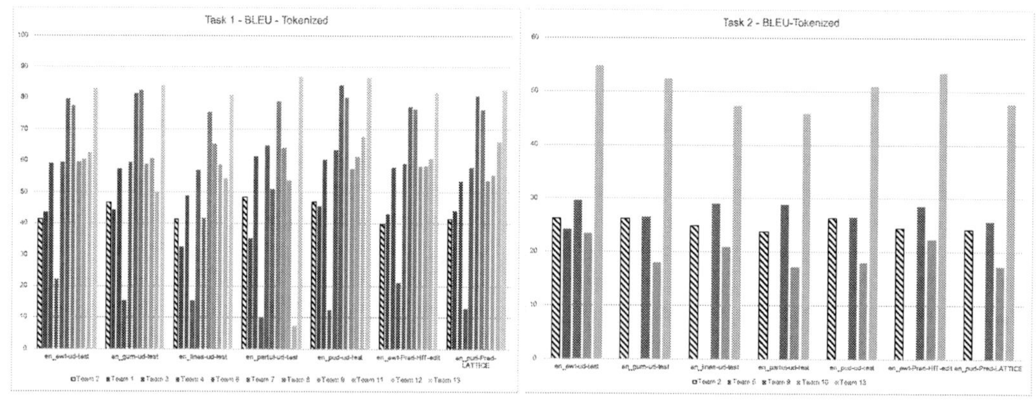

Figure 1: Comparison for BLEU scores for T1 (left) and T2 (right) on tokenized sentences from the English corpora for UD-SURFR (Team 2) shown as the first black stripped bar to the left compared with the scores obtained by other participants.

5 Conclusion

We have described a symbolic approach for tackling the tasks T1 and T2 of SR'19. We first described the development of UD-SURFR, a text realizer for standard UD input that can be used for checking the annotation. We then described UD-SURFR was modified to take into account the specificities of the shared task. The system has processed the training, development and test sets of the competition and obtained average results compared to other machine learning approaches. This is quite surprising given the fact, that the symbolic system only used a very small part of the training and development corpora. But more important, the experiment has revealed that task T1 (for English at least) is perhaps too easy and does not really correspond to a realistic input for a text realizer. T2 proved more challenging but the results are finally relatively similar.

References

Albert Gatt and Ehud Reiter. 2009. SimpleNLG: A realisation engine for practical applications. In *Proceedings of the 12th European Workshop on Natural Language Generation (ENLG 2009)*, pages 90–93, Athens, Greece. Association for Computational Linguistics.

Simon Mille, Anja Belz, Bernd Bohnet, Yvette Graham, and Leo Wanner. 2019. The Second Multilingual Surface Realisation Shared Task (SR'19): Overview and Evaluation Results. In *Proceedings of the 2nd Workshop on Multilingual Surface Realisation (MSR), 2019 Conference on Empirical Methods in Natural Language Processing (EMNLP)*, Hong Kong, China.

Simon Mille, Anja Belz, Bernd Bohnet, and Leo Wanner. 2018. Underspecified universal dependency structures as inputs for multilingual surface realisation. In *Proceedings of the 11th International Conference on Natural Language Generation*, pages 199–209, Tilburg University, The Netherlands. Association for Computational Linguistics.

Paul Molins and Guy Lapalme. 2015. JSrealB: A bilingual text realizer for web programming. In *Proceedings of the 15th European Workshop on Natural Language Generation (ENLG)*, pages 109–111, Brighton, UK. Association for Computational Linguistics.

Joakim Nivre, Marie-Catherine de Marneffe, Filip Ginter, Yoav Goldberg, Jan Hajič, Christopher D. Manning, Ryan McDonald, Slav Petrov, Sampo Pyysalo, Natalia Silveira, Reut Tsarfaty, and Daniel Zeman. 2016. Universal dependencies v1: A multilingual treebank collection. In *Proceedings of the Tenth International Conference on Language Resources and Evaluation (LREC 2016)*, pages 1659–1666, Portorož, Slovenia. European Language Resources Association (ELRA).

Aarne Ranta and Prasanth Kolachina. 2017. From universal dependencies to abstract syntax. In *Proceedings of the NoDaLiDa 2017 Workshop on Universal Dependencies (UDW 2017)*, pages 107–116, Gothenburg, Sweden. Association for Computational Linguistics.

Roy Schwartz, Jesse Dodge, Noah A. Smith, and Oren Etzioni. 2019. Green AI. arXiv-1907.10597.

IMSurReal: IMS at the Surface Realization Shared Task 2019

Xiang Yu, Agnieszka Falenska, Marina Haid, Ngoc Thang Vu, Jonas Kuhn
Institut für Maschinelle Sprachverarbeitung
Universität Stuttgart, Germany
`firstname.lastname@ims.uni-stuttgart.de`

Abstract

We introduce the IMS contribution to the Surface Realization Shared Task 2019. Our submission achieves the state-of-the-art performance without using any external resources. The system takes a pipeline approach consisting of five steps: linearization, completion, inflection, contraction, and detokenization. We compare the performance of our linearization algorithm with two external baselines and report results for each step in the pipeline. Furthermore, we perform detailed error analysis revealing correlation between word order freedom and difficulty of the linearization task.

1 Introduction

This paper presents our submission to the Surface Realization Shared Task 2019 (Mille et al., 2019). We participate in both shallow and deep track of the shared task, where the shallow track requires the recovery of the linear order and inflection of a dependency tree, and the deep track additionally requires the completion of function words.

We approach both tasks with very similar pipelines, consisting of linearizing the unordered dependency trees, completing function words (for the deep track only), inflecting lemmata to word forms, and contracting several words as one token, and finally detokenizing to obtain the natural written text. We use machine learning models for the first four steps and a rule-based off-the-shelf detokenizer for the final step.

In the evaluation on the tokenized text, our system achieves the highest BLEU scores for each individual treebank in both tracks, with an average of 79.97 for the shallow track and 51.41 for the deep track. In the human evaluation on four languages, we also rank the first in terms of readability and adequacy.

2 Surface Realization System

Our system takes a pipeline approach, which consists of up to five steps to produce the final detokenized text. The steps are: linearization (§2.2), completion (§2.3), inflection (§2.4), contraction (§2.5), and detokenization (§2.6), among which completion is used only in the deep track. All the steps except for the rule-based detokenization use the same Tree-LSTM encoder architecture (§2.1). As the multi-task style training hurt performance in the preliminary experiments, all the steps are trained separately.

Since the submission is mostly based on our system described in Yu et al. (2019b), here we mainly focus on the changes introduced for this shared task, and we refer the reader to Yu et al. (2019b) for more details, especially on the explanation and ablation experiments of the Tree-LSTM encoder and the linearization decoder.

2.1 Tree-LSTM Encoder

Representation of each token in the tree is based on its lemma, UPOS, morphological features, and dependency label. We use embeddings for the lemma, UPOS and dependency label, and employ an LSTM to process the list of morphological features.[1] We then concatenate all of the obtained vectors as the representation of each token ($\mathbf{v}°$).

The representation is further processed by a bidirectional Tree-LSTM to encode the tree structure information. The encoder is generally the same as described in Yu et al. (2019b), consisting of two passes of information: a bottom-up pass followed by a top-down pass. In the bottom-up pass, we use a Tree-LSTM (Zhou et al., 2016) to compose the bottom-up vector of the head from the vectors of the dependents, attended by the

---

[1] There could be better treatment of the morphological features, since they are not sequences in nature.

Proceedings of the 2nd Workshop on Multilingual Surface Realisation (MSR 2019), pages 50–58
Hong Kong, China, November 3rd, 2019. ©2019 Association for Computational Linguistics
https://doi.org/10.18653/v1/P17

token-level vector of the head, denoted as $\mathbf{v}^\uparrow$. The bottom-up vectors are then fed into a sequential LSTM for the top-down pass from the root to each leaf token, so that every token has access to all the descendants of all its ancestors, namely all tokens in the tree. The output vector is denoted as $\mathbf{v}^\downarrow$.

For linearization, we use the concatenation of $\mathbf{v}^\uparrow$ and $\mathbf{v}^\downarrow$ as the representation of each token. For the other tasks, where the sequence is already determined, we additionally use a sequential bidirectional LSTM to encode the sequence, with the tree-based vectors as input.

2.2 Linearization

The linearization algorithm is the same as in Yu et al. (2019b), which is in turn based on the linearizer described by Bohnet et al. (2010). The algorithm takes an *divide-and-conquer* strategy, which orders each subtree (a head and its dependents) individually, and then combines them into a fully linearized tree.[2]

The main improvement of our algorithm to Bohnet et al. (2010) is that instead of ordering the subtrees from left to right, we start from the head (thus called the head-first decoder), and add the dependents on both sides of the head incrementally. We also train a left-to-right and a right-to-left decoders to form an ensemble with a shared encoder, which is shown in Yu et al. (2019b) to achieve the best performance.

We use beam search to find the best linearization order of each subtree, where the best N partial hypotheses are kept to expand at each step. For the head-first decoder, we use two LSTMs to track the left and right expansion of the sequence (only one LSTM is needed for the left-to-right or right-to-left expansion), and the score of the sequence is calculated from the concatenation of the two LSTM states followed by an MLP.

Note that in the shared task some tokens are provided with information about the relative word order to its head.[3] We use these constraints in our decoder so that the hypotheses violating the constraints are ignored. Preliminary experiments

---

[2]This algorithm can only create projective trees. An method to bypass the projective constraints is described in Bohnet et al. (2012). However, we did not use this method and only produce projective trees due to limited time.

[3]The information are encoded in the morphological features, such as `lin=+2`, which means this token must appear after the token with the feature `lin=+1` after the head. They are provided for the cases that do not have a unique correct order, e.g., punctuation or coordinating conjunction.

showed that disregarding this word order information would decrease the BLEU score by 2-3 points.

2.3 Completion

The completion model for the deep track takes the output of the linearization model as input and insert function words into the linearized subtrees.

Similarly to the linearization algorithm, we also use a head-first strategy to complete each subtree. We use two pairs of LSTMs to encode the sequence: a pair of forward and backward LSTMs for the left dependents, and a pair for the right dependents, where "forward" means from the head to the end and "backward" means from the end towards the head. Since the two pairs are symmetrical, we only describe the decoding process to the right side of the head.

We use a pointer to indicate the current token, which initially points to the head. We use the backward LSTM to encode the upcoming sequence of linearized tokens, and the forward LSTM to encode the already processed tokens up to the pointer (which includes both the previously linearized tokens and the newly generated tokens).

At each decoding step, we concatenate the forward LSTM output of the current pointed token and the backward LSTM output of the next token, and calculate a softmax distribution of all possible function words, as well as a special symbol $\Rightarrow$, which moves the pointer to the next token. If a new token is generated, the pointer will point to the new token. If $\Rightarrow$ is predicted and the pointer already reached the last token in the sequence, then the completion process is terminated.

Figure 1 illustrate an example of the completion process to the right side of the head, where the linearized tokens are [h, $d^{(+1)}$, $d^{(+2)}$, \$], h is the head, $d^{(+1)}$ and $d^{(+2)}$ are right dependents, and \$ indicates the end of the subtree. In step (1) the symbol $\Rightarrow$ is predicted, therefore we move the pointer from the h to $d^{(+1)}$; in step (2) a new token f_1 is created and attached to $d^{(+1)}$; in step (3) another token f_2 is created and attached to f_1; in step (4) the pointer is moved to $d^{(+2)}$; in step (5) the pointer is moved again to \$, which terminates the process and outputs the sequence [h, $d^{(+1)}$, f_1, f_2, $d^{(+2)}$].

The left and right completion processes are independent of each other, since both forward LSTMs are only aware of the initial linearized tokens on both sides but not the newly generated tokens. We tried several variations in the prelimi-

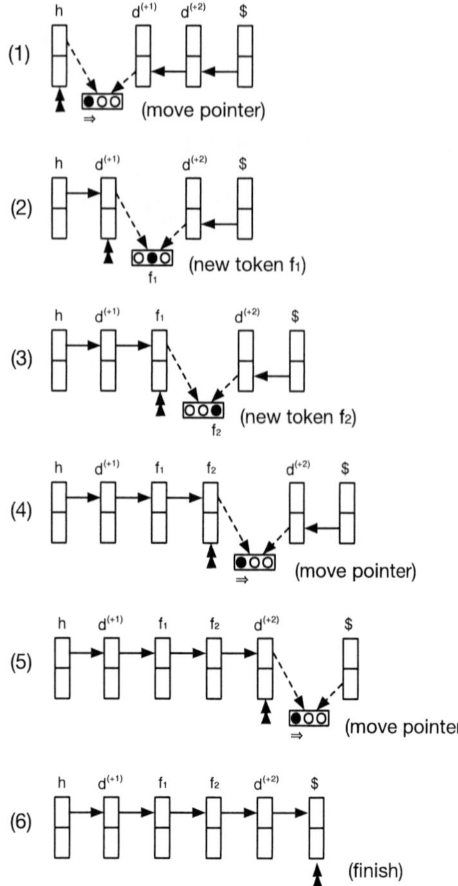

Figure 1: An example of the completion process to the right side, where the right arrows illustrate the forward LSTM, and the left arrows the backward LSTM.

nary experiments, including joint linearization and completion, interleaving the left and right completion processes, and beam-search for completion. All approaches yielded lower performance than the described method.[4] However, we note that the completion step seems to have the most potential to benefit from external language models. We observe that many generated function words are syntactically correct but semantically implausible, and the language models are generally good at capturing semantic coherence. We plan to incorporate language models in the future work.

---

[4]Admittedly, most of the experiments are rather brief, more careful design and thorough experiments might lead to different results.

2.4 Inflection

The inflection model is the same as in Yu et al. (2019b). It generates a sequence of edit operations that modifies the lemma into the inflected word form. The model takes the characters in the lemma as input and encodes through a bidirectional LSTM. A binary feature is concatenated to the vector of each character which functions as a pointer to indicate the input character currently to be processed. At each step, the decoder attends to the input vectors and predicts an output, which could be a symbol ✓ to copy the current input character, a symbol ✗ to ignore the current input character, or a character from the alphabet to generate a new one. When ✓ or ✗ is predicted, the input pointer will move one step forward, while if a character is generated, the input pointer does not move.

The ground truth of such sequence is calculated from the Levenshtein edit operations between the lemma and the word form, where only insertion and deletion is allowed (no substitution).

Our model is in a way similar to the hard monotonic attention in Aharoni and Goldberg (2017), but we use a much simpler source-target alignment (Levenshtein edit operations), and we use copy as an edit operation to avoid completion errors while they do not. Furthermore, our edit operations are associated with the moving of the pointer, while they treat moving the pointer as an atomic operation, which lead to longer prediction sequences. Generally, our model performs on a par with theirs, see the comparison in Yu et al. (2019b).

2.5 Contraction

In Yu et al. (2019b) we described a rule-based contraction method by constructing an automaton from the training data, which works reasonably well for most of the languages where the contraction is trivial. However, it works rather poorly for Arabic since the contraction is not just among closed class function words but also content words, so that the coverage of the rules is very small. It is also problematic for the verb-pronoun contraction in Spanish and Portuguese although they are much less frequent.

We therefore implement a character-based contraction model to alleviate this problem. The model works in two steps. First it predicts BIO tags to identify the groups of consecutive words that need to be contracted. Then it concatenates the group as a character sequence and predicts the contracted word form as output. We use a simple Seq2Seq model for the contraction due to limited time, although an edit based model similar to the one for inflection might yield better results.

2.6 Detokenization

The detokenization step is the same as described in Yu et al. (2019b), namely a rule-based tool MosesDetokenizer.[5] After the submission we realized that the tool removes all empty spaces in Korean texts, similar to Chinese and Japanese. However, Korean actually uses empty spaces to separate words, thus we expect lower score in the human evaluation for this language.

2.7 Discussion on Pipeline Order

In our pipeline, we choose the order of linearization, completion, and finally inflection. Our rationale for such order is as follows: (1) the inflection in some cases depends on the linearized sequence of lemmata, e.g., the English determiner "a/an" depends on whether the following noun begins with a vowel, therefore inflection is the last of the three steps; (2) the search-based linearization model is more reliable than the greedy completion model, therefore we first perform linearization to reduce error propagation.

However, this choice is only based on our intuition, and one could come up with arguments for the alternative orders. For example, since inflection is the easiest and most accurate task, performing it first might further reduce error propagation. Further experiments are needed to determine the best order in the pipeline. Alternatively, a carefully designed joint prediction might address the error propagation problem, however, our initial attempts did not yield positive outcome.

2.8 Implementation Details

All the neural models are implemented with the DyNet library(Neubig et al., 2017), and the full system is available at the first author's website.[6] We use the embedding size of 64 for lemma and character, and 32 for UPOS, XPOS, morphological features, and dependency labels. The output dimension of the bottom-up and top-down encoder

LSTMs, as well as all the decoder LSTMs, are equal to the input dimension. The beam size for the linearization is 32. We train the model up to 100000 steps without batching using the Adam optimizer (Kingma and Ba, 2014), test on the development set every 2000 steps, and stop training if there is no improvement 10 times in a row. All the hyperparameters are only minimally tuned to balance speed and performance, and kept the same for all languages.

The training and prediction of each treebank are run on single CPU cores. Depending on the treebank size, the training time of linearization models typically ranges from 1 to 10 hours. The completion, inflection, and contraction models are much faster, mostly under 1 hour, since they are all greedy models.

The prediction speed is around 10 sentence per second, which is not very fast, however, we did not perform any optimization toward speed (e.g. mini-batch, multi-processing, etc.) due to the experimental nature of our work.

3 Data

The training and test data in the shared task is based on Universal Dependencies (Nivre et al., 2016), see the overview paper for the details.

We do not use any external resources for our system, except that we concatenate the training treebanks for some languages (see Table 3 and 4). However, not all treebanks benefits from the concatenation, since the idiosyncrasies in the UD treebanks can hurt the performance as noted in Björkelund et al. (2017), where the concatenation of multiple UD treebanks also hurts parsing performance.

Evaluation in the shared task is also performed on out-of-domain datasets, namely the automatically parsed trees from some in-domain treebanks and the unseen PUD treebanks. We use the same model for the automatically parsed trees as for the gold ones, and use the model trained on concatenated treebanks for the PUD test data.

Some treebanks have XPOS tag set quite different from the UPOS, which could be useful as complementary information. We used XPOS as features when the tag set size is at least twice as large as the UPOS set size and smaller than 500 (to avoid sparsity). In fact, the XPOS tags in some treebanks could be decomposed as morphological features, e.g., Arabic, Indonesian, Korean. In

---

the submission, we only choose to decompose the XPOS for Korean because it can be easily split by the "+" delimiter and both Korean treebanks do not have morphological features otherwise. We also use the real stems in the Korean treebanks by removing the suffixes after the "+" delimiter in the lemmata, in order to reduce the out-of-vocabulary problem, and the information on the suffixes are well preserved in the morphological features derived from the XPOS.

Finally, since contraction appears only in Arabic, Spanish, French and Portuguese, we therefore only train contraction models for these languages.

4 Evaluation

The automatic evaluation results of our submission to the shared task are shown in Table 1 and Table 2 for the shallow and deep tracks, respectively. The first three columns contain the BLEU, DIST, and NIST scores of our system, and the fourth column is the difference of BLEU scores between our system and the best system among other participants for each treebank.

Our system achieve the best performance for all treebanks in both tracks. Comparing to the best scores of other teams, the differences range from single digits for the English treebanks to about 20 points for most other treebanks and 38 points for Arabic. In the out-of-domain scenario, our system performs very stable in most of the cases. However, comparing to the English and Japanese PUD treebanks, the performance drop on Russian PUD treebank is quite notable. Our conjecture is that the annotation of the PUD treebank is much closer to the GSD treebank than the SynTagRus treebank. Since we use both treebanks for training, the much larger size of SynTagRus might have dominated the training.

In the human evaluation (see Mille et al. (2019) for details), we also rank the first in all four languages (English, Russian, Chinese and Spanish) both for readability and adequacy.

5 Analysis

5.1 Pipeline Performance

Table 3 and 4 show the results on the development sets of the in-domain treebanks for the shallow track and deep track, respectively. We also provide the linearization baselines by Puduppully

	BLEU	NIST	DIST	Δ_{BLEU}
ar_padt	64.90	12.22	73.71	38.50
en_ewt	82.98	13.61	86.72	3.29
en_gum	83.84	12.69	83.49	1.45
en_lines	81.00	12.71	82.21	5.51
en_partut	87.25	11.01	85.68	8.27
es_ancora	83.70	14.69	79.82	7.23
es_gsd	82.98	12.77	79.45	12.83
fr_gsd	84.00	12.45	84.15	23.85
fr_partut	83.38	10.36	82.32	17.37
fr_sequoia	85.01	12.53	85.13	22.22
hi_hdtb	80.56	13.07	79.07	11.33
id_gsd	85.34	12.83	83.92	21.63
ja_gsd	87.69	12.42	87.17	24.10
ko_gsd	74.19	12.27	80.95	28.11
ko_kaist	73.93	13.00	78.69	26.70
pt_bosque	77.75	12.15	79.80	25.06
pt_gsd	75.93	13.07	79.33	23.43
ru_gsd	71.23	12.15	73.04	16.14
ru_syntagrus	76.95	15.08	78.66	16.96
zh_gsd	83.85	12.78	83.18	15.31
en_pud	86.61	13.47	87.00	2.54
ja_pud	86.64	13.02	84.04	20.12
ru_pud	58.38	10.91	77.12	6.01
en_ewt-pred	81.80	13.46	85.35	4.59
en_pud-pred	82.60	13.26	86.18	1.94
es_ancora-pred	83.31	14.61	81.14	6.03
hi_hdtb-pred	80.19	13.05	78.88	10.27
ko_kaist-pred	74.27	13.02	79.12	27.55
pt_bosque-pred	78.97	12.14	81.56	25.33
AVG	79.97	12.79	81.62	15.64

Table 1: Automatic Evaluation Results of the shallow track (T1) and the BLEU difference with the best system among other participants for each treebank.

	BLEU	NIST	DIST	Δ_{BLEU}
en_ewt	54.75	11.79	76.30	25.17
en_gum	52.45	11.04	73.07	25.85
en_lines	47.29	10.63	71.93	18.21
en_partut	45.89	9.03	67.45	17.04
es_ancora	53.13	12.38	68.58	16.15
es_gsd	51.17	10.82	68.85	16.52
fr_gsd	53.62	10.79	68.82	28.02
fr_partut	46.95	8.27	68.99	18.76
fr_sequoia	57.41	11.00	72.06	28.85
en_pud	51.01	11.45	72.31	24.45
en_ewt-pred	53.54	11.55	74.99	24.91
en_pud-pred	47.60	11.08	71.65	21.83
es_ancora-pred	53.54	12.36	70.02	16.13
AVG	51.41	10.94	71.16	21.68

Table 2: Automatic Evaluation Results of the deep track (T2) and the BLEU difference with the best system among other participants for each treebank.

	P16	B10	lin*	lin	inf	con	final
ar_padt	77.73	82.69	84.24	87.27	95.63	91.59	68.58
en_ewt	79.10	82.71	85.11	88.01	98.47		84.50
en_gum	74.03	82.36	83.69	87.29	98.23		84.35
en_lines(+)	69.47	75.69	78.39	82.40	97.86		79.05
en_partut	71.45	80.11	86.38	89.14	97.94		86.25
es_ancora	74.57	81.61	83.47	85.33	99.51	99.86	84.43
es_gsd(+)	78.28	82.32	83.53	86.18	99.18	99.09	84.04
fr_gsd(+)	82.99	85.26	87.02	89.74	98.63	99.47	86.98
fr_partut	71.46	83.92	87.07	90.08	96.95	99.44	84.17
fr_sequoia	74.16	83.66	87.09	90.39	98.20	99.58	86.51
hi_hdtb	79.83	82.03	82.79	85.25	98.11		81.62
id_gsd	74.68	78.27	81.23	86.05	99.51		84.62
ja_gsd	86.20	89.08	90.41	92.55	98.69		89.49
ko_gsd(+)	67.55	69.48	76.05	79.66	96.74		74.25
ko_kaist(+)	76.98	77.47	78.73	80.01	97.32		76.04
pt_bosque	76.97	80.30	82.48	84.35	99.31	98.23	80.75
pt_gsd	83.19	86.53	87.17	89.24	94.99	99.84	76.89
ru_gsd	68.32	74.04	74.64	79.09	95.98		73.66
ru_syntagrus(+)	73.58	77.01	78.52	80.97	97.84		76.28
zh_gsd	68.92	75.60	81.22	84.10	100.00		83.34
AVG	75.47	80.51	82.96	85.86	97.95		81.29

Table 3: Development results in the shallow track, including the linearization baselines.

	lin	comp	inf	con	final
en_ewt	80.17	67.70	97.98		55.27
en_gum(+)	76.14	61.44	97.72		50.53
en_lines(+)	76.63	60.47	97.16		47.17
en_partut(+)	73.80	60.63	97.63		44.59
es_ancora	77.88	66.95	98.25	99.85	53.57
es_gsd	77.98	69.72	97.85	99.71	53.81
fr_gsd(+)	81.36	73.20	97.63	99.26	57.46
fr_partut(+)	75.36	65.94	94.64	98.39	48.17
fr_sequoia(+)	80.03	73.01	97.04	99.60	58.27
AVG	77.40	66.42	97.24		51.70

Table 4: Development results in the deep track.

et al. (2016) (P16) and Bohnet et al. (2010) (B10).[7] The columns show different evaluation metrics on different targets. Except for the final column, each one evaluates on only one step assuming all previous steps are gold.

In Table 3, columns 1-4 are the BLEU scores of linearization evaluated on the lemmata, column 5 is the accuracy of inflection, column 6 is BLEU score on the contracted word form (empty cells means contraction is not applied), column 7 is the final BLEU score of the full pipeline. The column lin* shows the models trained on single treebanks and without using the word order information, which allows a fair comparison to the two baselines. The models marked with + are trained with concatenated treebanks for the submission, which performs slightly better than the single treebank, typically by 0.5-1 BLEU points. For each treebank, we either use the concatenated treebank to train all steps in the pipeline or use the single treebank for all steps, depending on the final BLEU score on the development set.

In Table 4, column 1 is the BLEU score on the lemmata of the given content words, columns 2 is the BLEU score on the lemmata including generated tokens, column 3 is the accuracy on word forms, column 4 is the BLEU score of contracted word forms, and column 5 is the BLEU score of the full pipeline. Similar to Table 3, the models marked with + are trained with concatenated treebanks.

In the shallow track, our linearization model outperforms the best baseline (Bohnet et al., 2010) by 2.5 BLEU points on average. The inclusion of word order information (and treebank concatenation to a much smaller extent) brings about 3 additional points. For the deep track, the BLEU score of linearization is much higher than completion, which motivates our decision to perform linearization before completion.

5.2 Word Order Preferences

In this section we analyze the relation between word order preferences of each language and the errors made by the linearizer,[8] characterized by

---

[7]We run the two baseline systems *as is*, where we only convert the input format to ensure all systems are using the same information and keep their default options.

[8]Note that an "error" is counted when the predicted order is different from the original order in the reference, however,

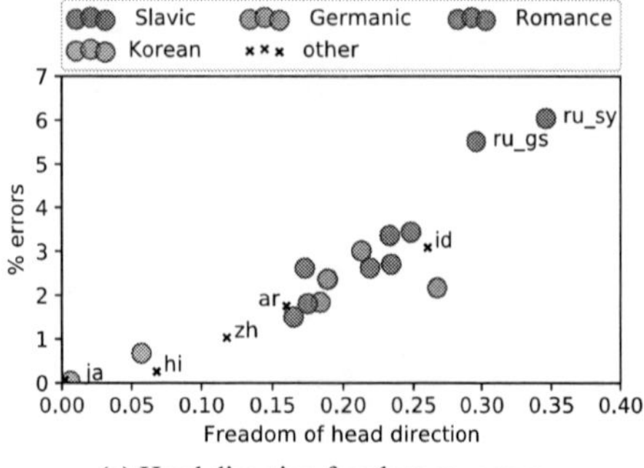
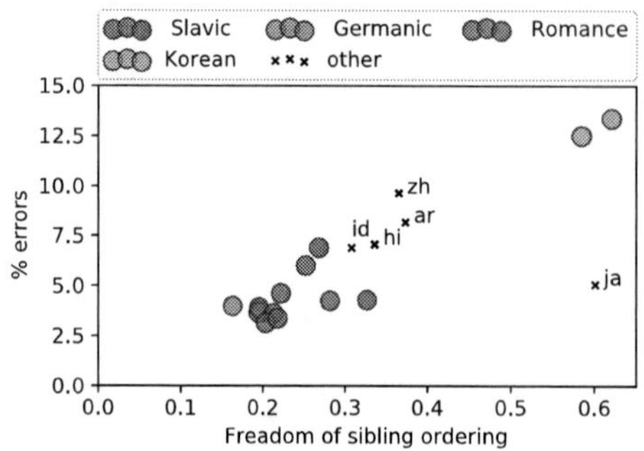

(a) Head direction freedom vs. errors.

(b) Sibling ordering freedom vs. errors.

Figure 2: The correlation of word order freedom and linearization errors. Different language families are marked with different colors.

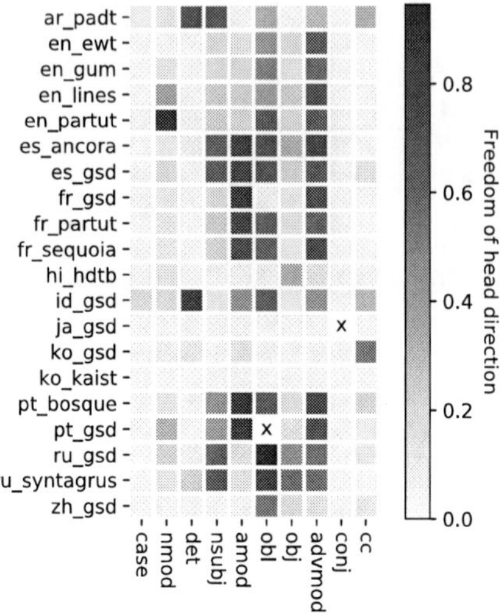
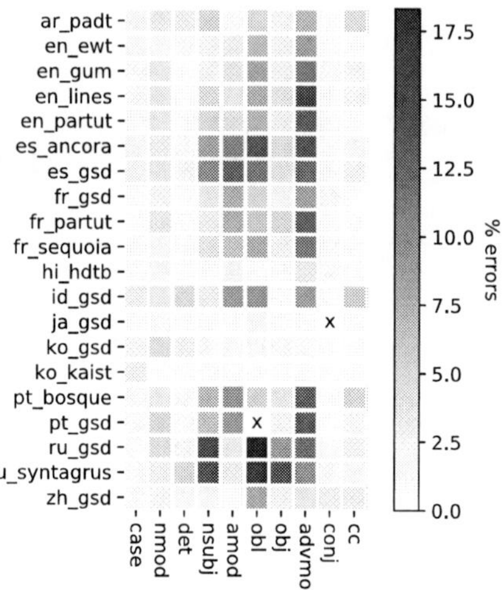

(a) Head direction freedom of each dependency relations in each training set.

(b) Head direction errors of each dependency relations in each development set.

Figure 3: Detailed visualization of head direction freedom vs. linearization errors of the 10 most frequent dependency relations in each treebank, where "x" means no such relation in the treebank.

two types of word order preferences as defined in Yu et al. (2019a):

head direction – whether the dependent appears to the left or the right side of the head;

sibling order – the order of a pair of dependents on the same side of the head.

We then define the freedom of these two types of word order preferences, namely the entropy of the word order of each dependency relation, which is described in details in Yu et al. (2019a)[9]. In both

types of word orders, higher freedom means less constraints on the word order.

We also calculate the error rate of the linearizer by the dependency relations:

head direction – whether the dependent appears on the correct side of the head;

sibling order – whether a pair of dependents on the same side of the head has the correct order.

Figure 2 shows the correlation of freedom and linearization errors of the two types of word orders. For both head direction (Figure 2a) and sibling ordering (Figure 2b), we can observe quite strong correlation of the freedom and linearization errors. For the head direction, both Russian treebanks have the highest freedom, and the linearizer

____

this does not mean that the predicted one is incorrect. The variation of word order in natural languages can not be trivially evaluated by the single reference BLEU score, human judgement is thus needed for a more accurate evaluation.

[9]Here we only use the dependency relations to characterize the word orders for simplicity of visualization, while Yu et al. (2019a) additionally use the UPOS tag, which is more

____

fine-grained.

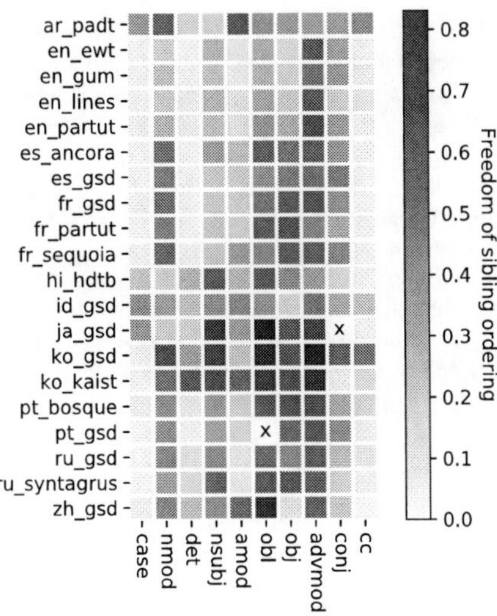

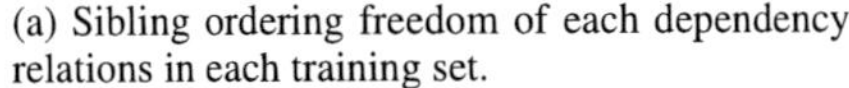

(a) Sibling ordering freedom of each dependency relations in each training set.

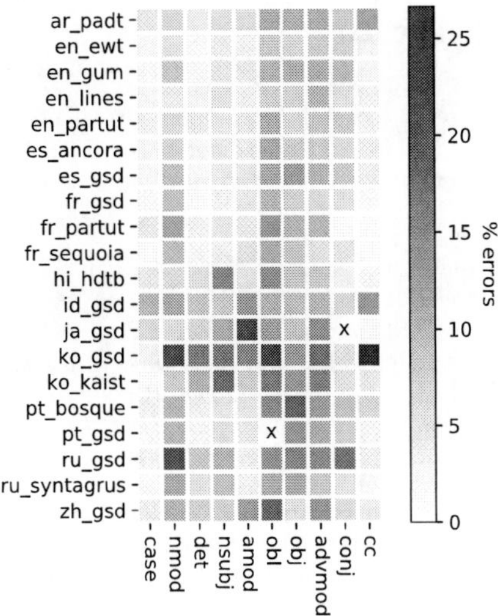

(b) Sibling ordering errors of each dependency relations in each development set.

Figure 4: Detailed visualization of sibling ordering freedom vs. linearization errors of the 10 most frequent dependency relations in each treebank, where "x" means no such relation in the treebank.

also makes the most errors. Verb final languages such as Korean, Japanese and Hindi, on the contrary, have the lowest freedom and the least errors. For the sibling ordering, both Korean treebanks have the highest freedom and linearization error rate. However, there are no treebanks with very low freedom or error rate, which suggests that the ordering of arguments are generally less strict than the head direction in all languages.

We then look into the errors of our system in more details. We take ten most common dependency relations in all the treebanks (we map the language-specific relation subtypes to their general type, e.g., nmod:poss is mapped to nmod) and calculate their freedom and the linearization error rate. Figure 3 presents results for the head direction constraint, where the intensity patterns of the freedom and error rate align very well. Interestingly, the verb-final languages have very low freedom and error rate across almost all relations, not only verb arguments. For the most other languages, obl and advmod are difficult; amod is difficult for Romance languages; and nsubj is difficult for Russian.

Figure 4 shows the freedom and error rate for sibling ordering. The freedom of particular relations (Figure 4a) and their linearization errors (Figure 4b) also show quite similar patterns, although less clear than the head direction.

In particular, some relations with very high free-

dom do not have high error rate, e.g. many verb arguments in Japanese. This suggests that the lexicalized linearization model can capture more sophisticated word order information than the coarse word order preferences defined by the dependency relations.

6 Conclusion

We have presented our surface realization system, which performs both shallow and deep completion. The system achieves state-of-the-art results without any external data.

As future work, we plan to focus on improving the completion model, since it is currently the performance bottleneck of the deep generation task, which is a more realistic task for NLG applications. We also plan to incorporate ranking methods with and without external language models to further improve the linearization, since the described results suggest that there is room for improvement.

Acknowledgements

This work was in part supported by funding from the Ministry of Science, Research and the Arts of the State of Baden-Württemberg (MWK), within the CLARIN-D research project.

References

Roee Aharoni and Yoav Goldberg. 2017. Morphological Inflection Generation with Hard Monotonic Attention. In *Proceedings of the 55th Annual Meeting of the Association for Computational Linguistics (Volume 1: Long Papers)*, pages 2004–2015.

Anders Björkelund, Agnieszka Falenska, Xiang Yu, and Jonas Kuhn. 2017. IMS at the CoNLL 2017 UD Shared Task: CRFs and Perceptrons Meet Neural Networks. In *Proceedings of the CoNLL 2017 Shared Task: Multilingual Parsing from Raw Text to Universal Dependencies*, pages 40–51, Vancouver, Canada. Association for Computational Linguistics.

Bernd Bohnet, Anders Björkelund, Jonas Kuhn, Wolfgang Seeker, and Sina Zarrieß. 2012. Generating Non-Projective Word Order in Statistical Linearization. In *Proceedings of the 2012 Joint Conference on Empirical Methods in Natural Language Processing and Computational Natural Language Learning*, pages 928–939.

Bernd Bohnet, Leo Wanner, Simon Mille, and Alicia Burga. 2010. Broad Coverage Multilingual Deep Sentence Generation with a Stochastic Multi-Level Realizer. In *Proceedings of the 23rd International Conference on Computational Linguistics*, pages 98–106. Association for Computational Linguistics.

Diederik P. Kingma and Jimmy Ba. 2014. Adam: A Method for Stochastic Optimization.

Simon Mille, Anja Belz, Bernd Bohnet, Yvette Graham, and Leo Wanner. 2019. The Second Multilingual Surface Realisation Shared Task (SR'19): Overview and Evaluation Results. In *Proceedings of the 2nd Workshop on Multilingual Surface Realisation (MSR), 2019 Conference on Empirical Methods in Natural Language Processing (EMNLP)*, Hong Kong, China.

Graham Neubig, Chris Dyer, Yoav Goldberg, Austin Matthews, Waleed Ammar, Antonios Anastasopoulos, Miguel Ballesteros, David Chiang, Daniel Clothiaux, Trevor Cohn, et al. 2017. Dynet: The Dynamic Neural Network Toolkit. *arXiv preprint arXiv:1701.03980*.

Joakim Nivre, Marie-Catherine De Marneffe, Filip Ginter, Yoav Goldberg, Jan Hajic, Christopher D Manning, Ryan McDonald, Slav Petrov, Sampo Pyysalo, Natalia Silveira, et al. 2016. Universal Dependencies v1: A Multilingual Treebank Collection. In *Proceedings of the Tenth International Conference on Language Resources and Evaluation (LREC 2016)*, pages 1659–1666.

Ratish Puduppully, Yue Zhang, and Manish Shrivastava. 2016. Transition-based Syntactic Linearization with Lookahead Features. In *Proceedings of the 2016 Conference of the North American Chapter of the Association for Computational Linguistics: Human Language Technologies*, pages 488–493.

Xiang Yu, Agnieszka Falenska, and Jonas Kuhn. 2019a. Dependency Length Minimization vs. Word Order Constraints: An Empirical Study On 55 Treebanks. In *Proceedings of the First Workshop on Quantitative Syntax (Quasy, SyntaxFest 2019)*, pages 89–97, Paris, France. Association for Computational Linguistics.

Xiang Yu, Agnieszka Falenska, Ngoc Thang Vu, and Jonas Kuhn. 2019b. Head-first linearization with tree-structured representation. In *Proceedings of the 12th International Conference on Natural Language Generation*, Tokyo, Japan.

Yao Zhou, Cong Liu, and Yan Pan. 2016. Modelling Sentence Pairs with Tree-structured Attentive Encoder. In *Proceedings of COLING 2016, the 26th International Conference on Computational Linguistics: Technical Papers*, pages 2912–2922.

Surface Realization Shared Task 2019 (SR'19): The Tilburg University Approach

Thiago Castro Ferreira[1,2] and **Chris van der Lee**[1] and **Emiel Krahmer**[1]

[1]Tilburg center for Cognition and Communication (TiCC), Tilburg University, The Netherlands
[2]Federal University of Minas Gerais (UFMG)
{tcastrof,e.j.krahmer}@tilburguniversity.edu

Abstract

This study describes the approach developed by the Tilburg University team to the shallow track of the Multilingual Surface Realization Shared Task 2019 (SR'19) (Mille et al., 2019). Based on Ferreira et al. (2017) and on our 2018 submission Ferreira et al. (2018), the approach generates texts by first preprocessing an input dependency tree into an ordered linearized string, which is then realized using a rule-based and a statistical machine translation (SMT) model. This year our submission is able to realize texts in the 11 languages proposed for the task, different from our last year submission, which covered only 6 Indo-European languages. The model is publicly available[1].

1 Introduction

This study presents the approach developed by the Tilburg University team for the shallow track of the Multilingual Surface Realization Shared Task 2019 (SR'19) (Mille et al., 2019). Given a lemmatized dependency tree without word order information, the goal of this task consists of linearizing the lemmas in the correct order and realizing them as a surface string with the proper morphological form.

Our approach is similar to our submission for the 2018 version of the shared-task (Ferreira et al., 2018). It is based on the surface realization approach described in Ferreira et al. (2017), where a semantic graph structure is first preprocessed into a preordered linearized form, which is subsequently converted into text using a Statistical Machine Translation (SMT) model implemented in

Moses (Koehn et al., 2007). The difference is that, instead of a semantic structure, our approach preprocesses the lemmas of the dependency tree into an ordered linearized version, which is then converted into text using rules and an SMT model.

Different from our last submission where our approach covered only some of the proposed languages (6 out of 10), this year it is able to generate text in all of the 11 languages proposed in the shared-task: Arabic, Chinese, English, French, Hindi, Indonesian, Japanese, Korean, Portuguese, Russian and Spanish. For these languages, parallel datasets were provided with alignment information between source and target sides.

Regarding the languages covered in the previous version of the shared-task, our submission introduced promising results for English, French, Portuguese and Spanish, with BLEU scores higher than 40. For the newly covered languages, results appear promising for realizing Hindi and Indonesian output, with BLEU scores higher than 50. However, the approach appeared to work poorly for Arabic and Russian, and had problems to generate texts in the Asian languages Chinese, Japanese and Korean.

In the remainder of this paper, we better describe our method: Section 2 describes the general approach, Section 3 describes the results and discussion of our approach and Section 4 concludes the study, also describing future work which can be done to improve the model.

2 Model

Following our submission of last year (Ferreira et al., 2018), our model is based on the NLG approach introduced in Ferreira et al. (2017), where a semantic graph structure is first preprocessed into a preordered linearized form, which is then converted into its textual counterpart using an SMT

---

[1]https://github.com/ThiagoCF05/Dep2Text

59

Proceedings of the 2nd Workshop on Multilingual Surface Realisation (MSR 2019), pages 59–62
Hong Kong, China, November 3rd, 2019. ©2019 Association for Computational Linguistics
https://doi.org/10.18653/v1/P17

model implemented with Moses. However for this task, instead of a semantic structure, our approach takes as input a lemmatized dependency tree, which is linearized and converted into its final version by a rule-based and an SMT model. In the next sections, we explain the linearization and realization phases in more detail.

2.1 Linearization

This method aims to linearize a dependency tree input without punctuation nodes into an ordering string format. Our approach is similar to the 2-step classifier introduced in Ferreira et al. (2017) and is depicted in Algorithm 1.

The approach starts by deciding which first-order child nodes are most likely to be before and after its head node (lines 1-13). It uses a maximum entropy classifier ϕ_1, trained for each language based on the relevant aligned training set. As features, this classifier uses the lemmas as well as the dependency and part-of-speech tags of the head and child nodes.

Once the nodes are split into a group of nodes before and another group of nodes after their heads, each one of these groups is ordered with an algorithm similar to the MergeSort one (lines 14-24 and function $SORT$). To decide the order of two child nodes of a same group, we use a second maximum entropy classifier ϕ_2, also trained for each language based on the corresponding aligned training set. As features (line 44), it uses the lemmas as well as the dependency and part-of-speech tags of the head and the two child nodes involved in each comparison.

2.2 Realization

Once the dependency trees are linearized, two methods were used to surface realize the lemmas: a rule-based and a statistical machine translation (SMT) model.

Rule-based For all the 11 covered languages, this approach uses a lexicon created based on the aligned information extracted from the datasets. Given a lemma and its features, our approach looks for the most frequent morphological form in the lexicon.

SMT For 4 languages (English, French, Portuguese and Spanish), after linearizing the dependency tree and realizing the lemmas using a rule-based strategy, we trained a phrase-based machine translation to convert this representation into the

---

Algorithm 1 Linearization method

Require: depTree
 1: **function** LINEAR(root, orderId)
 2:     before ← ∅
 3:     after ← ∅
 4:     edges ← getEdges(depTree, root)
 5:     **for all** edge ∈ edges **do**
 6:         node ← edge.node
 7:         features$_1$ ← f$_1$(depTree, root, node)
 8:         **if** ϕ_1(features$_1$) == before **then**
 9:             before ← before ∪ node
10:         **else**
11:             after ← after ∪ node
12:         **end if**
13:     **end for**
14:     before ← SORT(before)
15:     **for all** node ∈ before **do**
16:         orderId ← LINEAR(node, orderId)
17:     **end for**
18:     root.orderId ← orderId
19:     orderId ← orderId + 1
20:     after ← SORT(after)
21:     **for all** node ∈ after **do**
22:         orderId ← LINEAR(node, orderId)
23:     **end for**
24:     **return** orderId
25: **end function**
26:
27: **function** SORT(nodes)
28:     **if** |nodes| < 2 **then**
29:         **return** nodes
30:     **end if**
31:     half ← |nodes|/2
32:     end ← |nodes|
33:     nodes$_1$ ← SORT(nodes[0,half))
34:     nodes$_2$ ← SORT(nodes[half,end])
35:     ordNodes ← ∅
36:     i$_1$, i$_2$ ← 0, 0
37:     **while** i$_1$ < |nodes$_1$| or i$_2$ < |nodes$_2$| **do**
38:         **if** |nodes$_1$| = 0 **then**
39:             ordNodes ← ordNodes ∪ POP(nodes$_2$)
40:             i$_2$ ← i$_2$ + 1
41:         **else if** |nodes$_2$| = 0 **then**
42:             ordNodes ← ordNodes ∪ POP(nodes$_1$)
43:             i$_1$ ← i$_1$ + 1
44:         **else**
45:             node$_1$ ←POP(nodes$_1$)
46:             node$_2$ ←POP(nodes$_2$)
47:             features$_2$ ← f$_2$(depTree, node$_1$, node$_2$)
48:             **if** ϕ_2(features$_2$) = before **then**
49:                 ordNodes ← ordNodes ∪ node$_1$
50:                 i$_1$ ← i$_1$ + 1
51:             **else**
52:                 ordNodes ← ordNodes ∪ node$_2$
53:                 i$_2$ ← i$_2$ + 1
54:             **end if**
55:         **end if**
56:     **end while**
57:     **return** ordNodes
58: **end function**
59:
60: LINEAR($depTree.root$, 0)

Language	Model	In/Out-Dom.	File	BLEU	DIST	NIST
Arabic	Rule	in-domain	ar_padt	19.01	6.40	53.82
Chinese	Rule	in-domain	zh_gsd	0.16	0.05	58.78
English	SMT	in-domain	en_ewt	56.28	10.88	74.39
		in-domain	en_gum	57.37	10.41	70.54
		in-domain	en_lines	53.78	10.09	67.88
		in-domain	en_partut	62.08	9.19	67.08
		out-domain	en_pud	60.04	11.04	71.75
		predicted	en_ewt	56.25	10.89	73.33
		predicted	en_pud	55.67	10.83	67.99
French	SMT	in-domain	fr_gsd	45.42	9.20	63.46
		in-domain	fr_partut	60.04	8.55	72.35
		in-domain	fr_sequoia	50.14	9.47	66.37
Hindi	Rule	in-domain	hi_hdtb	61.09	12.26	65.73
		predicted	hi_hdtb	61.90	12.37	66.21
Indonesian	Rule	in-domain	id_gsd	52.55	10.51	71.77
Japanese	Rule	in-domain	ja_gsd	0.14	0.01	55.37
		out-domain	ja_pud	0.08	0.01	52.86
Korean	Rule	in-domain	ko_gsd	0.00	0.00	31.35
		in-domain	ko_kaist	0.00	0.00	31.50
		predicted	ko_kaist	0.00	0.00	34.07
Portuguese	SMT	in-domain	pt_bosque	46.31	9.37	63.79
		in-domain	pt_gsd	35.43	9.00	59.89
		predicted	pt_bosque	47.85	9.60	64.76
Russian	Rule	in-domain	ru_gsd	6.65	4.50	50.58
		in-domain	ru_syntagrus	29.59	10.07	57.28
		out-domain	ru_pud	15.54	6.41	59.11
Spanish	SMT	in-domain	es_ancora	54.64	11.73	63.27
		in-domain	es_gsd	49.00	9.86	62.70
		predicted	es_ancora	55.04	11.73	63.5

Table 1: BLEU, DIST and NIST scores of our approach in the original (non-tokenized) test sets.

final realized text. The SMT model was built using the Moses toolkit (Koehn et al., 2007).

The settings were copied from the Statistical MT system introduced in Ferreira et al. (2017). At training time, we extract and score phrases up to the size of nine tokens. As feature functions, we used direct and inverse phrase translation probabilities and lexical weighting, as well as word, unknown word and phrase penalties. These feature functions were trained using alignments from the training set obtained by MGIZA (Gao and Vogel, 2008). Model weights were tuned on the development data using 60-batch MIRA (Cherry and Foster, 2012) with BLEU as the evaluation metric. A distortion limit of 6 was used for the reordering models. We used two lexicalized reordering models: a phrase-level (phrase-msd-bidirectional-fe) (Koehn et al., 2005) and a hierarchical-level one (hier-mslr-bidirectional-fe) (Galley and Manning, 2008). At decoding time, we used a stack size of 1000. To rerank the candidate texts, we used a 5-gram language model trained on the EuroParl corpus (Koehn, 2005) using KenLM (Heafield, 2011).

3 Results and Discussion

Concerning the languages covered in the previous version of the shared-task, our approach introduced promising results for English, French, Portuguese and Spanish, with BLEU scores higher than 40. For the newly covered languages, results were promising for the realization of Hindi and Indonesian texts, with BLEU scores higher than 50. On the other hand, our approach obtained low results for Arabic and Russian, and had problems to generate texts in the Asian languages Chinese, Japanese and Korean. For Chinese and Japanese, the problem arose from the fact we did not manage the tokenization/detokenization process well, which had a drastic negative influence on the final results.

4 Conclusion

This study described a shallow surface realizer for the 11 target languages in the Surface Realization Shared Task 2019 (SR'19). In future work, we aim to fix the problems for the Asian languages Chinese, Japanese and Korean. Specifically, for Chinese and Japanese, we require a proper method to tokenize/detokenize the results produced by our approach. Moreover, we aim to design the task based on novel pipeline architectures for Natural Language Generation (Ferreira et al., 2019).

Acknowledgments

This work is part of the research program "Discussion Thread Summarization for Mobile Devices" (DISCOSUMO) which is financed by the Netherlands Organization for Scientific Research (NWO).

References

Colin Cherry and George Foster. 2012. Batch tuning strategies for statistical machine translation. In *Proceedings of the 2012 Conference of the North American Chapter of the Association for Computational Linguistics: Human Language Technologies*, NAACL-HLT'12, pages 427–436, Montreal, Canada. Association for Computational Linguistics.

Thiago Castro Ferreira, Iacer Calixto, Sander Wubben, and Emiel Krahmer. 2017. Linguistic realisation as machine translation: Comparing different mt models for amr-to-text generation. In *Proceedings of the 10th International Conference on Natural Language Generation*, pages 1–10. Association for Computational Linguistics.

Thiago Castro Ferreira, Chris van der Lee, Emiel van Miltenburg, and Emiel Krahmer. 2019. Neural data-to-text generation: A comparison between pipeline and end-to-end architectures. *arXiv preprint arXiv:1908.09022*.

Thiago Castro Ferreira, Sander Wubben, and Emiel Krahmer. 2018. Surface realization shared task 2018 (SR18): The Tilburg university approach. In *Proceedings of the First Workshop on Multilingual Surface Realisation*, pages 35–38, Melbourne, Australia. Association for Computational Linguistics.

Michel Galley and Christopher D. Manning. 2008. A simple and effective hierarchical phrase reordering model. In *Proceedings of the 2008 Conference on Empirical Methods in Natural Language Processing*, EMNLP'08, pages 848–856, Honolulu, Hawaii. Association for Computational Linguistics.

Qin Gao and Stephan Vogel. 2008. Parallel implementations of word alignment tool. In *Software Engineering, Testing, and Quality Assurance for Natural Language Processing*, SETQA-NLP'08, pages 49–57, Columbus, Ohio. Association for Computational Linguistics.

Kenneth Heafield. 2011. Kenlm: Faster and smaller language model queries. In *Proceedings of the Sixth Workshop on Statistical Machine Translation*, WMT '11, pages 187–197, Stroudsburg, PA, USA. Association for Computational Linguistics.

Philipp Koehn. 2005. Europarl: A parallel corpus for statistical machine translation. In *MT summit*, volume 5, pages 79–86.

Philipp Koehn, Amittai Axelrod, Alexandra Birch, Chris Callison-Burch, Miles Osborne, and David Talbot. 2005. Edinburgh System Description for the 2005 IWSLT Speech Translation Evaluation. In *International Workshop on Spoken Language Translation*.

Philipp Koehn, Hieu Hoang, Alexandra Birch, Chris Callison-Burch, Marcello Federico, Nicola Bertoldi, Brooke Cowan, Wade Shen, Christine Moran, Richard Zens, Chris Dyer, Ondřej Bojar, Alexandra Constantin, and Evan Herbst. 2007. Moses: Open source toolkit for statistical machine translation. In *Proceedings of the 45th Annual Meeting of the ACL on Interactive Poster and Demonstration Sessions*, ACL'07, pages 177–180, Prague, Czech Republic. Association for Computational Linguistics.

Simon Mille, Anja Belz, Bernd Bohnet, Yvette Graham, and Leo Wanner. 2019. The Second Multilingual Surface Realisation Shared Task (SR'19): Overview and Evaluation Results. In *Proceedings of the 2nd Workshop on Multilingual Surface Realisation (MSR), 2019 Conference on Empirical Methods in Natural Language Processing (EMNLP)*, Hong Kong, China.

The Concordia NLG Surface Realizer at SR'19

Farhood Farahnak and **Laya Rafiee** and **Leila Kosseim** and **Thomas Fevens**
Dept. of Computer Science and Software Engineering
Concordia University
Montreal, Canada
`firstname.lastname@concordia.ca`

Abstract

This paper presents the model we developed for the shallow track of the 2019 NLG Surface Realization Shared Task. The model reconstructs sentences whose word order and word inflections were removed. We divided the problem into two sub-problems: reordering and inflecting. For the purpose of reordering, we used a pointer network integrated with a transformer model as its encoder-decoder modules. In order to generate the inflected forms of tokens, a Feed Forward Neural Network was employed.

1 Introduction

The goal of Natural Language Generation (NLG) is to produce natural texts given structured data. Typically, NLG is sub-divided into two tasks: Content Planning and Surface Realization (Hovy et al., 1996; Reiter and Dale, 2000). While Content Planning focuses on selecting the most appropriate content to convey, Surface Realization produces the linear form of the text from this selected data following a given grammar.

Although the field of Natural Language Processing (NLP) has witnessed significant progress in the last few years, NLG, and surface realization in particular, still performs significantly below human performance.

Recently, several shared tasks have been proposed to improve the state of the art in specific NLG tasks (eg. Dušek et al. (2019); May and Priyadarshi (2017)). In particular, the Surface Realization Shared Task 2019 (SR'19) (Mille et al., 2019) aims to provide common-ground datasets for developing and evaluating NLG systems. Similarly to SR'18 (Mille et al., 2018), SR'19 proposed two tracks: a shallow track and a deep track. In the shallow track, unordered and lemmatized tokens with universal dependency (UD) structures (de Marneffe et al., 2014) were provided to participants and systems were required to reorder and inflect the tokens to produce final sentences. The deep track is similar to the shallow track but functional words and surface-oriented morphological information were removed as well. In addition to determining token order and inflections, systems participating in the deep track also had to determine the omitted words.

We decided to only participate in the shallow track. We used a model based on the transformer encoder-decoder architecture (Vaswani et al., 2017) combined with a pointer network (Vinyals et al., 2015) to reconstruct the word order from the input provided and a Feed Forward Neural Network to produce inflections. Based on the human evaluation, our model has an average score of 48.1% and 60.9% on all the English datasets for Readability/Quality and Meaning Similarity respectively.

2 Background

Pointer networks are types of encoder-decoder models where the output corresponds to a position in the input sequences (Vinyals et al., 2015). One of the main advantages of pointer networks compared to standard sequence-to-sequence models is that the number of output classes depends on the length of the input. This feature can be useful to address problems involving sorting variable sized sequences such as required at SR'19.

In Vinyals et al. (2015), Recurrent Neural Networks (RNNs) are used as encoder and decoder. RNNs compute the context representation based on the order of the input sequences. In cases where there is no information regarding the correct order of the input sequences, using an RNN-based encoder cannot provide a proper context representation for the decoder.

63

Proceedings of the 2nd Workshop on Multilingual Surface Realisation (MSR 2019), pages 63–67
Hong Kong, China, November 3rd, 2019. ©2019 Association for Computational Linguistics
https://doi.org/10.18653/v1/P17

Transformer models constitute an alternative to RNNs as they entirely rely on the self-attention mechanism (Vaswani et al., 2017). Transformer models have achieved state of the art performance in many NLP tasks such as machine translation (Vaswani et al., 2017) and language modeling (Devlin et al., 2019; Radford et al., 2019).

The encoder and decoder modules of transformer models consist of multiple layers of stacked self-attention and point-wise fully connected layers. The encoder of the transformer consists in several encoder layers, each of which is composed of two sub-layers. The first sub-layer has a multi-head attention which consists of several layers of self-attention computing on the same input, and the second sub-layer is a feed-forward network. The output of each sub-layer is added with a residual connection from their input followed by a normalization layer. The decoder module consists of several layers similar to the encoder, where the decoder layers have an extra sub-layer of encoder-decoder attention.

Transformer models have no information regarding the order of the input sequence. Hence "Mary killed John" and "John killed Mary" have the same internal representations. To alleviate this issue, Vaswani et al. (2017) considered using positional encoding summed to the embedding of each word. Because the transformer without positional encoding does not rely on the order of the input sequence, this architecture constitutes a promising option for the SR'19 where the correct order of the input sequence were removed (see Section 3).

3   Dataset

For the shallow track, training and development sets were provided for 11 different languages. These were taken from the Universal Dependency (UD) datasets (de Marneffe et al., 2014). The correct token order within the sentences was removed by shuffling the tokens. In total, 7 features were provided by the organizers. Out of these features, FEATS contained more than 40 morphological sub-features from the universal feature inventory and the relative linear order with respect to the governor (Lin). Table 1 lists the 8 features used by our model: 6 features of the UD structure, in addition to 2 features for Lin (the Lin feature divided into its absolute value and its sign).

In particular, we worked only on the En-

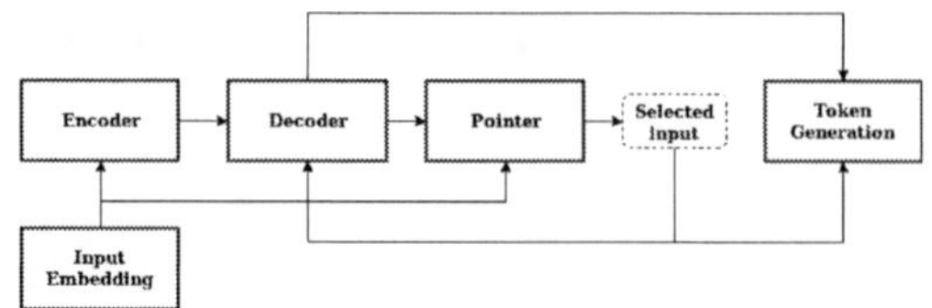

Figure 1: The model architecture used for the shallow track at SR'19

glish datasets, which consists of four training and development pairs. We concatenated all four training sets (en_ewt-ud-train, en_gum-ud-train, en_lines-ud-train and en_partut-ud-train) into a single one containing 19,976 sentences, with the longest sentence containing 209 words.

Because the development sets provided by the SR'19 organizers are not labeled, we divided the training data in two parts; training $(18,000$ sentences) and validation $(1,967$ sentences). We removed all sentences longer than 100 tokens for efficiency reasons.[1]

4   Model

Inspired by previous work from SR'18 (Mille et al., 2018) that used pointer networks to reconstruct unordered sentences (Elder and Hokamp, 2018), we developed a similar model using a pointer network integrated with a transformer as its encoder and decoder. As shown in Figure 1, our model is composed of five modules: input embedding, encoder, decoder, pointer, and token generation. In the following, we describe each module in more detail.

4.1   Input embedding

In order to train the model, we embedded each feature separately into vectors and then concatenated them. Table 1 indicates the embedding size of each feature. For the token embeddings, we employed the GloVe pretrained embeddings of size 300 (Pennington et al., 2014), while the remaining feature embeddings are trained from scratch. At the end, the concatenated vector (of size 393) is linearly mapped into the desired embedding size (512 in our case, see Section 5).

4.2   Encoder

The embedded input is fed into the encoder to compute its representation. The encoder mod-

---

[1]This removed 9 sentences from the training sets.

#	Feature	Feature description	Embedding size
1	Token	Lemma or stem of word form	300
2	UPOS	Universal part-of-speech tag	10
3	XPOS	Language-specific part-of-speech tag	10
4	Deprel	Universal dependency relation to the Head	10
5	Head	Head of the current word	20
6	Index	Word index	20
7	Lin	Relative linear order with respect to the governor	20
8	Lin sign	The sign of the Lin feature	3
	All	Concatenation of all features	393

Table 1: The 8 features used in our model with their corresponding embedding sizes

ule uses the transformer architecture described in Vaswani et al. (2017). Since the input data does not provide any ordering information, we directly feed the embedded input into the encoder without summing it with the positional encoding of the tokens.

4.3 Decoder

The decoder in the transformer model receives the previously generated tokens alongside the encoded representation from the encoder as its input to generate the next token. However, since our task is to produce an ordering rather than generate tokens, we decided to feed the same embeddings used for the encoder (see Section 4.1) in its correct order. Since the correct order for the previously generated tokens is determined in the decoding phase, we add the positional encoding with the embedded input.

4.4 Pointer

To find the next token, we deploy the attention mechanism described in Vaswani et al. (2017) and in Equation 1.

$$\text{Attention}(Q, V, K) = \text{softmax}\left(\frac{QK^T}{\sqrt{d_k}}\right) V \quad (1)$$

In each decoding step, the keys (K) and values (V) come from the embedded input and the query (Q) is defined by the output of the decoder (in this setup the keys and query have a dimension of d_k). The pointer selects the most probable embedded input as the next input to the decoder. During test time, we mask out the previously selected embedded inputs so that they are not selected again.

4.5 Token generation

The Pointer Network orders the given lemmatized tokens based on the input features. However, the desired output should be the inflected form of the input tokens. To this end, the token generation

module (see Figure 1) is designed to generate the inflected form of the tokens, where its input is the concatenation of the selected embedded input token with the decoder's output. The output of this module is the probability over all the words in the vocabulary. This module consists of two feed-forward layers with a ReLU activation function. The last layer is initialized with pretrained GloVe embeddings in order to provide a better generalization on unseen tokens.

5 Experiments and Results

5.1 Model Configuration

The model submitted to SR'19, under the team name CLaC, has the following configuration optimized on the validation set.

The encoder and decoder of the model have 4 layers each with 8 heads (number of attention in each layer). All the embedding sizes of the encoder and decoder layers as well as input embedding are set to 512.

To preserve the GloVe embeddings, we froze the weights of both token embeddings and the last layer of the token generation module.

We suspected that the Head and Index features (see Table 1) constituted valuable information regarding the dependency tree structure of the sentences. Therefore, to ensure the model does not memorize the actual value of these features, but rather their relationship, in each training iteration, we randomly changed the values of these features while keeping the tree structure relationship intact.

The model was trained using two cross-entropy loss functions: order loss for the pointer and token loss for the generation module. We observed training with the order loss and then fine tuning on both losses increased the performance of the model.

The final model trained for 60 epochs, where training on the order loss is done for 30 epochs, and fine tuning the order and token losses were

#		Dataset	Tokenized			Detokenized		
			BLEU	**NIST**	**DIST**	**BLEU**	**NIST**	**DIST**
1		en_ewt-ud-test	**22.08**	9.77	45.99	14.62	7.21	44.7
2	In-domain	en_gum-ud-test	15.32	8.64	38.13	10.55	6.53	36.97
3		en_lines-ud-test	15.30	8.23	40.40	9.81	6.10	39.08
4		en_partut-ud-test	10.07	7.14	36.21	7.45	5.57	35.32
5	Out-of-domain	en_pud-ud-test	12.36	8.83	36.26	9.11	6.66	35.23
6	Predicted	en_ewt-Pred-HIT-edit	21.21	9.69	43.59	14.14	7.23	42.41
7		en_pud-Pred-LATTICE	12.89	8.82	36.67	9.29	6.69	35.53

Table 2: Results of our submission in the shallow track task of SR'19

done on the remaining 30 epochs. The initial learning rate was set to 1×10^{-4}. We also took advantage of learning rate decay with the factor of 0.5 when there is no improvement on the validation loss. A dropout rate of 0.3 was used on the encoder, decoder, and input embedding module.

The model was implemented using the PyTorch 1.1 framework. For the transformer encoder and decoder, we modified the fairseq transformer implementation of Ott et al. (2019).

In the test phase, we used tokens generated by the model as the final output. When encountering unknown tokens, the model uses the input token where the pointer points at.

5.2 Results

At SR'19, three types of test sets were given: In-domain, Out-of-domain, and Predicted. The In-domain datasets share the same domain as the training data, while Out-of-domain dataset does not. The Predicted datasets are those where the annotation were built using parser outputs from the Universal Dependency Parsing shared task 2018 (Zeman et al., 2018) instead of the gold syntactic annotations. Evaluation was performed in both a tokenized and detokenized fashion.

Table 2 shows the results of our model on the test data. As shown in Table 2, our model achieved its highest performance on the en_ewt-ud-test dataset with a BLEU score of 22.08 for tokenized among the In-domain datasets. Whereas the lowest score is for en_partut-ud-test with a BLEU of 10.07. Clearly, the performance of the model on these four datasets is directly related to the relative size of corresponding training set in the concatenated training set used to train our model. For example, the en_ewt-ud-train dataset accounts for the greatest proportion of our training set (63%) and achieves the highest BLEU; whereas en_partut-ud-train accounts for only 9% of the training samples yielding the lowest BLEU

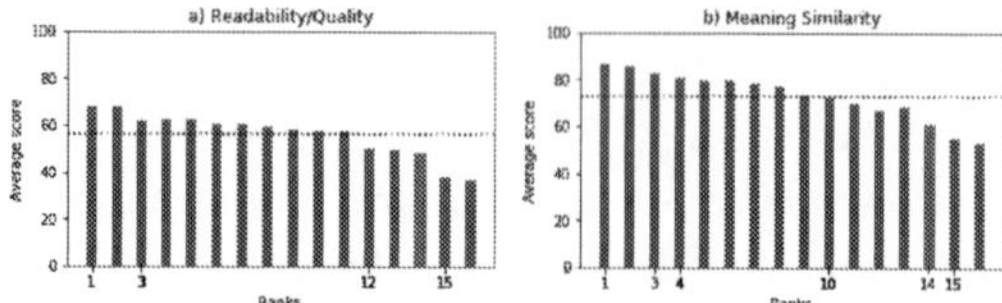

Figure 2: Human evaluation results compared to all participants of the shallow track at SR'19

of 10.07 with en_partut-ud-test.

Based on human evaluation, our submitted system achieved average Readability/Quality score of 48.1% and a Meaning Similarity score of 60.9% with the rank of 12 and 14 respectively among the 16 participating systems. The results are shown in the Figure 2.

6 Conclusions

In this paper, we have presented the model we developed for SR'19. The proposed system is composed of a pointer network where its encoder and decoder modules borrowed from transformer, aim to reconstruct the tokens' order and inflection. The model achieved its best performance on the English datasets with the average scores of 48.1 and 60.9 for the Readability/Quality and Meaning Similarity respectively. Although this performance is lower than expected, the lack of training data is observable. It was noticeable that training the model in an end-to-end fashion without feature engineering could not lead the model to learn meaningful representation of the input features.

As future work, it would be interesting to investigate further the model's sensitivity to the training size, as we noted in our submission's results, by training it on a much larger dataset. We will also further investigate the use of other features provided in the universal dependency structure. Another avenue worth looking into is the use of pretrained language models. Finally, a thorough error analysis would provide us with hints as to where the model is weaker, in the ordering task or in the inflection task.

Acknowledgements

The authors would like to thank the anonymous reviewers for their comments on an earlier version of this paper.

This work was financially supported by the Natural Sciences and Engineering Research Council of Canada (NSERC).

References

Jacob Devlin, Ming-Wei Chang, Kenton Lee, and Kristina Toutanova. 2019. BERT: Pre-training of deep bidirectional transformers for language understanding. In *Proceedings of the 2019 Conference of the North American Chapter of the Association for Computational Linguistics: Human Language Technologies, Volume 1 (NAACL/HLT 2019)*, pages 4171–4186, Minneapolis, Minnesota. Association for Computational Linguistics.

Ondřej Dušek, Jekaterina Novikova, and Verena Rieser. 2019. Evaluating the state-of-the-art of end-to-end natural language generation: The E2E NLG Challenge. *arXiv preprint arXiv:1901.11528.*

Henry Elder and Chris Hokamp. 2018. Generating high-quality surface realizations using data augmentation and factored sequence models. In *Proceedings of the First Workshop on Multilingual Surface Realisation*, pages 49–53, Melbourne, Australia. Association for Computational Linguistics.

Eduard Hovy, Gertjan van Noord, Guenter Neumann, and John Bateman. 1996. Language generation. *Survey of the State of the Art in Human Language Technology*, pages 131–146.

Marie-Catherine de Marneffe, Timothy Dozat, Natalia Silveira, Katri Haverinen, Filip Ginter, Joakim Nivre, and Christopher D. Manning. 2014. Universal Stanford dependencies: A cross-linguistic typology. In *Proceedings of the Ninth International Conference on Language Resources and Evaluation (LREC-2014)*, pages 4585–4592, Reykjavik, Iceland. European Languages Resources Association (ELRA).

Jonathan May and Jay Priyadarshi. 2017. SemEval-2017 task 9: Abstract meaning representation parsing and generation. In *Proceedings of the 11th International Workshop on Semantic Evaluation (SemEval-2017)*, pages 536–545, Vancouver, Canada. Association for Computational Linguistics.

Simon Mille, Anja Belz, Bernd Bohnet, Yvette Graham, and Leo Wanner. 2019. The Second Multilingual Surface Realisation Shared Task (SR'19): Overview and Evaluation Results. In *Proceedings of the 2nd Workshop on Multilingual Surface Realisation (MSR), 2019 Conference on Empirical Methods in Natural Language Processing (EMNLP)*, Hong Kong, China.

Simon Mille, Anja Belz, Bernd Bohnet, and Leo Wanner. 2018. Underspecified universal dependency structures as inputs for multilingual surface realisation. In *Proceedings of the 11th International Conference on Natural Language Generation*, pages 199–209, Tilburg University, The Netherlands. Association for Computational Linguistics.

Myle Ott, Sergey Edunov, Alexei Baevski, Angela Fan, Sam Gross, Nathan Ng, David Grangier, and Michael Auli. 2019. fairseq: A fast, extensible toolkit for sequence modeling. In *Proceedings of the 2019 Conference of the North American Chapter of the Association for Computational Linguistics (NAACL/HLT 2019): Demonstrations*, pages 48–53, Minneapolis, Minnesota. Association for Computational Linguistics.

Jeffrey Pennington, Richard Socher, and Christopher Manning. 2014. GloVe: Global Vectors for Word Representation. In *Proceedings of the 2014 Conference on Empirical Methods in Natural Language Processing (EMNLP 2014)*, pages 1532–1543, Doha, Qatar. Association for Computational Linguistics.

Alec Radford, Jeffrey Wu, Rewon Child, David Luan, Dario Amodei, and Ilya Sutskever. 2019. Language models are unsupervised multitask learners. *OpenAI Blog*, 1(8).

Ehud Reiter and Robert Dale. 2000. *Building Natural Language Generation Systems*. Cambridge University Press, New York, NY, USA.

Ashish Vaswani, Noam Shazeer, Niki Parmar, Jakob Uszkoreit, Llion Jones, Aidan N Gomez, Ł ukasz Kaiser, and Illia Polosukhin. 2017. Attention is all you need. In I. Guyon, U. V. Luxburg, S. Bengio, H. Wallach, R. Fergus, S. Vishwanathan, and R. Garnett, editors, *Advances in Neural Information Processing Systems 30 (NIPS 2017)*, pages 5998–6008. Curran Associates, Inc.

Oriol Vinyals, Meire Fortunato, and Navdeep Jaitly. 2015. Pointer Networks. In C. Cortes, N. D. Lawrence, D. D. Lee, M. Sugiyama, and R. Garnett, editors, *Advances in Neural Information Processing Systems 28 (NIPS 2015)*, pages 2692–2700. Curran Associates, Inc.

Daniel Zeman, Filip Ginter, Jan Hajič, Joakim Nivre, Martin Popel, and Milan Straka. 2018. CoNLL 2018 Shared Task: Multilingual Parsing from Raw Text to Universal Dependencies. In *Proceedings of the CoNLL 2018 Shared Task: Multilingual Parsing from Raw Text to Universal Dependencies*, Brussels, Belgium. Association for Computational Linguistics.

The OSU-Facebook Realizer for SR '19:
Seq2seq Inflection and Serialized Tree2Tree Linearization

Kartikeya Upasani,[1] **David L. King,**[2] **Jinfeng Rao,**[1]
Anusha Balakrishnan,[1] **and Michael White**[12]
[1]Facebook Assistant, Menlo Park, CA, USA
{kart,raojinfeng,anushabala,mwhite14850}@fb.com
[2]Department of Linguistics, The Ohio State University
The Ohio State University, Columbus, OH, USA
king.2138@osu.edu, mwhite@ling.osu.edu

Abstract

We describe our exploratory system for the shallow surface realization task, which combines morphological inflection using character sequence-to-sequence models with a baseline linearizer that implements a tree-to-tree model using sequence-to-sequence models on serialized trees. Results for morphological inflection were competitive across languages. Due to time constraints, we could only submit complete results (including linearization) for English. Preliminary linearization results were decent, with a small benefit from reranking to prefer valid output trees, but inadequate control over the words in the output led to poor quality on longer sentences.

1 Introduction

With our entry in the shallow surface realization shared task, we aimed to (1) implement an up-to-date morphological inflection model based on the approach of Faruqui et al. (2016) and Kann and Schütze (2016), and (2) conduct exploratory experiments with linearization using the constrained decoding approach of Balakrishnan et al. (2019) adapted to dependency trees.

Our system is a pipeline that begins by generating inflected wordforms from uninflected terminals in the tree using character seq2seq models. We then serialize these inflected syntactic trees as constituent trees by converting the relations to non-terminals. The serialized constituent trees are fed to seq2seq models (including models with copy and with tree-LSTM encoders), whose outputs also contain tokens marking the tree structure. We obtain n-best outputs for orderings and choose the highest confidence output sequence with a valid tree—i.e., one where the input and output trees are isomorphic up to sibling order—in order to obtain a projective linearization where possible, given that the vast majority of gold linearizations are projective.[1]

While we found that this validity checking step provided a small benefit, fully adapting the constrained decoding approach to dependency trees would have required adding a step to ensure that all and only the input words appeared in the output tree, and enforcing these constraints during beam search. Due to time constraints, however, we were only able to obtain preliminary linearization results for English without these word-level checks.

Development results for morphological inflection were competitive across languages as compared to previous implementations (King and White, 2018; Puzikov and Gurevych, 2018). With linearization, the preliminary results were decent, but showed substantial degradation for longer sentences where problems with lack of control over the output words became more severe.

In the rest of the paper, we describe our inflection and linearization components in more detail, along with our experimental results.

2 Inflection

Our pipeline begins by producing fully inflected word forms from the citation forms pro-

---

[1]To handle non-projective cases, the arc-lifting method of Bohnet et al. (2012) could be applied as a preprocessing step.

Proceedings of the 2nd Workshop on Multilingual Surface Realisation (MSR 2019), pages 68–74
Hong Kong, China, November 3rd, 2019. ©2019 Association for Computational Linguistics
https://doi.org/10.18653/v1/P17

vided in the UD input. In a sense, at this stage, the system has to be able to perform the wug test (Berko, 1958): having never seen a word before, we need to have the ability to produce the correct form for a given paradigm cell. We utilize sequence-to-sequence models (Bahdanau et al., 2014) in keeping with previous successful approaches (Kann and Schütze, 2016; Faruqui et al., 2016; King and White, 2018). Additionally, we reimplemented Kann and Schütze's 2016 approach in PyTorch.[2]

We also follow Kann and Schütze's approach by training our inflection model at the languages level and not at the level of individual paradigm cells as originally proposed by Faruqui et al. More formally, our LSTMs (Hochreiter and Schmidhuber, 1997) create an encoding, producing hidden state h_t which is dependent on the input x_t, the hidden state from the previous time step h_{t-1}, and nonlinear function f. c is the context of all previous time steps. Additionally, we set h_j to be the concatenated forward and backward encodings since we use bidirectional LSTMs.

$$h_t = f(x_t, h_{t-1}) \tag{1}$$

$$c = q(h_1, ..., h_{T_x}) \tag{2}$$

$$h_j = \left[\overrightarrow{h_j^T}, \overleftarrow{h_j^T}\right]^T \tag{3}$$

During inference (i.e. decoding), output y depends on the input sequence and previous inference steps. We also use the same attention as described by Bahdanau et al. and Kann and Schütze:

$$p(y|x) = \prod_{t=1}^{T_y} p(y_t|\{y_1, ..., y_t - 1\}, s_t, c_t) \tag{4}$$

$$c_i = \sum_{j=1}^{T_x} \alpha_{ij} h_j \tag{5}$$

$$\alpha_{ij} = \frac{exp(e_{ij})}{\sum_{k=1}^{T_x} exp(e_{ik})} \tag{6}$$

$$e_{ij} = a(s_{i-1}, hj) \tag{7}$$

As seen in Table 1, uncased results are almost always higher than cased. This should not surprise us as, operating on the word-internal level, any sequence-to-sequence model

---

[2]Freely available here: `https://github.com/davidlking/med-pytorch`

would have no access to syntagmatic information outside of how UDs encode that information in the morphosynctactic feature sets. Also Arabic, Hindi, and Japanese do not have cased orthography and therefore have no difference in their case/uncased accuracies.

As for feature sets, we include the same set as described by King and White. In addition to using the morphosyntactic features provided by the UD schema, we also used the POS tag and dependency name as input to the system. Differing from previous shared tasks (Cotterell et al., 2016, 2017), we do not alter the token frequencies. In traditional SIGMORPHON inflection tasks, each system only sees a word form once per epoch. We found that this causes the system to miss irregulars. Since irregular forms tend to occur with higher frequency, allowing the system to see more examples during each epoch increased performance on irregular forms. We also found that adding a rule for English specifically designed to account for the "to be" paradigm raises accuracy for English another 0.6% to 98.5%.

Finally, for Korean and Chinese, we simply write rule sets for their morphology. The Korean dataset exclusively uses concatenation. The input forms list items and their corresponding affixes, in order, and simply removing the morpheme boundary token (a "+") yielded 100% accuracy. For Chinese, the plural marker "们" (*men*) only ever occurred with "人" (*rén*, "person"), "我" (*wǒ*, "I"), "F" (*tā*, "it" [animals]), "它" (*tā*, "it" [inanimate]), "她" (*tā*, "she"), and "他" (*tā*, "he"). Writing a rule that adds "们" when any of the character co-occur with the `Num=Plur` feature also gives us 100% accuracy for Chinese.

3 Linearization

To help assess the potential of using tree-to-tree models with constrained decoding (Balakrishnan et al., 2019) for linearization and guide future work in this direction, we conducted exploratory experiments using off-the-shelf sequence-to-sequence models where the input and output trees are represented as sequences using non-terminal tokens corresponding to dependency relations. In these serialized trees, each non-terminal token is followed by the inflected form, its dependents,

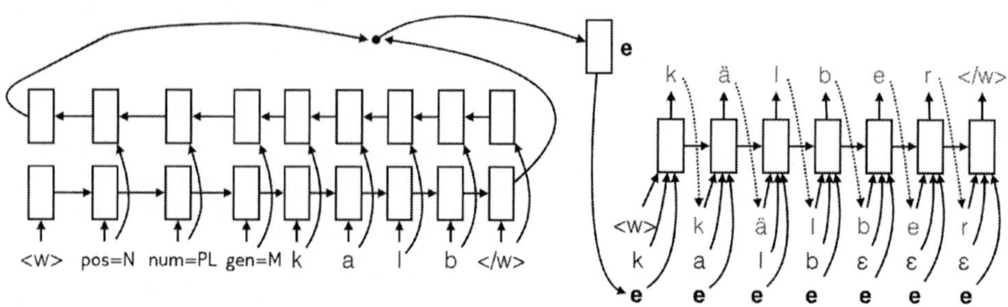

Figure 1: A graphical representation of the architecture originally introduced by Faruqui et al. (2016) and adapted by Kann and Schütze (2016). A bidirectional LSTM creates an encoding of the input wordform and supplied features. That encoding is subsequently fed to the decoder LSTM along with the original input wordform.

Model	Language										
	ar	en	es	fr	hi	id	ja	ko	pt	ru	zh
Cased	92.2	91.1	91.3	89.2	97.3	86.4	99.6	N/A	87.1	90.0	N/A
Uncased	92.2	97.9	93.5	95.3	97.3	98.9	99.6	N/A	91.4	96.9	N/A

Table 1: Morphological inflection results on the development set. Although we only submitted results for the English due to time constraints, we did train inflection models for each language.

Input: **[root** behind **[advmod** badly **] [advmod** now **] [cop** are **] [nsubj** we **] [obl** matter **[case** in **] [det** this **]] [punct** . **]]**

Target: **[root [nsubj** we **] [cop** are **] [advmod** badly **]** behind **[advmod** now **] [obl [case** in **] [det** this **]** matter **] [punct** . **]]**

Figure 2: Example of serialized tree representation used for linearization.

and finally a closing-bracket indicating the end of the non-terminal's span, as exemplified in Figure 2 shows an example of serialized inputs and outputs.

We experimented with three different variants of sequence-to-sequence models:

Seq2Seq: Simple encoder-decoder model with attention (Bahdanau et al., 2014). Both the encoder and decoder are LSTMs.

Tree2Seq: Similar to Seq2Seq, but we use a variant of the N-ary tree-LSTM (Tai et al., 2015) as the encoder, as described in Rao et al. (2019), thereby potentially taking better advantage of the input tree structure.

Seq2Seq-Copy: Seq2Seq model with a pointer-generator mechanism (See et al., 2017) for copying tokens from input. The decoder can choose to either generate a word from the vocabulary or copy an input token instead. We did not have an off-the-shelf implementation for a Tree2Seq-Copy model, though our experiments suggest it would be worth developing one.

Additionally, we also experimented with constrained decoding (Balakrishnan et al., 2019) with each of the above model. Using this method, in each step of beam search, we check for and remove candidates whose tree structures deviate from that of the input tree. The constraints include ensuring that a parent node only accepts valid children, and that all its children have been generated before it can accept a closing bracket, thereby helping to ensure a projective realization. However, as noted in the introduction, we did not have time to extend the constraints to ensure that all and only the input words appeared in the output, so we did not expect this method to work as well as we would have liked. As such, we also experimented with reranking an n-best list to select the highest-scoring output with a valid tree (i.e., one that matches the tree of the input, up to sibling ordering).

4   Results

We picked the approach that gave the best performance on dev set. We combined samples of all English train sets, training on all sets together gave better dev BLEU scores than training individually. Table 2 shows a comparison of the different models that we tried.

Model	en_gum-ud	en_partut-ud
Seq2Seq	0.180	0.163
Tree2Seq	0.585	0.275
Seq2Seq-Copy	0.870	0.902

Table 2: Dev set BLEU scores (calculated along with non-terminals), using gold inflected forms

In the table, the BLEU scores are calculated with the non-terminals included in both input and output sequences, inflating them somewhat relative to regular BLEU scores. Gold inflected forms were also used.

Table 3 compares the constrained and unconstrained versions of the Seq2Seq-Copy (again with non-terminals in the output and gold inflected forms). Since we did not have time to implement word-level constraints, the results seem to be mixed. In the end, we chose the constrained model on datasets where dev BLEU was higher than its unconstrained counterpart. Table 4 shows the gains obtained by doing validity reranking (again with gold inflected forms); here the scores shown are calculated without non-terminals.

Given our time constraints, we only submitted English results for evaluation. Although we generated inflected forms for all languages in the T1 task, we could only obtain linearization results for English. Our results are decent (with the exception of the en_partut-ud-test dataset), suggesting that the approach may represent a viable starting point for future work. In particular, in the human evaluation results for English in the shared task overview paper (Mille et al., 2019), our system was ranked in the middle group of systems for meaning preservation and in the large group of systems tied for third–twelfth place in readability. Consistent with the human evaluation, the automatic scores for our system (Table 5) were also in the middle of the pack. Note that the test scores are lower than the dev scores at least in part because only the former are calculated with generated inflected forms.

5   Discussion

Regarding the en_partut-ud-test dataset, our preliminary error analysis seems to indicate that the inflection model overfit the dev set. Although the model outputs relatively sane er-

Model	en_ewt-ud	en_gum-ud	en_partut-ud
Seq2Seq-Copy Unconstr	0.8239	0.8731	0.8984
Seq2Seq-Copy Constr	0.8499	0.8337	0.8847

Table 3: Preliminary BLEU scores for constrained decoding (calculated along with non-terminals), using gold inflected forms

Dataset	w/o reranking	w/ reranking
en_ewt	0.8328	0.8405
en_gum	0.8294	0.8289
en_lines	0.7655	0.7778
en_partut	0.7891	0.7909

Table 4: BLEU scores on dev sets before and after reranking, using gold inflected forms

Test set	BLEU	NIST	DIST
en_ewt-ud-test	62.38	11.29	77.93
en_gum-ud-test	49.91	8.5	66.88
en_lines-ud-test	54.56	9.89	71.07
en_partut-ud-test	7.37	3.21	54.27
en_pud-ud-test	67.91	11.74	78.12
en_ewt-Pred-HIT-edit	60.58	10.96	74.64
en_pud-Pred-LATTICE	66.18	11.7	76.8

Table 5: Test set results for English from the organizers

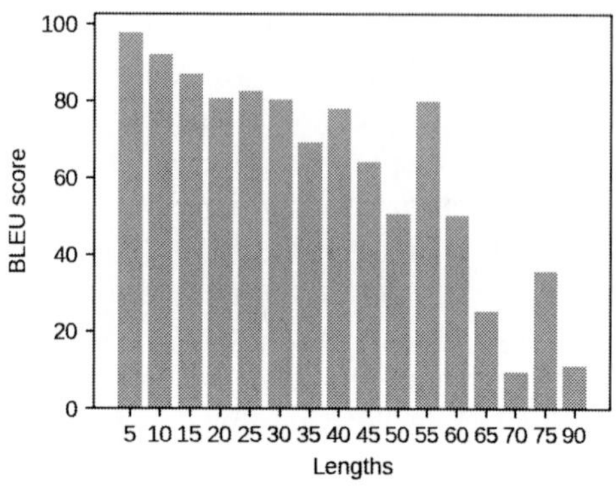

Figure 3: BLEU score plotted against gold sequence lengths for en-gum-ud dev set.

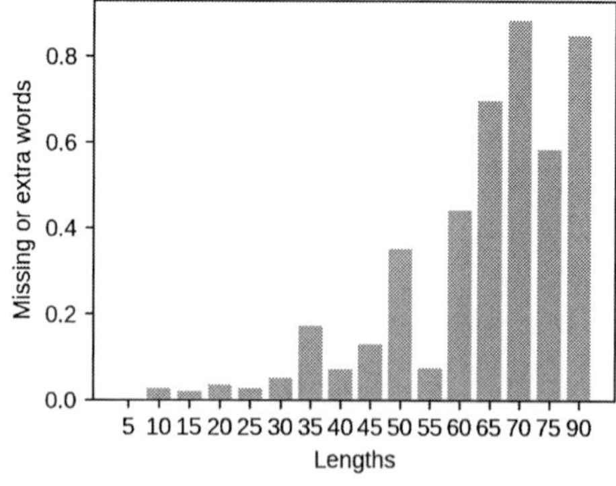

Figure 4: Extra or missing words normalized by length, plotted against gold sequence lengths for en-gum-ud dev set.

rors with the other test sets, errors with this particular set are much noisier. For example, in another file the model emits "multichart" as "multichartart". This kind of error is extremely consistent with errors regarding the attention mechanism. In fact, Faruqui et al. explicitly feed the lemma into their decoder for this very reason. That said, errors from the en_partut-ud-test file are not as clear (e.g. "copyright" → "Sropopyright").

Turning to linearization, Seq2Seq-Copy does much better than the other models. We believe this is due to the architectural prior of copying words from the input, as nearly all output words are present in the input (modulo words whose inflected forms are sensitive to adjacent words). Figure 3 shows that BLEU scores significantly decrease as sequence length increases. Figure 4 shows that the number of extra or missing words increases with lengths, which could explain the drop in BLEU. Such mistakes could perhaps have been avoided by adding word-level constraints to constrained decoding. Other errors are due to picking the correct words but in the incorrect order. Out of 366 mismatches on the en-gum dev set, 193 (53%) are cases of mismatched word order with the correct words.

Figure 5 shows examples of linearization model predictions. In 1, the model misses the word "summer" and repeats "olympic" instead. This can potentially be alleviated by constraining the generation of a word based on the number of times it appears in the input. In 2, the model picks the right set of words but in an order that is different from the gold order. In 3, the model fails by stuttering, i.e. it repeats the same phrase again and again.

6 Conclusions and Future Work

Our exploratory experiments show that combining a morphological inflection with a baseline linearizer achieves decent results. Our pipeline for the shallow surface realization shared task first produces inflected wordforms from lemmas using a character level sequence-to-sequence model. We then use those forms in serialized trees as input to a tree-to-tree model, which is also implemented using a sequence-to-sequence architecture, yielding serialized trees as output. This allows outputs to be filtered for validity in most cases, enforcing projective outputs. Due to time limitations we could only submit fully linearized results for English, and we were not able to implement word-level constraints, so we consider these preliminary baseline results. Given our error analysis, in future work it may be fruitful to update the attention mechanism in the inflection model (Aharoni and Goldberg, 2017), and to use a tree encoder + copy mechanism in the linearizer together with word-level constraints in decoding.

References

Roee Aharoni and Yoav Goldberg. 2017. Morphological inflection generation with hard monotonic attention. In *Proceedings of the 55th Annual Meeting of the Association for Computational Linguistics (Volume 1: Long Papers)*, volume 1, pages 2004–2015.

Dzmitry Bahdanau, Kyunghyun Cho, and Yoshua Bengio. 2014. Neural machine translation by jointly learning to align and translate. *arXiv preprint arXiv:1409.0473*.

Anusha Balakrishnan, Jinfeng Rao, Kartikeya Upasani, Michael White, and Rajen Subba. 2019. Constrained decoding for neural NLG from compositional representations in task-oriented dialogue. In *Proceedings of the 57th Annual Meeting of the Association for Computational Linguistics*, pages 831–844, Florence, Italy. Association for Computational Linguistics.

Jean Berko. 1958. The child's learning of english morphology. *Word*, 14(2-3):150–177.

Bernd Bohnet, Anders Björkelund, Jonas Kuhn, Wolfgang Seeker, and Sina Zarriess. 2012. Generating non-projective word order in statistical linearization. In *Proceedings of the 2012 Joint Conference on Empirical Methods in Natural Language Processing and Computational Natural Language Learning*, pages 928–939, Jeju Island, Korea. Association for Computational Linguistics.

Ryan Cotterell, Christo Kirov, John Sylak-Glassman, Géraldine Walther, Ekaterina Vylomova, Patrick Xia, Manaal Faruqui, Sandra Kübler, David Yarowsky, Jason Eisner, and Mans Hulden. 2017. CoNLL-SIGMORPHON 2017 Shared Task: Universal morphological reinflection in 52 languages. *CoRR*, abs/1706.09031.

Ryan Cotterell, Christo Kirov, John Sylak-Glassman, David Yarowsky, Jason Eisner, and Mans Hulden. 2016. The SIGMORPHON 2016 Shared Task—Morphological Reinflection. In *Proceedings of the 2016 Meeting of SIGMORPHON*, Berlin, Germany. Association for Computational Linguistics.

Manaal Faruqui, Yulia Tsvetkov, Graham Neubig, and Chris Dyer. 2016. Morphological inflection generation using character sequence to sequence learning. In *Proc. of NAACL*.

Sepp Hochreiter and Jürgen Schmidhuber. 1997. Long short-term memory. *Neural computation*, 9(8):1735–1780.

Katharina Kann and Hinrich Schütze. 2016. MED: The LMU system for the SIGMORPHON 2016 shared task on morphological reinflection. *ACL 2016*, page 62.

David L King and Michael White. 2018. The osu realizer for srst' 18: Neural sequence-to-sequence inflection and incremental locality-based linearization. *ACL 2018*, page 39.

Simon Mille, Anja Belz, Bernd Bohnet, Yvette Graham, and Leo Wanner. 2019. The Second Multilingual Surface Realisation Shared Task (SR'19): Overview and Evaluation Results. In *Proceedings of the 2nd Workshop on Multilingual Surface Realisation (MSR), 2019 Conference on Empirical Methods in Natural Language Processing (EMNLP)*, Hong Kong, China.

1. **Gold**: athens hosted the 2004 summer olympic games .
   Pred: athens hosted the olympic olympic 2004 games .

2. **Gold**: and it has , because it is spring and inside the ground something is stirring .
   Pred: and it has because it is spring , and something is stirring inside the ground .

3. **Gold**: ok well i have a crush on 2 guys but unforchunitly it is almost valentine s day afnd i just broke up with my and i have dated one of the guys i like and one guy lives in my naborhood guy i need your help i am a girl but i need a guy s help what shoul i do ?
   Pred: well i have a crush on 2 guy and i have almost dated one of the guys i like and i have almost dated one of the guys i like and i have almost dated one of the guys i like and i have almost dated one of the guys i like and i have almost dated one of the guys i like ?

Figure 5: Examples of linearization predictions with BLEU score < 0.6.

Yevgeniy Puzikov and Iryna Gurevych. 2018. BinLin: A simple method of dependency tree linearization. In *Proceedings of the First Workshop on Multilingual Surface Realisation*, pages 13–28, Melbourne, Australia. Association for Computational Linguistics.

Jinfeng Rao, Kartikeya Upasani, Anusha Balakrishnan, Michael White, Anuj Kumar, and Rajen Subba. 2019. A tree-to-sequence model for neural nlg in task-oriented dialog. In *Proceedings of the 12th International Conference on Natural Language Generation (to appear)*.

Abigail See, Peter J. Liu, and Christopher D. Manning. 2017. Get to the point: Summarization with pointer-generator networks. In *Proceedings of the 55th Annual Meeting of the Association for Computational Linguistics (Volume 1: Long Papers)*, pages 1073–1083, Vancouver, Canada. Association for Computational Linguistics.

Kai Sheng Tai, Richard Socher, and Christopher D. Manning. 2015. Improved semantic representations from tree-structured long short-term memory networks. In *Proceedings of the 53rd Annual Meeting of the Association for Computational Linguistics and the 7th International Joint Conference on Natural Language Processing (Volume 1: Long Papers)*, pages 1556–1566, Beijing, China. Association for Computational Linguistics.

Improving Language Generation from Feature-Rich Tree-Structured Data with Relational Graph Convolutional Encoders

***†Xudong Hong, †Ernie Chang, †Vera Demberg**
*Dept. of Computer Vision and Machine Learning, MPI Informatics
†Dept. of Language Science and Technology, Saarland University
{xhong,cychang,vera}@coli.uni-saarland.de

Abstract

The Multilingual Surface Realization Shared Task 2019 focuses on generating sentences from lemmatized sets of universal dependency parses with rich features. This paper describes the system design and the results of our participation in the deep track. The core innovation in our approach is to use a graph convolutional network to encode the dependency trees given as input. Upon adding morphological features, our system achieves the second rank in the deep track without using data augmentation techniques or additional components (such as a re-ranker).

1 Introduction

The goal in the Multilingual Surface Realization Shared Task 2019 (MSR'19) is to generate fluent text from Universal Dependencies (UD) structures. The task makes available UD-annotated resources in 11 languages for the shallow task, and three languages (English, Spanish, French) for the deep track. Developing surface generation systems that are largely language-independent is a central objective of the shared task (Mille et al., 2018). To generate sentences based on the UD structure and morphological features, recent neural approaches mainly adopt neural sequence-to-sequence architectures (Cabezudo and Pardo, 2018; Madsack et al., 2018; Elder and Hokamp, 2018). While representing the feature-rich data in a linearized manner proved to be a viable option, we argue that these linear sequences do not optimally exploit the input information. We therefore propose to encode the dependency trees using a graph convolutional network (GCN) and find that this GCN encoder leads to a substantial boost in performance, compared to a sequential encoder.

The datasets in the deep track consist of semantic representations induced from syntactic dependency parses, see Figure 1 for an example. This

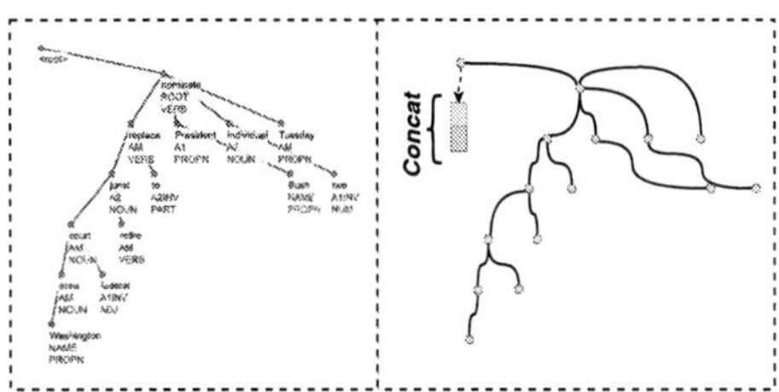

Figure 1: An example of a UD structure with concatenated feature embeddings from the MSR'19 deep task.

task is reflects the information that's realistically available in real-world natural language generation task.

Our method works as follows: We first apply delexicalization to the datasets, replacing rare tokens with placeholders. Next, encode the dependency trees using graph representation learning techniques (Li et al., 2015; Xu et al., 2018a), in order to improve the encoding of structured data within the encoder-decoder architecture. Our model hence learns a mapping between graph inputs and sequence outputs. Our ablation study in the evaluation demonstrates that encoding UD structure in this manner does embed additional semantic information and subsequently improves the performance across the three languages available for the deep track (i.e. English, French, and Spanish). Finally, we use an LSTM decoder with copy mechanism and attention to generate surface text.

Our contributions are as follows:

1. We show that a GCN encoder for UD input structures outperforms sequential encoders.

2. We propose to use a variant of relational GCN (R-GCN) to better represent edge labels in the graph, and show that this boosts overall performance.

3. We show that structural encoding with the GCN benefits all three languages in the task.

Proceedings of the 2nd Workshop on Multilingual Surface Realisation (MSR 2019), pages 75–80
Hong Kong, China, November 3rd, 2019. ©2019 Association for Computational Linguistics
https://doi.org/10.18653/v1/P17

2   Related Work

2.1   Neural NLG

Systems proposed as part of the Surface Realization Shared Task 2018 are largely sequence-to-sequence models targeting the Shallow Task. Most systems in the past contain two separate components: 1) preprocessing of the UD dataset, and the 2) neural generator with the encoder-decoder architecture.

Most neural generators combine features by concatenating the aligned feature sequences and feed them as a single sequence into the neural generator (Elder and Hokamp, 2018; Madsack et al., 2018). In these systems, a pre-trained embedding is typically used to represent each lemmas, before concatenated with embeddings of surface-level morphological categories and dependency relations. A form of Recurrent Neural Network (RNN) are utilized to map the input to a latent space, and another RNN then decodes into target output. Examples of common RNN usage include Long Short-Term memory (LSTM) or the Bi-directional LSTM as used in Elder and Hokamp (2018); Madsack et al. (2018).

2.2   Graph-to-text Generation

Considering the fact that a dependency tree is a special case of a directed acyclic graph, surface realization is a graph-to-text generation tasks. Graph neural networks have been successfully applied to different graph to text generation task like SQL to text generation (Xu et al., 2018b), AMR-to-text generation (Beck et al., 2018) and semantic machine translation (Song et al., 2019). LSTM can be modified to model graph-level information (Song et al., 2018). Graph Convolutional Networks (GCN), originally designed for semi-supervised learning of node representations in graphs (Kipf and Welling, 2017), explicitly exploit tree structure data and outperform LSTM and TreeLSTM on AMR-to-text generation (Damonte and Cohen, 2019). To also model different types of edges in graphs, Relational Graph Convolutional Networks (R-GCN) represent each type of edge with a corresponding parameter matrix (Schlichtkrull et al., 2018). We leverage the R-GCN by grouping in-edge and out-edge together and apply to a graph-to-text generation task.

3   Our Approach

3.1   Feature Representations

The input format of the MSR'19 deep track is multi-source in the sense that each type of feature corresponds to a sequence of features, i.e., part-of-speech tags (POS), morphological features etc. As shown in Figure 1, we transform the tree-structured data into a graph. We construct node representations by simply concatenating token and its features. Then we use an embedding matrix to map the representations into low-dimensional vector space.

To handle rare words in input tokens, we firstly perform delexicalization for all datasets as follows:

1. Replace tokens that have part-of-speech tags of *NAME, PROPN, NUM* and *X* with placeholders jointly indexed by the number of head and the number of entities.

2. Build a dictionary from placeholders to original tokens for each input-output pair.

After obtaining the model output, we lexicalize the text by looking up each generated placeholder in the corresponding dictionary and insert the original token.

For our official submission to the shared task, we did not make use of features, in order to see whether the dependency tree is informative enough for surface realization. However, we performed additional experiments to show the effectiveness of GCN encoder with selected concatenated features, see Table 1.

3.2   Model

The graph-to-text generation task has a directed acyclic graph as input $G = \{V, E\}$, where V is a set of nodes and E is a set of directed edges e between nodes. In this paper, a node is an embedding vector containing a token and its features. An edge is the dependency relation between two nodes. The output Y is a sequence of tokens which form a sentence expressing the input. We extend the architecture by Marcheggiani and Perez-Beltrachini (2018) which combines a graph convolutional encoder and attentional LSTM decoder as described in Figure 2.

Graph Convolutional Encoder We use R-GCN, a variant of GCN (Schlichtkrull et al., 2018) assigning parameters for edges in a graph, to model

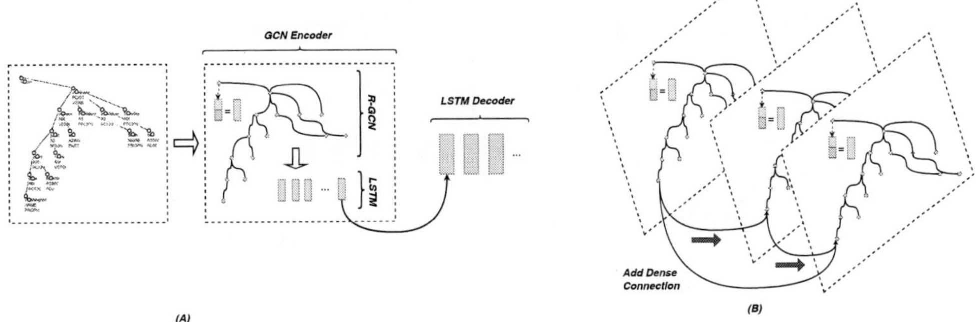

Figure 2: **(A)**: depicts the conceptual relationship between the GCN encoder and LSTM decoder. **(B)**: Addition of a dense layer is analogous to adding extra connections between multiple layers of graphical representation.

graph-structure input explicitly. Given a directed graph G, we represent each node with an embedding vector $\mathbf{x}_v \in \mathbb{R}^d$. Then the l-th R-GCN layer compute the hidden representation for node v in $(l + 1)$-th layer as follows:

$$\mathbf{h}_v^{l+1} = f(\mathbf{W}\mathbf{h}_v^l + \sum_{u \in N(v)} \mathbf{W}_e \mathbf{h}_u^l) \qquad (1)$$

where $\mathbf{W}, \mathbf{W}_e \in \mathbb{R}^{d \times h}$ and $e \in E$. f is the linear rectifier (ReLU), a non-linear activation function. $N(v)$ is the set of all neighbours of node v. This design is over-parameterized and there is no parameter sharing between similar edge labels. Therefore we redesign the update rule to:

$$\mathbf{h}_v^{l+1} = f(\mathbf{W}\mathbf{h}_v^l + \sum_{u \in N(v)} \mathbf{W}_{dir(e)} \mathbf{h}_u^l \circ \mathbf{r}_e) \qquad (2)$$

where "$\circ$" is the Hadamard production, $\mathbf{W}_{r(u,v)} \in \mathbb{R}^{d \times h}$, $dir(e) \in \{in, out\}$ represents direction of the edge $e_{u,v}$ and $\mathbf{r}_e \in \mathbb{R}^h$ is an embedding vector of the label of $e_{u,v}$.

Each layer aggregates the direct neighbours of each node. To model neighbours of neighbours, we stack L GCN layers where L is set to the average radius of all graphs (here, average depth of all trees). Stacking GCN into deep neural networks could lead to gradient vanishing problem, thus we add residual connections (He et al., 2016) or dense connections (Huang et al., 2017) for each layer.

LSTM Decoder We apply stacked LSTM layers (Hochreiter and Schmidhuber, 1997) as the decoder on top of the GCN. The first layer is an input-feed LSTM (Luong et al., 2015) that aggregates the hidden representations of nodes into one hidden vector $\mathbf{h}_C$ for the whole graph. The second LSTM layer decodes the hidden vector and

generates the representations of output token at each time step. We use global attention (Luong et al., 2015) to re-weight the hidden representations from the first layer and merge them into a global hidden vector $\mathbf{h}_G$. In order to generate the placeholder directly from the input, we apply the copying mechanism (Gu et al., 2016), which is effective when using lexcalization. The probability of token y_t conditioned on input G and previous token $y_{1:t-1}$ is obtained by applying a softmax layer on the decoder output as $P(y_t|y_{1:t-1}, G) = softmax(g(\mathbf{h}_G, \mathbf{h}_C))$, where g is a perceptron. The model is trained to maximize the likelihood function $L = \prod_{|Y|}^{t=1} P(y_t|y_{1:t-1}, G)$.

Encoder	BLEU	NIST	DIST
GCN (*)	23.0	6.88	42
LSTM	28.8	8.13	44.48
BiLSTM	31.2	8.53	46.86
GCN	35.9	8.73	52.86
R-GCN (*residual*)	39.81	9.24	55.45
R-GCN (*dense*)	**41.01**	**9.43**	**56.49**

(*) denotes system without morphological features, which is also our official submission to the shared task.

Table 1: Ablation study: results of models on the MSR'19 validation set of UD English EWT (enewt-ud-dev) corpus. We compare different encoders while keeping decoder constant, i.e., LSTM decoder with copy mechanism and coverage attention. For beam search we maintain a constant use of blocking 3-gram.

3.3 Experiments

We built our system on a variant of OpenNMT-py (Klein et al., 2017) from Marcheggiani and Perez-Beltrachini (2018) with customized encoders. We construct the training and validation datasets by concatenating corresponding splits of all available corpora for each language. We stack 4 R-GCN

Encoder	Output
BiLSTM	President Bush threw two members to replace manufacturers in the Washington area to replace manufacturers in federal nations.
GCN	In Tuesday, President Bush commissioned two connections to replace the federal individual of federal statements in the Washington area.
RGCN	In Tuesday, President Bush nominated two individuals to replace jurist trials to the Washington area.
Gold	President Bush on Tuesday nominated two individuals to replace retiring jurist on federal courts in the Washington area.

Table 2: Comparison of outputs from systems with encoder variants given the graph in Figure 1 as input. We highlighted obvious erroneous blocks of text for contrast. Note that the only variants are the encoders, all other configurations remain the same.

Corpus	Dev		Test	
	GCN (*)	R-GCN (dense)	GCN (*)	R-GCN (dense)
en_ewt-ud	23.0	41.01	23.35	18.37
en_gum-ud	17.71	34.47	17.97	14.6
en_lines-ud	18.32	12.7	20.96	14.89
en_partut-ud	18.54	35.3	17.19	12.85
es_ancora-ud	21.09	37.2	18.59	36.85
es_gsd-ud	20.56	33.39	18.69	35.92
fr_gsd-ud	20.48	35.12	15.83	10.65
fr_partut-ud	19.16	33.57	14.06	6.07
fr_sequoia-ud	21.07	34.49	18.52	10.22
en_pud-ud	-	-	18.11	12.31
en_ewt-Pred-HIT	-	-	22.42	39.05
en_pud-Pred-LATTICE	-	-	17.3	35.85
es_ancora-Pred-HIT	-	-	21.1	37.2

(*) denotes our submission to the shared task, which doesn't use morphological features

Table 3: Evaluation of our submissions to MSR'19 **Deep Task** across all corpora on both Test and Dev sets. Numbers are BLEU scores.

layers with dense connections as encoder and train the model with dropout rate of 0.5. We perform early stopping when the training accuracy is higher than the validation accuracy and choose the checkpoint before over-fitting for evaluation.

4 Results and Analysis

4.1 Encoder Model Selection

As indicated in Table 1, we compare R-GCN with different encoders. Systems are evaluated on the validation set of UD English EWT (enewt-ud-dev) corpus. With the same linearized inputs, we began with a LSTM encoder before moving on to bi-directional LSTM (BiLSTM). With 2.4 BLEU points improvement, BiLSTM appeared to be the option in terms of sequential encoder. Next, we employed the variant of GCN by Marcheggiani and Perez-Beltrachini (2018) with four fully-connected layers. We observed that this change gave an additional 4.7 BLEU points boost, which outperforms sequential encoders significantly. We then compare our R-GCN model to the GCN, which obtains additional 3.91 BLEU points. We further add dense conenctions to R-GCN, termed the *dense*, that eventually result in 41.01 BLEU points on the validation set. This was an overall 12 BLEU points improvement from the initial LSTM encoder.

4.2 Ablation Study: Decoder

We intend to investigate if the LSTM decoder can be further modified for improvement. Two of such changes are the **copy mechanism** and **coverage**

attention. The copy mechanism was shown to be beneficial in numerous similar tasks such as data-to-text generation (Li and Wan, 2018). With the addition of copy mechanism while keeping the encoder unchanged, an average of 1 BLEU score improvement can be observed; reusing the global attention for copying mechanism gave the system another 5 BLEU point boost.

4.3 Discussion

Our analysis shows that structural encoding of the UD trees leads to substantial improvements in performance. It also shows that including morphological features is crucial to performance of the surface realizer — without these features, we observe many errors in tense and agreement.

We also analyzed the system outputs to look for evidence to substantiate the intuition that a structural encoder can better represent the a priori linguistic information. One of such examples is shown in Table 2, where we observe fluency improvements going from BiLSTM encoder to GCN, and finally to R-GCN, where an overall improvement in fluency is conspicuous.

We report the results of our submissions in Table 3. Comparing to the validation results, **GCN(*)** trained without morphological features performs similarly across validation and test datasets of each corpus, however **R-GCN(dense)** has a significant drop from validation to test and experiences over-fitting. Importantly, we notice substantial BLEU rise and drop going from **GCN(*)** to **R-GCN(dense)** on the test datasets. We postulate that addition of relational modeling of edges (R-GCN) on top of rich features constrain the model to learn specific subset of a priori linguistic structures, thereby mitigating the overall performance.

5 Conclusion

We have shown that without additional modules such as re-ranker or data augmentation, the traditional encoder-decoder architecture can still be competitive by exploiting the existing structural input information. For future work, we intend to see if the performance can be further improved with pre-trained language models such as GPT-2 (Radford et al.).

Acknowledgements

This research was funded in part by the German Research Foundation (DFG) as part of SFB 1102 "Information Density and Linguistic Encoding" and SFB 248 "Foundations of Perspicuous Software Systems". Xudong Hong is supported by International Max Planck Research School for Computer Science (IMPRS-CS) of Max-Planck Institute for Informatics (MPI-INF). We sincerely thank the anonymous reviewers for their insightful comments that helped us to improve this paper.

References

Daniel Beck, Gholamreza Haffari, and Trevor Cohn. 2018. Graph-to-Sequence Learning using Gated Graph Neural Networks.

Marco Antonio Sobrevilla Cabezudo and Thiago Pardo. 2018. Nilc-swornemo at the surface realization shared task: Exploring syntax-based word ordering using neural models. In *Proceedings of the First Workshop on Multilingual Surface Realisation*, pages 58–64.

Marco Damonte and Shay B. Cohen. 2019. Structural Neural Encoders for AMR-to-text Generation. pages 3649–3658.

Henry Elder and Chris Hokamp. 2018. Generating high-quality surface realizations using data augmentation and factored sequence models. In *Proceedings of the First Workshop on Multilingual Surface Realisation*, pages 49–53.

Jiatao Gu, Zhengdong Lu, Hang Li, and Victor OK Li. 2016. Incorporating copying mechanism in sequence-to-sequence learning. *arXiv preprint arXiv:1603.06393*.

Kaiming He, Xiangyu Zhang, Shaoqing Ren, and Jian Sun. 2016. Deep residual learning for image recognition. In *Proceedings of the IEEE conference on computer vision and pattern recognition*, pages 770–778.

Sepp Hochreiter and Jürgen Schmidhuber. 1997. Long short-term memory. *Neural computation*, 9(8):1735–1780.

Gao Huang, Zhuang Liu, Laurens Van Der Maaten, and Kilian Q Weinberger. 2017. Densely connected convolutional networks. In *Proceedings of the IEEE conference on computer vision and pattern recognition*, pages 4700–4708.

Thomas N. Kipf and Max Welling. 2017. Semi-supervised classification with graph convolutional networks. In *Iclr*, pages 1–11.

Guillaume Klein, Yoon Kim, Yuntian Deng, Jean Senellart, and Alexander Rush. 2017. Opennmt: Open-source toolkit for neural machine translation. In *Proceedings of ACL 2017, System Demonstrations*, pages 67–72.

Liunian Li and Xiaojun Wan. 2018. Point precisely: Towards ensuring the precision of data in generated texts using delayed copy mechanism. In *Proceedings of the 27th International Conference on Computational Linguistics*, pages 1044–1055.

Yujia Li, Daniel Tarlow, Marc Brockschmidt, and Richard Zemel. 2015. Gated Graph Sequence Neural Networks.

Minh-Thang Luong, Hieu Pham, and Christopher D Manning. 2015. Effective approaches to attention-based neural machine translation. *arXiv preprint arXiv:1508.04025*.

Andreas Madsack, Johanna Heininger, Nyamsuren Davaasambuu, Vitaliia Voronik, Michael Käufl, and Robert Weißgraeber. 2018. Ax semantics submission to the surface realization shared task 2018. In *Proceedings of the First Workshop on Multilingual Surface Realisation*, pages 54–57.

Diego Marcheggiani and Laura Perez-Beltrachini. 2018. Deep graph convolutional encoders for structured data to text generation. *arXiv preprint arXiv:1810.09995*.

Simon Mille, Anja Belz, Bernd Bohnet, Yvette Graham, Emily Pitler, and Leo Wanner. 2018. The first multilingual surface realisation shared task (sr18): Overview and evaluation results. In *Proceedings of the First Workshop on Multilingual Surface Realisation*, pages 1–12.

Alec Radford, Jeffrey Wu, Rewon Child, David Luan, Dario Amodei, and Ilya Sutskever. Language models are unsupervised multitask learners.

Michael Schlichtkrull, Thomas N. Kipf, Peter Bloem, Rianne van den Berg, Ivan Titov, and Max Welling. 2018. Modeling Relational Data with Graph Convolutional Networks. *Lecture Notes in Computer Science (including subseries Lecture Notes in Artificial Intelligence and Lecture Notes in Bioinformatics)*, 10843 LNCS(1):593–607.

Linfeng Song, Daniel Gildea, Yue Zhang, Zhiguo Wang, and Jinsong Su. 2019. Semantic neural machine translation using amr. *Transactions of the Association for Computational Linguistics*, 7:19–31.

Linfeng Song, Yue Zhang, Zhiguo Wang, and Daniel Gildea. 2018. A Graph-to-Sequence Model for AMR-to-Text Generation. pages 1616–1626.

Kun Xu, Lingfei Wu, Zhiguo Wang, Yansong Feng, Michael Witbrock, and Vadim Sheinin. 2018a. Graph2Seq: Graph to Sequence Learning with Attention-based Neural Networks. pages 1–18.

Kun Xu, Lingfei Wu, Zhiguo Wang, Mo Yu, Liwei Chen, and Vadim Sheinin. 2018b. Sql-to-text generation with graph-to-sequence model. *arXiv preprint arXiv:1809.05255*.

The DipInfoUniTo Realizer at SR'19: Learning to Rank and Deep Morphology Prediction for Multilingual Surface Realization

Alessandro Mazzei
Dipartimento di Informatica
Universit degli Studi di Torino
Corso Svizzera 185, 10153 Torino
mazzei@di.unito.it

Valerio Basile
Dipartimento di Informatica
Universit degli Studi di Torino
Corso Svizzera 185, 10153 Torino
basilei@di.unito.it

Abstract

We describe the system presented at the SR'19 shared task by the DipInfoUnito team. Our approach is based on supervised machine learning. In particular, we divide the SR task into two independent subtasks, namely word order prediction and morphology inflection prediction. Two neural networks with different architectures run on the same input structure, each producing a partial output which is recombined in the final step in order to produce the predicted surface form. This work is a direct successor of the architecture presented at SR'19.

1 Introduction

Surface Realisation (SR) is one of the main tasks involved in Natural Language Generation. SR focuses the final macro-step of the standard NLG pipeline defined by Reiter and Dale (2000), therefore involving the production of producing natural language sentences and longer documents from formal abstract representations. Such input is assumed to come from an external source, such as a macro-planning and micro-planning pipeline, and therefore it will contain all the necessary information to create the final natural language output. Generating a **correct** and **fluent** output in a target natural language is the main responsibility of the SR component. In this paper, we report on the system submitted to the second edition of the Surface Realization Shared Task (Mille et al., 2019, SR'19), organized in the context of the Multilingual Surface Realization Workshop in 2019.

The SR task, in the version proposed at SR'19, considers the surface realization of Universal Dependency (UD) trees, i.e., syntactic structures where the words of a sentence are linked by labeled directed arcs. In particular, UD represents natural language syntax with trees where each node is a word. The labels on the arcs indicate the syntactic relation holding between each word and its dependent words — see an example in Figure 1a. Our approach to the SR task is based on supervised machine learning. In particular, we draw inspiration from Basile (2015), subdividing the task into two independent subtasks, namely **word order prediction** and **morphology inflection prediction**. Two neural networks with different architectures run on the same input structure, each producing a partial output which is recombined in the final step in order to produce the predicted surface form. This work is a direct successor of the architecture presented at last year's edition of the shared task (Mille et al., 2018) and experimented in more detail in (Basile and Mazzei, 2018b). With respect to the last year previous system, there are two major differences: i) we took advantage of a high-performance computing public platform (see acknowledgments) in order to optimize the learning parameters and avoid overfitting; ii) we select the best model by using the Kendall's Tau (Kendall, 1938, τ), a rank correlation measure used to score the word order at the subtree level predicted by the model, at different training epochs (Basile and Mazzei, 2018b). By following the approach of (Basile, 2015), the fitness of the model at each epoch is computed by using the number of incorrect item inversions (intrinsic evaluation), rather than on the downstream task score (see Section 3).

In the following, we refer to our system by using the name *DipInfo-UniTo realizer*.

2 Method

In this section, we detail the two main components developed to approach word order prediction (2.1) and morphology inflection (2.2).

Proceedings of the 2nd Workshop on Multilingual Surface Realisation (MSR 2019), pages 81–87
Hong Kong, China, November 3rd, 2019. ©2019 Association for Computational Linguistics
https://doi.org/10.18653/v1/P17

2.1 Word Ordering

We formulate the task of predicting the correct order of words in a sentence in terms of reordering the subtrees in its syntactical structure. The algorithm works in three steps:

1. splitting the unordered tree into single-level unordered subtrees;

2. predicting the local word order for each subtree;

3. recomposing the single-level ordered subtrees into a single multi-level ordered tree to obtain the global word order.

The first step splits the input UD tree into several single-level unordered trees composed by a head (the root) and all its dependents (the children), similarly to Bohnet et al. (2012).

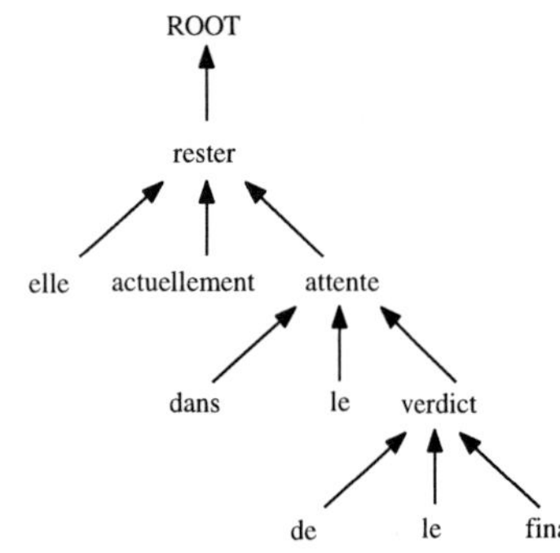
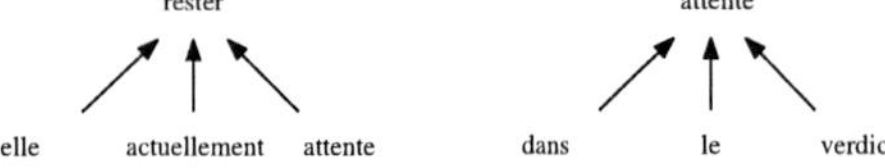

(a) Tree corresponding to the French sentence "Elle reste actuellement dans l'attente de le verdict final." (*"She is currently waiting for the final verdict."*)

(b) Two subtrees extracted from the main tree.

Figure 1: Splitting the input tree into subtrees to extract lists of items for learning to rank.

An example is shown in Figure 1: from the (unordered) tree representing the sentence *"Elle reste actuellement dans l'attente de le verdict final."* (1a), each of its component subtrees (limited to one-level dependency) is considered separately (1b). The head and the dependents of each subtree form an unordered list of lexical items. We leverage the flat structure of the subtrees to extract structures that are suitable as input to the learning to rank approach we propose, carried out by the next step of the pipeline.

The second step of the algorithm predicts the relative order of the head and the dependents of each subtree with a *learning to rank* approach. We employ the list-wise learning to rank algorithm *ListNet* (Cao et al., 2007). The limited cardinality of the lists to rank makes it advantageous to use a list-wise approach, as opposed to pair-wise or point-wise approaches, without an unmanageable increase of the computation load. ListNet is a generalized version of the pairwise learning to rank algorithm RankNet (Burges et al., 2005). ListNet employ a list-wise loss function based on the *top-one probability*, i.e., the probability of an element of being the first one in the ranking. The top-one probability model approximates the *permutation probability* model that assigns a probability to each possible permutation of an ordered list. This approximation is necessary to keep the problem tractable by avoiding the exponential explosion of the number of permutations. Formally, the top-one probability of an object j is defined as

$$P_s(j) = \sum_{\pi(1)=j,\pi\in\Omega_n} P_s(\pi)$$

that is, the sum of the probabilities of all the possible permutations of n objects (denoted as Ω_n) where j is the first element. $s = (s_1, ..., s_n)$ is a given list of *scores*, i.e., the position of elements in the list. Considering two permutations of the same list y and z (in the case of the SR task, the predicted order and the reference order) their distance is computed using cross entropy. The distance measure and the top-one probabilities of the list elements are used to compute the loss function:

$$L(y, z) = -\sum_{j=1}^{n} P_y(j)log(P_z(j))$$

A linear neural network model provides the learning environment, using the list-wise loss function above. ListNet takes as input a sequence of ordered lists of feature encoded as numeric vectors. The weights of the network are updated over several epochs by computing distance between the reference ranking and the prediction of the model (list-wise cost function) and passing its value to the gradient descent algorithm for optimization. We used an implementation of ListNet[1] that was previously applied in a surface realization task

---

[1] https://github.com/valeriobasile/
listnet

with a similar supervised setting (Basile, 2015). On top of the core ListNet algorithm, this implementation features a regularization parameter to prevent overfitting.

We manually engineer the features for the supervised learning in the word order module. We use several word-level features encoded as one-hot vectors, namely: the universal POS-tag, the treebank specific POS tag, the morphology features and the head-status of the word (head of the single-level tree vs. leaf). We also include vectorial word representations of two different kinds. Content words are open-class word lemmas, and are represented by language-specific, pre-trained word embeddings. In particular, we employ the multilingual model Polyglot (Al-Rfou' et al., 2013). Function words are closed-class word lemmas, and are encoded as one-hot bag-of-words vectors. An implementation of the feature encoding for the word ordering module of our architecture is available online[2].

The third step of the word ordering algorithm reconstructs the global order (i.e., at the sentence level) from the local order of the one-level trees. Note that this approach works under the hypothesis of *projectivity*. The DipInfo-UniTo realizer cannot predict the correct word order for non-projective sentences. If the local reordering of the one-level tree T_1^h with root h and children $c_1...c_M$ produces an order of nodes $n_1 n_2...n_{M+1}$, the hypothesis of projectivity implies that in the global word order the position of all the children of the node n_j will be after the position of the node n_{j-1} and before the position of the node n_{j+1}. So, the node global order (O) of a k-level tree T_k^h rooted by the node h and with children $c_1...c_M$ can be rewritten formally in terms of the local order as:

$$O(T_k^h) = \begin{cases} h & \text{if } k=0 \\ O_{ln}(h, c_1, ..., c_M) & \text{if } k=1 \\ O_{ln}(h, O(T_{k-1}^{c_1}), ..., O(T_{k-1}^{c_M})) & \text{if } k>1 \end{cases}$$

where $O_{ln}(h, c_1, ..., c_M)$ is the permutation learned by the ListNet algorithm from the training set and parametrized over the feature set $F(h, c_1, ..., c_M)$, that is

$$O_{ln}(h, c_1, ..., c_M) \stackrel{def}{=} P_{ListNet}^{F(h,c_1,...,c_M)}(h, c_1, ..., c_M)$$

---

[2] https://github.com/alexmazzei/ud2ln

2.2 Morphology Inflection

The second half of our proposed architecture is the morphology inflection component. We consider this task an alignment problem at the level of character, and approach it with a *sequence-to-sequence* supervised model. We employ the deep neural network based on a hard attention mechanism introduced by Aharoni and Goldberg (2017). The model consists of a neural network in an encoder-decoder setting. At each training step, the model can either write a symbol to the output sequence, or move the attention pointer to the next state of the sequence. This architecture models the monotonic alignment between the input and output sequences, allowing the freedom to condition the output on the entire sequence in input.

We employ all the morphological features provided by the UD annotation and the dependency relation between the target word and its head. We transform the training CONLL files into a set of $((lemma, features), form)$ tuples, in order to learn the neural inflectional model associating a $(lemma, features)$ to the corresponding $form$. An example of training instance for the morphology inflection module is the following:

```
lemma: rester
features:
  uPoS=VERB
  rel=root
  Number=Sing
  Mood=Ind
  Person=3
  Tense=Pres
  VerbForm=Fin
form: reste
```

Corresponding to the word form *reste*, an inflected form (3rd person, present, indicative) of the lemma *rester* (to remain, to stay).

3 Experiments

Since our approach does not rely on language specific procedures or hand-made rules, we tested it on three languages, namely English, French and Chinese, in order to cover different families of languages. We were not able to provide results for other language for computational time constraints. For word ordering, we ran the system on a virtualized GNU/Linux box with 16-core and 64GB of RAM. The computation time of the word ordering component was around one hour per epoch for the English language, which had the larger data set among the three languages that we considered. For morphology inflection, we used a GNU/Linux box with NVIDIA Tesla K40c GPU computing capability. Similarly to word ordering, the computation time for each epoch in morphology inflection was around one hour for the English language.

3.1 Pipelines

We designed two processing pipelines for the training and testing phase, as depicted in Figure 2. We applied the pipelines separately for each of the tested languages (EN-FR-ZH).

In the training pipeline, we created two distinct files starting from the UD treebank training files. The first file contains morphological information (that is $((lemma, features), form)$, see Section 2.2), used to create the morphological inflection model with the deep learning architecture described in Section 2.2. The second file contains the vector representation of the tree features (word embeddings or one-hot for function words, morphological features, etc.) and it is used to create the word order model by using the linear neural network architecture described in Section 2.1.

In the testing pipeline, we created two distinct files starting from the test files provided from the organizers. Both files are created with the same procedures of the training pipelines. The first file was used to test the morphological neural model and to create a mapping from the lemma-features pair to the inflected form. The second file was used to test the word order model by providing the local word orders of the subtrees and the global word order at the sentence level. In a subsequent step, the information from the morphological map and from the word ordered trees are merged into one single complete, CONLL-compliant tree structure. Finally, the trees are *detokenized* (see 3.3) in order to produce the sentences that are submitted as the final output of the system.

3.2 Datasets

The rules of the shallow track for the SR'19 do not allow to use external resources to train the surface realizer. However, of lexical resources such as word embedding and neural language models are allowed. In order to investigate about the syntactic information contained in the Universal Dependency format and its appropriateness for the SR task, we decided to focus on information derived from the Universal Dependency project

(Nivre et al., 2016), with the only exception of pre-compiled embeddings to encode of the open-class words.

The task organizers provided twenty training files and twenty development files, derived from the version 2.2 of the UD dataset for the eleven languages included in the shallow track. In particular, modified versions of the original treebanks were provided, where the information about the original word order was replaced by a random ordering. Moreover, the original UD feature set was enriched with new features, i.e. `original_id` containing the original position of the word in the sentence. For a number of specific parts of speech (e.g. `PUNCT`, punctuation), the feature `lin` is added, containing the original relative position of the word with respect to its head. Note that the `lin` feature, in contrast to the `original_id` feature, is present in the test file too.

We decided not to use the `lin` feature, therefore we employ the original versions 2.2 of the treebank files (provided by the shared task organizer) since they contain both the gold word order and the inflected forms of the word. However, during the conversion of the dependency trees into a vector form (see Section 2.1), we ignored the information about word ordering and inflected forms.

For all the three language processed, we decided to use an *holistic* approach to learning, that is, we built one single probabilistic model (i.e. one for word ordering and one for morphology inflection) by using one single training file obtained by merging together all the training file for a specific language.

3.3 Detokenization

In order to produce the final result of the realization, one needs to transform the UD tree produced by the DipInfoUniTo realizer into a single string containing the sentence. Since the final goal of the task is to reproduce an output sentence close to the original sentence, in detokenized form, we post-processed the English and French syntax trees, in two additional phases, namely *contraction* and *space removal*.

In contraction, the sentence was modified in order to produce the contracted form for some specific multi-word constructions. In particular, in French there are two linguistic phenomena to account for, typical of romance languages, namely *articulated preposition* and *clitics*. Since they are

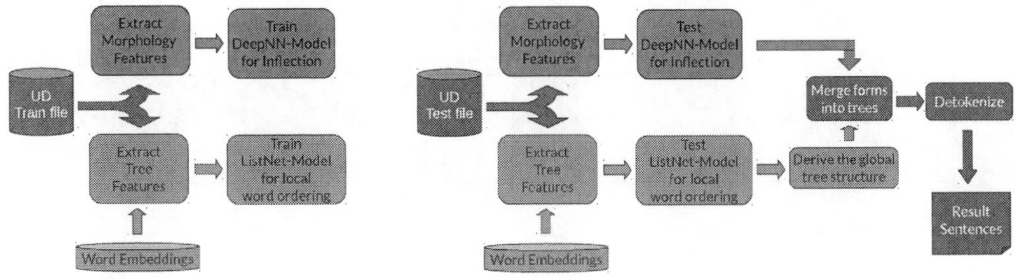

Figure 2: The training and testing pipelines, originally reported in (Basile and Mazzei, 2018a).

special case of multi-word expressions, both articulated prepositions and clitics have a special annotation status into UD treebanks, that we exploited to obtain the contracted form (see (Basile and Mazzei, 2018a) for details).

Moreover, each language has additional specific rules for the treatment of space between words and punctuation. In order to treat this specific cases we used the detokenizer script provided in the *moses* project[3]. The detokenizer provides specific rules for English and French.

3.4 Results

The final results have been produced by training the neural models for word ordering and morphology inflection for exactly 100 epochs and by using the development set provided by the organizer to select the best model. Note that the morphology inflection deep neural network uses a standard accuracy measure to select the best epoch-model. In contrast, the performance of word ordering is measured in terms of average Kendall's Tau (Kendall, 1938, τ), a rank correlation measure used to score the rankings predicted by a specific epoch model for every subtree (cf. (Basile and Mazzei, 2018b)). τ measures the similarity between two rankings by counting how many pairs of elements are swapped with respect to the original ordering out of all possible pairs of n elements:

$$\tau = \frac{\#concordant\_pairs - \#discordant\_tpairs}{\frac{1}{2}n(n-1)}$$

---

[3]`https://github.com/moses-smt/mosesdecoder/blob/master/scripts/tokenizer/detokenizer.perl`

In Table 1 the official scores of the DipInfoUniTo system for English, French and Chinese datasets are reported, computed in terms of the automatic metrics BLUE, NIST, and DIST. With respect to the other teams, our results score are in the lower half of the leaderboard, raking between $8th$ and $9th$ position depending on metrics and detokenization over the 12 teams participating to the T1-shared task. Since there is no notable difference in the ranking of our system in tokenized and detokenized ranks, we hypothesize that our detokenization procedure is similar to that of the others teams.

It is interesting to note the the best values for BLEU and NIST have been obtained on the `en_pud-ud-test` test file. This fact seems to suggest that our model does not overfit on a specific domain, which could be a consequence of our design choice to produce domain-agnostic models for each language.

Moreover, since the performance of the system for English and French does not correlate to the dataset size, we speculate that there are other linguistic features influencing the performance of the system, e.g., average length of the sentences, or the complexity of the lexicon. More experimentation is necessary to investigate on this speculation.

4 Conclusions and Future Work

In this paper, we described the DipInfoUnito realizer and its participation to the SR'19 competition. With respect to the previous year, we have introduced the evaluation of the models produced

	Detokenized			Tokenized		
	BLEU	NIST	DIST	BLEU	NIST	DIST
en_ewt-ud-test	37.88	10.03	60.10	43.5	11.56	60.13
en_gum-ud-test	39.59	9.82	56.28	44.24	11.15	56.04
en_lines-ud-test	26.83	8.56	52.97	32.42	10.05	53.21
en_partut-ud-test	29.47	7.81	51.03	35.11	9.08	51.15
fr_gsd-ud-test	25.86	8.19	47.48	27.04	9.58	47.33
fr_partut-ud-test	36.77	7.84	55.08	37.69	8.57	54.85
fr_sequoia-ud-test	27.4	8.49	49.13	28.95	9.72	48.70
zh_gsd-ud-test	0.02	0.01	32.10	32.87	11.16	50.57
en_pud-ud-test (OoD)	40.73	10.43	53.53	45.61	11.81	53.26
en_ewt-Pred-HIT-edit (Pred)	0.00	0.00	0.00	43.23	11.44	58.72
en_pud-Pred-LATTICE (Pred)	39.63	10.28	54.61	44.06	11.67	54.42

Table 1: The official scores of the DipInfoUniTo system for English, French and Chinese datasets, in terms of the automatic metrics BLUE, NIST, and DIST. Note that the label OoD stands for *out of domain* and the label Pred stands for *predicted* values of the features values.

at each epoch by the word ordering neural network in the training pipeline in terms of Kendall's Tau. Due to computational constraints, we have been able to run our systems on three languages only, namely English, French and Chinese. The final results rank our system in the the mid-lower part of the final ranking. We believe that a more efficient implementation of the word ordering, i.e., the neural network implementing the ListNet algorithm, could improve the results.

With respect to the problem of generalizing our approach to account for non-projective structure, we intend to develop our work in two directions. First, decomposing the original dependency tree into structures with a wider *domain of locality*. By following the direction by Joshi and Rambow (2003), we plan to model the prediction of local order with more complex structures. Second, as pointed out in (Basile, 2015, Chapter 7), learning the global order of the words rather (or in addition to) their local order. However, learning the word order globally may impact the transparency of the system, therefore a careful balance between performance and explainability must be achieved. On the other hand, global order may alleviate the problem of non-projective sentences, that is currently an issue with the local ordering approach. In future work, we plan to devise a two-step approach to leverage both approaches and learn jointly from both global and local order, e.g., in a multi-task learning fashion.

Aknowledgment

We thank the GARR consortium for the use of GARR Cloud Platform[4]. Valerio Basile was partially funded by Progetto di Ateneo/CSP 2016 (*Immigrants, Hate and Prejudice in Social Media*, S1618_L2_BOSC_01).
Alessandro Mazzei was partially supported by the HPC4AI project, funded by the Region Piedmont POR-FESR 2014-20 programme (INFRA-P call).

References

Roee Aharoni and Yoav Goldberg. 2017. Morphological inflection generation with hard monotonic attention. In *Proceedings of the 55th Annual Meeting of the Association for Computational Linguistics, ACL 2017*, pages 2004–2015.

Rami Al-Rfou', Bryan Perozzi, and Steven Skiena. 2013. Polyglot: Distributed word representations for multilingual nlp. In *CoNLL*, pages 183–192. ACL.

Valerio Basile. 2015. *From Logic to Language : Natural Language Generation from Logical Forms*. Ph.D. thesis, University of Groningen, Netherlands.

Valerio Basile and Alessandro Mazzei. 2018a. The dipinfo-unito system for srst 2018. In *Proceedings of the First Workshop on Multilingual Surface Realisation*, pages 65–71. Association for Computational Linguistics.

Valerio Basile and Alessandro Mazzei. 2018b. Neural surface realization for italian. In *Proceedings of the*

---

[4] https://cloud.garr.it

Fifth Italian Conference on Computational Linguistics (CLiC-it 2018), Torino, Italy, December 10-12, 2018.

Bernd Bohnet, Anders Björkelund, Jonas Kuhn, Wolfgang Seeker, and Sina Zarrieß. 2012. Generating non-projective word order in statistical linearization. In *Proceedings of the 2012 Joint Conference on Empirical Methods in Natural Language Processing and Computational Natural Language Learning*, pages 928–939. Association for Computational Linguistics.

Chris Burges, Tal Shaked, Erin Renshaw, Ari Lazier, Matt Deeds, Nicole Hamilton, and Greg Hullender. 2005. Learning to rank using gradient descent. In *Proceedings of the 22Nd International Conference on Machine Learning*, ICML '05, pages 89–96, New York, NY, USA. ACM.

Zhe Cao, Tao Qin, Tie-Yan Liu, Ming-Feng Tsai, and Hang Li. 2007. Learning to rank: From pairwise approach to listwise approach. In *Proceedings of the 24th International Conference on Machine Learning*, ICML '07, pages 129–136, New York, NY, USA. ACM.

Aravind K. Joshi and Owen Rambow. 2003. A formalism for dependency grammar based on tree adjoining grammar.

M. G. Kendall. 1938. A new measure of rank correlation. *Biometrika*, 30(1/2):81–93.

Simon Mille, Anja Belz, Bernd Bohnet, Yvette Graham, Emily Pitler, and Leo Wanner. 2018. The first multilingual surface realisation shared task (sr'18): Overview and evaluation results. In *Proceedings of the First Workshop on Multilingual Surface Realisation*, pages 1–12. Association for Computational Linguistics.

Simon Mille, Anja Belz, Bernd Bohnet, Yvette Graham, and Leo Wanner. 2019. The Second Multilingual Surface Realisation Shared Task (SR'19): Overview and Evaluation Results. In *Proceedings of the 2nd Workshop on Multilingual Surface Realisation (MSR), 2019 Conference on Empirical Methods in Natural Language Processing (EMNLP)*, Hong Kong, China.

Joakim Nivre, Marie-Catherine de Marneffe, Filip Ginter, Yoav Goldberg, Jan Hajic, Christopher D. Manning, Ryan T. McDonald, Slav Petrov, Sampo Pyysalo, Natalia Silveira, Reut Tsarfaty, and Daniel Zeman. 2016. Universal dependencies v1: A multilingual treebank collection. In *Proceedings of the Tenth International Conference on Language Resources and Evaluation LREC 2016, Portorož, Slovenia, May 23-28, 2016.*

Ehud Reiter and Robert Dale. 2000. *Building Natural Language Generation Systems*. Cambridge University Press, New York, NY, USA.

LORIA / Lorraine University at Multilingual Surface Realisation 2019

Anastasia Shimorina
LORIA / Lorraine University
anastasia.shimorina@loria.fr

Claire Gardent
LORIA / CNRS
claire.gardent@loria.fr

Abstract

This paper presents the LORIA / Lorraine University submission at the Multilingual Surface Realisation shared task 2019 for the shallow track. We outline our approach and evaluate it on 11 languages covered by the shared task. We provide a separate evaluation of each component of our pipeline, concluding on some difficulties and suggesting directions for future work.

1 Introduction

SR'19 (Mille et al., 2019) is the second edition of the multilingual surface realisation task ran in 2018 (Mille et al., 2018). It aims at developing surface realisers in the multilingual setting. Given an input tree, a well-formed sentence should be produced. The input tree can be either an unordered dependency tree (shallow track), or a tree with a predicate-argument structure (deep track).

The predecessor of the task is SR'11 (Belz et al., 2011), which dealt with surface realisation for English using data from Penn Treebank. Then, most approaches were based on statistical and rule-based methods. In SR'18, most participants used neural-based components, however, most teams (7 out of 8) used a pipeline approach, where they dealt separately with word ordering and morphological inflection (Basile and Mazzei, 2018; Castro Ferreira et al., 2018; Elder and Hokamp, 2018; King and White, 2018; Madsack et al., 2018; Puzikov and Gurevych, 2018; Singh et al., 2018; Sobrevilla Cabezudo and Pardo, 2018).

In this paper, we present a brief overview of the LORIA / Lorraine University system. We participated in the shallow track, and delivered solutions for all the languages proposed by the organisers. We also participated in generating output for all the types of corpora: in-domain, out-of-domain, and predicted by syntax parsers. Re-

sults on the development set are presented, and the system performance for each step of surface realisation is evaluated and discussed. All the code and experiments are available at https://gitlab.com/shimorina/msr-2019.

2 Data

We used only the data provided by the organisers. If several corpora were available for a language, they were mixed to the one training and development dataset. We used original UD files for creating target files for training the word ordering component, i.e. we extracted a sequence of tokens (the field `token` in the CoNLL format) instead of using a reference sentence.

3 Model

We made use of the model introduced in Shimorina and Gardent (2019) with some slight modifications. This model, developed for the SR'18 shared task data, is a pipeline approach to the surface realisation task, which has separate modules for word ordering, morphological inflection, and contraction generation. A brief outline is provided below; for more details about the model, we refer the reader to Shimorina and Gardent (2019).

3.1 Word Ordering (WO)

Word ordering is modelled as a sequence-to-sequence task, where an input tree is linearised. Linearisation differs from our previous approach in that it was augmented with information about the relative order of some elements, a feature that was introduced for this year edition of the shared task. So nodes were linearised using the depth-first search, and then elements with the relative order feature were reordered to match the added information.

Proceedings of the 2nd Workshop on Multilingual Surface Realisation (MSR 2019), pages 88–93
Hong Kong, China, November 3rd, 2019. ©2019 Association for Computational Linguistics
https://doi.org/10.18653/v1/P17

All input lemmas were delexicalised, i.e. replaced by identifiers both in the source and target, and enriched with features, or factors. A neural, factored encoder-decoder model was trained for each language, where factors are dependency relations, POS tags, and parent node identifiers (Elder and Hokamp, 2018; Alexandrescu and Kirchhoff, 2006).

During relexicalisation, all the identifiers were replaced by inflected lemmas. For the word ordering evaluation, we also relexicalised identifiers using the corresponding lemmas (see Section 4).

3.2 Morphological Realisation (MR)

Morphological paradigms were learned from pairs of (lemma, POS+features) extracted from the training data (the `upos` and `features` fields from CoNLL) using Aharoni and Goldberg (2017)'s model. Lemmas with no morphological features were not used. Since features are not provided for Chinese, Japanese, and Korean treebanks, the morphological realisation module was not trained for those languages. Instead, during the inflection phase (a) for Chinese, analytic language, lemmas were copied verbatim to the ouput; (b) for Korean, agglutinative language, morphemes in a lemma were glued together, and then the lemma was copied; (c) for Japanese, synthetic language, a dictionary of the form (lemma+POS: wordform) was constructed from the training data and looked up. If a key 'lemma+POS' was not present in the dictionary, the lemma was copied to the output verbatim. The same rule applies for any other lemma with no morphological features in any treebank (e.g., URLs, foreign words, numbers, punctuation signs, etc.)[1].

3.3 Contraction Generation (CG)

Contraction generation was implemented for French and Portuguese to handle clitic attachment, contractions, and elision. In the following, we will refer to the MR component as including the contraction generation module as well.

Eventually, one may also include detokenisation, a task of glueing tokens together, in this last step, as each language requires specific detokenisation rules to produce a final well-formed sentence, which can be shown to an end-user. We

lang	Acc.	Amb. %	Amb. count
ar	90.87	7.29	1,815
en	96.35	0.84	226
es	98.85	0.85	418
fr	98.40	1.48	430
hi	89.95	6.46	569
id	98.52	0.55	47
ja	NA	3.62	800
ko	NA	0.86	945
pt	98.95	0.85	233
ru	97.25	0.72	933
zh	NA	0	0

Table 1: Accuracy of the morphological realisation component. NA: no MR component was developed. Percentage and count of lemmas with ambiguous forms found in the training data.

used the `sacremoses`[2] library to perform detokenisation. Besides, it was also used to tokenise reference sentences; we need that for the automatic scoring.

4 Results and Discussion

We evaluate each module separately. For WO, we compared a generated sequence of lemmas with a gold sequence of lemmas extracted from UD (Section 4.1). For MR, we calculated wordform prediction accuracy, and also applied MR to a gold sequence of lemmas instead of predicted sequence of lemmas (Section 4.2). Finally, we performed the overall evaluation, where our system predictions were compared to reference sentences (Section 4.3)[3].

4.1 WO Evaluation

Table 3 shows the results of WO. BLEU scores vary from 30 to 66 depending on the language and corpus ($mean = 56.98, median = 60.01$).

We surmised that low scores for Arabic, Chinese, Indonesian are due to small sizes of training corpora (6K, 4K, 4.5K, respectively), which are not enough for neural systems. Other languages' scores show a smaller variation, ranging from 51 to 66; we conjecture that the variations between languages are due to different syntactic phenom-

---

[1] We deleted features for foreign words in ru_gsd_ud for it to be consistent with ru_syntagrus_ud.

[2] `https://github.com/alvations/sacremoses`

[3] After the official submission, we fixed a bug in MR for Japanese and Korean. In this paper we are reporting improved results.

Corpus	BLEU	DIST	NIST
ar_padt-ud	40.07	47.23	8.25
en_ewt-ud	80.88	80.22	12.90
en_gum-ud	90.73	98.74	12.80
en_lines-ud	86.78	97.03	12.74
en_partut-ud	86.31	96.46	10.23
es_ancora-ud	93.82	98.47	14.88
es_gsd-ud	89.31	99.23	13.93
fr_gsd-ud	90.53	98.12	14.04
fr_partut-ud	87.07	96.61	9.82
fr_sequoia-ud	91.00	96.38	12.38
hi_hdtb-ud	91.88	96.89	13.67
id_gsd-ud	94.46	98.91	12.90
ja_gsd-ud	77.85	99.70	11.40
ko_gsd-ud	60.38	94.38	9.45
ko_kaist-ud	97.13	99.67	13.44
pt_bosque-ud	94.09	99.10	12.68
pt_gsd-ud	57.04	91.12	10.54
ru_gsd-ud	86.87	96.89	12.18
ru_syntagrus-ud	91.25	98.15	15.53
zh_gsd-ud	99.16	99.81	13.33

Table 2: The MR module applied to the gold word ordering input. Predictions and reference sentences are both tokenised. Results on the development set.

ena occurring in each language and the variations between corpora are due to different annotation guidelines.

4.2 MR+CG Evaluation

The inflection module was initially measured by accuracy of producing a correct word form given a lemma and its POS together with morphological features (cf. Table 1, second column). The average accuracy is 96.14 across 8 languages, which corresponds to the state-of-the-art results in inflection tasks (Cotterell et al., 2016).

We also calculated a number of lemmas, which can have different word forms, given the same set of POS and morphological features (Table 1, third column). For example, the lemma *people* with `pos=NOUN, Number=Plur` as features have two word forms in the training data: *people* and *peoples*. Those ambiguous forms may stem from different sources: language variation (as in the example above) including spelling, non-standard forms and typos; annotation mistakes; underspecified morphological features. The example of the latter is an adjective in Russian, which can have different forms in the accusative case depending on animacy of the noun it modifies (animacy in that case is an underspecified feature).

To measure the effect on scores, when converting a sequence of lemmas into a sentence, we applied MR+CG to gold sequences of lemmas (they have the same word order as the reference). Results are shown in Table 2. In general, high accuracies of MR alone (word level, Table 1) do not guarantee good performance while evaluating on the sentence level.

That type of evaluation enabled us to have more insight into the data used. Some of our findings are listed below.

- English: a discrepancy in performance across datasets. The sources of the en_ewt_ud corpus are blogs, social networks, reviews, emails, where the use of contractions (*isn't*, *ain't*, etc) is dominant comparing to formal style. Since the contraction generation was not applied for English, scores for this particular dataset are lower than for others.

- Arabic. We conjecture low scores for the high variability of forms (cf. Table 1) and contractions (We did not develop a module for handling contractions in Arabic.). For instance, some diacritics are optional (e.g., hamza with alif), so a word form can be written with or without them, being a valid word form in both cases.

- Japanese. MR module was not developed for Japanese, so a look-up dictionary based on training data was not sufficient to handle the morphology. The high number of ambiguous forms also impacted the scores, as in the case of Arabic.

- Portuguese. The pt_gsd_ud corpus is not annotated with morphological features, hence 57.04 score in BLEU compared to 94.09 in pt_bosque-ud.

- Korean. We do not read Korean, so we were not able to explain the difference between the two Korean corpora (97.13 vs. 60.38 BLEU). Some annotation disparity may well be the explanation.

4.3 Surface Realisation Evaluation

The performance of the overall surface realisation model is shown in Table 4. Automatic scores

Corpus	BLEU	DIST	NIST
ar_padt-ud	30.45	54.72	8.86
en_ewt-ud	66.71	84.18	12.57
en_gum-ud	62.92	80.61	11.53
en_lines-ud	61.89	75.76	11.67
en_partut-ud	62.38	75.87	9.82
es_ancora-ud	59.43	75.03	12.69
es_gsd-ud	61.83	74.94	12.80
fr_gsd-ud	60.58	78.66	12.74
fr_partut-ud	61.24	82.37	9.35
fr_sequoia-ud	55.22	74.18	10.86
hi_hdtb-ud	63.07	59.87	11.74
id_gsd-ud	46.09	76.07	9.99
ja_gsd-ud	56.53	62.41	10.33
ko_gsd-ud	53.73	53.01	11.69
ko_kaist-ud	66.43	63.19	12.85
pt_bosque-ud	52.88	81.98	11.13
pt_gsd-ud	51.01	72.59	11.82
ru_gsd-ud	59.11	62.30	11.72
ru_syntagrus-ud	62.37	67.88	14.03
zh_gsd-ud	45.67	56.01	10.23

Table 3: WO component performance on the development set. Predictions and references (sequences of lemmas) are both tokenised.

Corpus	BLEU	DIST	NIST
ar_padt-ud	18.06	43.86	6.49
en_ewt-ud	54.45	65.45	11.32
en_gum-ud	58.17	79.68	11.16
en_lines-ud	52.53	73.48	10.79
en_partut-ud	54.79	73.98	9.10
es_ancora-ud	56.99	73.78	12.53
es_gsd-ud	59.63	74.07	12.32
fr_gsd-ud	51.94	70.43	11.63
fr_partut-ud	51.72	74.74	8.47
fr_sequoia-ud	49.08	70.27	10.13
hi_hdtb-ud	58.48	61.13	11.42
id_gsd-ud	45.28	75.50	9.88
ja_gsd-ud	46.30	62.31	9.37
ko_gsd-ud	32.21	49.43	8.73
ko_kaist-ud	64.58	61.21	12.69
pt_bosque-ud	59.35	83.84	11.20
pt_gsd-ud	35.44	69.47	9.17
ru_gsd-ud	52.90	60.59	11.13
ru_syntagrus-ud	57.97	66.87	13.70
zh_gsd-ud	45.48	55.91	10.21

Table 4: Automatic metrics on the development set (WO + MR). Predictions and reference sentences are both tokenised.

show a drop compared to the WO component performance (Table 3), which is consistent with the errors of the MR+CG module, described in Section 4.2.

Figure 1 aggregates the BLEU scores, shown in Tables 2, 3, 4. For each corpus, BLEU for each module (X axis) is mapped to the final BLEU score (Y axis). The scatterplots show a strong, positive association between the two variables: Pearson's $\rho = 0.83$ and $\rho = 0.86$ for WO and MR on gold data respectively.

During test time, we also ran our system on out-of-domain and machine-generated data. For all languages concerned, automatic scores remain stable, which demonstrates the portability of our approach.

5 Conclusion

We presented the LORIA / Lorraine University submission to the SR'19 shared task. Our main takeaways are as follows. The WO component is easily transferrable between languages, and it will not require much effort for applying it to unseen languages. In contrast, the MR component requires a lot of attention, and needs to be tuned for each language separately. That is mainly due to the different approaches for language annotation across UD treebanks, and, what is more unexpected, across UD treebanks for the same language, not to speak of the detokenisation process, which is different for each language, and which should also be implemented separately.

Having those particularities in mind, we think that for future work MR (including contraction generation, and possibly detokenisation) would benefit for including context information, i.e. doing inflection and necessary character transformations on a whole sentence, rather than word by word. As for word ordering, it remains a tough problem for sequence-to-sequence architectures, and it is worth exploring other ways of encoding tree structure.

We also would like to highlight the importance of modular evaluation. If a system design allows it, system outputs may be tested against a sequence of lemmas, not only a reference sentence, thanks to the UD annotations. We encourage future participants not to neglect this type of evaluation to gain deeper insight into their system and data.

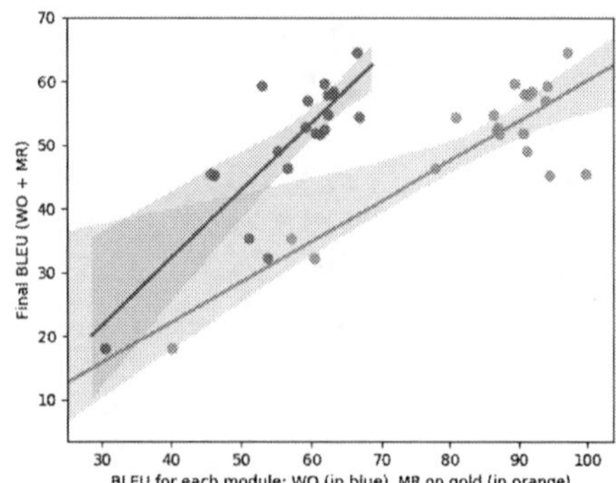

Figure 1: Linear regression between BLEU scores for each module and final BLEU scores. Data points are corpora. In orange: MR on gold data vs. final BLEU (WO + MR); in blue: WO vs. final BLEU (WO + MR).

References

Roee Aharoni and Yoav Goldberg. 2017. Morphological inflection generation with hard monotonic attention. In *Proceedings of the 55th Annual Meeting of the Association for Computational Linguistics (Volume 1: Long Papers)*, pages 2004–2015, Vancouver, Canada. Association for Computational Linguistics.

Andrei Alexandrescu and Katrin Kirchhoff. 2006. Factored neural language models. In *Proceedings of the Human Language Technology Conference of the NAACL, Companion Volume: Short Papers*, pages 1–4. Association for Computational Linguistics.

Valerio Basile and Alessandro Mazzei. 2018. The dipinfo-unito system for srst 2018. In *Proceedings of the First Workshop on Multilingual Surface Realisation*, pages 65–71. Association for Computational Linguistics.

Anja Belz, Mike White, Dominic Espinosa, Eric Kow, Deirdre Hogan, and Amanda Stent. 2011. The first surface realisation shared task: Overview and evaluation results. In *Proceedings of the 13th European Workshop on Natural Language Generation*, pages 217–226. Association for Computational Linguistics.

Thiago Castro Ferreira, Sander Wubben, and Emiel Krahmer. 2018. Surface realization shared task 2018 (sr18): The tilburg university approach. In *Proceedings of the First Workshop on Multilingual Surface Realisation*, pages 35–38. Association for Computational Linguistics.

Ryan Cotterell, Christo Kirov, John Sylak-Glassman, David Yarowsky, Jason Eisner, and Mans Hulden. 2016. The SIGMORPHON 2016 shared Task—Morphological reinflection. In *Proceedings of the 14th SIGMORPHON Workshop on Computational Research in Phonetics, Phonology, and Morphology*, pages 10–22, Berlin, Germany. Association for Computational Linguistics.

Henry Elder and Chris Hokamp. 2018. Generating high-quality surface realizations using data augmentation and factored sequence models. In *Proceedings of the First Workshop on Multilingual Surface Realisation*, pages 49–53. Association for Computational Linguistics.

David King and Michael White. 2018. The osu realizer for srst '18: Neural sequence-to-sequence inflection and incremental locality-based linearization. In *Proceedings of the First Workshop on Multilingual Surface Realisation*, pages 39–48. Association for Computational Linguistics.

Andreas Madsack, Johanna Heininger, Nyamsuren Davaasambuu, Vitaliia Voronik, Michael Käufl, and Robert Weißgraeber. 2018. Ax semantics' submission to the surface realization shared task 2018. In *Proceedings of the First Workshop on Multilingual Surface Realisation*, pages 54–57. Association for Computational Linguistics.

Simon Mille, Anja Belz, Bernd Bohnet, Yvette Graham, Emily Pitler, and Leo Wanner. 2018. The first multilingual surface realisation shared task (sr'18): Overview and evaluation results. In *Proceedings of the First Workshop on Multilingual Surface Realisation*, pages 1–12. Association for Computational Linguistics.

Simon Mille, Anja Belz, Bernd Bohnet, Yvette Graham, and Leo Wanner. 2019. The Second Multilingual Surface Realisation Shared Task (SR'19): Overview and Evaluation Results. In *Proceedings of the 2nd Workshop on Multilingual Surface Realisation (MSR), 2019 Conference on Empirical Methods in Natural Language Processing (EMNLP)*, Hong Kong, China.

Yevgeniy Puzikov and Iryna Gurevych. 2018. Binlin: A simple method of dependency tree linearization. In *Proceedings of the First Workshop on Multilingual Surface Realisation*, pages 13–28. Association for Computational Linguistics.

Anastasia Shimorina and Claire Gardent. 2019. Surface Realisation Using Full Delexicalisation. In *2019 Conference on Empirical Methods in Natural Language Processing and 9th International Joint Conference on Natural Language Processing*, Hong Kong, China.

Shreyansh Singh, Ayush Sharma, Avi Chawla, and A.K. Singh. 2018. Iit (bhu) varanasi at msr-srst 2018: A language model based approach for natural language generation. In *Proceedings of the First Workshop on Multilingual Surface Realisation*, pages 29–34. Association for Computational Linguistics.

Marco Antonio Sobrevilla Cabezudo and Thiago Pardo. 2018. Nilc-swornemo at the surface realization shared task: Exploring syntax-based word ordering using neural models. In *Proceedings of the First Workshop on Multilingual Surface Reali-sation*, pages 58–64. Association for Computational Linguistics.

Back-Translation as Strategy to Tackle the Lack of Corpus in Natural Language Generation from Semantic Representations

Marco Antonio Sobrevilla Cabezudo♣   **Simon Mille**♠
Thiago Alexandre Salgueiro Pardo♣
♣ Interinstitutional Center for Computational Linguistics (NILC)
Institute of Mathematical and Computer Sciences, University of São Paulo. São Carlos/SP, Brazil
♠ Universitat Pompeu Fabra. Barcelona, Spain
msobrevillac@usp.br, simon.mille@upf.edu, taspardo@icmc.usp.br

Abstract

This paper presents an exploratory study that aims to evaluate the usefulness of back-translation in Natural Language Generation (NLG) from semantic representations for non-English languages. Specifically, Abstract Meaning Representation and Brazilian Portuguese (BP) are chosen as semantic representation and language, respectively. Two methods (focused on Statistical and Neural Machine Translation) are evaluated on two datasets (one automatically generated and another one human-generated) to compare the performance in a real context. Also, several cuts according to quality measures are performed to evaluate the importance (or not) of the data quality in NLG. Results show that there are still many improvements to be made but this is a promising approach.

1 Introduction

Natural Language Generation (NLG) is the research area that aims to give to the computers the ability to generate texts in human language from some underlying representation of information (Reiter and Dale, 2000). This area has gained relevance in the Natural Language Processing community and in the industry in the last years.

There are several works and efforts in NLG for English.[1] Recently, shared-tasks focused on NLG from semantic representations have gained the attention of the NLG community. Thus, several representations have emerged for attending different contexts. For example, the RDF-based representation presented by Gardent et al. (2017) in its WebNLG challenge, the dialog-act-based representation presented by Novikova et al. (2016), and Abstract Meaning Representation (Banarescu et al., 2013).

There are not as many works for languages other than English: in 2018, the first multilingual surface realization was proposed (Mille et al., 2018). This event proposed two tasks, one focused on reordering a dependency tree and generating inflected words (called shallow track), and the other one focused on generating sentences from a deep-syntax representation similar to a semantic representation (called deep track). It is important to note that while NLG methods were evaluated in corpora for ten different languages in the shallow track, the deep track was limited to evaluating NLG methods on three languages (English, Spanish, and French). The fact that there are less datasets in the deep track is directly related to the higher complexity of the conversion compared to the shallow track, for which a superficial processing (basically order randomization) is sufficient.

Among the efforts to build or adapt semantic representations for non-English languages, it is possible to cite Abstract Meaning Representation (AMR) as an example. Although AMR was not born as an interlingua, several works have tried to use it in that way to annotate sentences in other languages like Chinese and Czech (Xue et al., 2014), Italian, Spanish, and German (Damonte and Cohen, 2018) and Brazilian Portuguese (Anchiêta and Pardo, 2018). Other works have tried to adapt the English AMR guidelines to Spanish and Brazilian Portuguese with some success (Migueles-Abraira et al., 2018; Sobrevilla Cabezudo and Pardo, 2019). However, most of these works report a small number of AMR-annotated sentences (compared to the English corpus) and are restricted to some domains like tales ("The Little Prince"). To the best of our knowledge, the only AMR-annotated corpus comparable (in terms of size) to the English corpus[2] is the

---

[1]Most of the work may be found at https://aclweb.org/anthology/sigs/siggen/.

[2]Available at https://catalog.ldc.upenn.

Proceedings of the 2nd Workshop on Multilingual Surface Realisation (MSR 2019), pages 94–103
Hong Kong, China, November 3rd, 2019. ©2019 Association for Computational Linguistics
https://doi.org/10.18653/v1/P17

Chinese corpus, containing 10,149 annotated sentences in its first version.[3]

This difficulty to get large corpora with this kind of annotation (due to the difficult and expensive annotation task that it represents) constrains the development of research in other languages. Consequently, it is difficult to achieve the same performance as in English or to replicate state-of-the-art works.

In general, a strategy to overcome the lack of corpora is to translate English corpora to non-English ones. This involves the use of Machine Translation (MT) systems, leveraging the good performance obtained by MT systems that work on English as a source or target language. However, the quality of the translations depends on the language pair. Thus, it is important to filter out some translations according to their quality. This may be accomplished by applying back-translation and performing a quality evaluation (using some quality measures like BLEU or METEOR) in English. In Machine Translation, Back-translation consists of translating a target sentence (in our case, Portuguese) into a source language (in our case, English).

This approach has shown good performance in some classification tasks like Sentiment Analysis and Word Sense Disambiguation (Klinger and Cimiano, 2015; Monsalve et al., 2019). Furthermore, Monsalve et al. (2019) show that despite the introduction of sentences with low quality (according to quality measures), the performance of the classifiers continues improving. Also, this approach has been successful in the context of neural machine translation (Sennrich et al., 2016). In the case of NLG from semantic representations, it would be expected that quality is critical since low-quality sentences may lead to models learning incorrect language. Additionally, other issues that may impact the performance of this task are the translation of the semantic representation and the alignments between language pairs.

In this context, this paper presents an exploratory study that aims to evaluate the usefulness of back-translation in NLG from semantic representations for non-English languages. Specifically, AMR and Brazilian Portuguese (BP) are chosen as semantic representation and language, respectively. Two methods (SMT-based and NMT-based) are evaluated on two datasets (one automatically generated and one human-generated) in order to compare the performance in a real context. Also, several cuts[4] according to quality measures are performed to evaluate the importance (or not) of the data quality in NLG.

This paper is organized as follows: §2 describes some work that applied back-translation to produce corpus in non-English languages. Then, §3 introduces Abstract Meaning Representation (our target representation) and works performed for English and non-English languages on it. Our methodology for generating corpus and the experiments performed are presented in §4. Furthermore, §5 contains the results and a discussion about the results. Finally, the conclusions and future work are presented in §6.

2 Related Work

Several works have proven the usefulness of translating corpora to increase the dataset size and improve the performance of their models. For example, Klinger and Cimiano (2015) used Phrase-based MT and some quality estimation measures to build a corpus with the best translations and use it in Sentiment Analysis. Misu et al. (2012) and Gaspers et al. (2018) explored back-translation in Natural Language Understanding systems using different measures. Misu et al. (2012) showed that BLEU is not a good quality measure and Gaspers et al. (2018) used measures from alignments, machine translation and language models to select the best sentences to be included in the corpus.

Monsalve et al. (2019) also explored some quality measures (BLEU and METEOR) to select the best sentences and build a non-English corpus for Reading Comprehension and Word Sense Disambiguation. Among the results, they showed that despite the introduction of low-quality sentences, the performance is still continually improving. However, their main goal was to get a well-translated corpus and not to get the best results in both tasks.

About the tasks that involve language generation, it is noted that back-translation has been widely, and successfully, used in neural machine translation. The aim was to generate synthetic source sentences to increase the parallel training dataset (Sennrich et al., 2016; Edunov et al.,

---

[3]Available at https://catalog.ldc.upenn.edu/LDC2019T07

[4]A cut consists of a set of sentences of the corpus with a similar quality.

2018). Also, Prabhumoye et al. (2018) applied back-translation to perform style transfer with good results.

Concerning the described work, a question emerges: How can back-translation influence NLG from semantic representations? It is important to note that not only English sentences will be translated into BP ones, but its corresponding semantic representations will be translated to handle representations for Portuguese. Thus, several issues related to alignments may affect the performance (in addition to the quality translation). The following sections show the influence of back-translation in NLG.

3 Abstract Meaning Representation

Abstract Meaning Representation (AMR) is a semantic formalism that aims to encode the meaning of a sentence with a simple representation in the form of a directed rooted graph (Banarescu et al., 2013). This representation includes information about semantic roles, named entities, spatial-temporal information, and co-references, among other information. AMR-annotated sentences may be represented using logic forms, PENMAN notation, and graphs (Figure 1).

AMR has gained relevance in the research community due to its attempt to abstract away from syntactic idiosyncrasies[5] and its wide use of other comprehensive linguistic resources, such as Prop-Bank (Palmer et al., 2005).[6]

The current AMR-annotated corpus for English contains 39,260 sentences. Some efforts have been performed to build a corpus for Non-English languages leveraging the alignments and the parallel corpora that exist and trying to consider AMR an interlingua (Xue et al., 2014; Damonte and Cohen, 2018; Anchiêta and Pardo, 2018). Other works tried to adapt the AMR guidelines to other languages (Migueles-Abraira et al., 2018; Sobrevilla Cabezudo and Pardo, 2019).

For Brazilian Portuguese, there are two AMR-annotated corpora, one automatically built from the alignments between the sentences of the "The Little Prince" book in English and Portuguese (Anchiêta and Pardo, 2018), and the other one that contains news texts sentences manually annotated

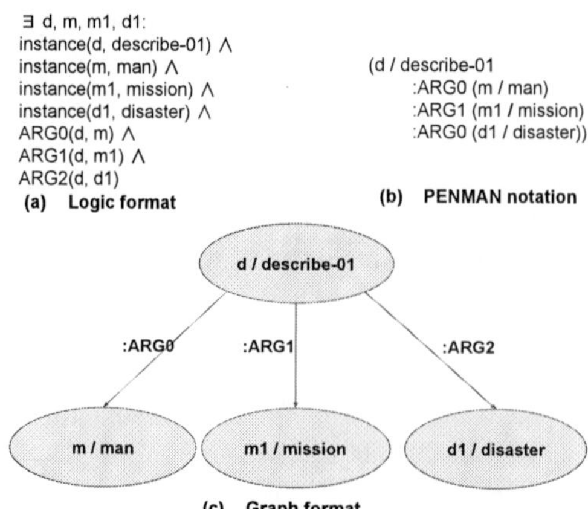

Figure 1: AMR example for the sentence "The man described the mission as a disaster"

using an adaptation of the AMR guidelines (Sobrevilla Cabezudo and Pardo, 2019). The lexical resource used to annotate some concepts in both corpora was the Verbo-Brasil (Duran and Aluísio, 2015), which is analogous to the PropBank lexical repository.

Concerning the Little Prince corpus, the style of the sentences reflects a rather unusual genre (tales) and the vocabulary is restricted to the story. Also, this corpus only contains 1,527 annotated sentences. In relation to the second corpus, although annotated sentences belong to news texts, the corpus size is still small, containing 299 annotated sentences. Besides, only the sentences that contain lexical units found in Verbo-Brasil were annotated, excluding those that are not represented in it. As a result, the current limitations of the corpora in terms of genre, size and richness of annotations hinders the development or adaptation of methods that target general purpose and semantics-oriented NLG tasks.

4 Methodology

In order to deal with the lack of corpus in the AMR-to-Text generation task, firstly, a corpus generation process was developed to build an AMR dataset for Brazilian Portuguese (BP) from an English one. This process involved back-translation and some MT measures to select the high-quality BP sentences that are comprised in the dataset. Secondly, several experiments using well-known methods for AMR-to-Text generation were used to evaluate the performance of each method, measure the influence of the qual-

---

[5]In Figure 1, there are other possible sentences like "The man's description about the mission: a disaster" that could generate the same representation despite syntactic difference.

[6]In Figure 1, the frameset "describe-01" belongs to the PropBank lexical repository.

ity of the translated sentences, determine the most useful MT measure to select high-quality BP sentences, and verify if the results obtained with the translated datasets are comparable with a curated dataset (gold dataset).

4.1 Corpus generation

The corpus generation was divided in two phases: the first one focused on filtering and splitting the original English corpus and the second one focused on translating the concepts of the AMR graph according to the alignments between English and Portuguese tokens in the sentences.[7]

4.1.1 Corpus Filtering and Splitting

The corpus filtering phase consisted of the following steps:

- select the sentences in the English corpus. This step focused on selecting English sentences which have a similar size to those annotated in the BP corpus, i.e., 23 tokens maximum. The number of sentences after this step was 27,464.

- apply the back-translation. This strategy consisted of translating English sentences into BP sentences and then translating those BP sentences into English sentences to measure the quality of the translation in Portuguese via English (since the Portuguese references did not exist). To achieve this goal, the Machine Translation model provided by Google Translate API was used;[8]

- evaluate the sentences according to automatic quality measures. In the same way as Monsalve et al. (2019), F[9] and METEOR were used to automatically measure the quality of the sentences. The quality scores of BP sentences were calculated applying the quality measures to their respective English sentences. This generated a dataset for each quality measure (F and METEOR), where each instance of each dataset comprised the BP sentence and its respective quality score, aiming to define some sets.

- define the development and test sets.[10] To achieve this step, firstly, a set of sentences with a quality higher than the mean plus one standard deviation of all sentences according to each quality measure was selected, generating two sub-sets. Secondly, the sentences included in the intersection of the sub-sets were selected in order to filter the highest-quality sentences. Finally, the development and test sets were defined as 25% of the sentences in the intersection. In total, 1,073 sentences were used for development and test sets, respectively.

- define cuts according to quality measures. Finally, the remaining sentences in the translated BP datasets were sorted decreasingly according to each quality measure. Then, five cuts of 5,000 sentences each were performed for each quality measure, thus, the first cut contained the 5,000 best sentences according to one quality measure and the last cut contained the 5,000 worst sentences. Table 1 shows the mean and standard deviation (std) of each cut for each dataset (for quality measure). These datasets and cuts constitute the training set.

Measure		1	2	3	4	5
F	mean	0.92	0.74	0.60	0.32	0.00
	std	0.07	0.04	0.04	0.20	0.00
METEOR	mean	0.98	0.58	0.48	0.41	0.30
	std	0.03	0.09	0.01	0.01	0.08

Table 1: Statistics of all cuts performed in the AMR Corpus

4.1.2 Target Corpus Generation

In order to get the AMR-annotated corpus in Brazilian Portuguese (BP), it was also necessary to convert the English AMR graphs into Portuguese ones.

This conversion was performed leveraging the alignments between English and BP sentences and the alignments between the English sentences and the AMR graphs provided by the corpus. Thus, Fast Align (Dyer et al., 2013) was applied to obtain the alignments between the sentences. Then,

---

[7]In this work, the LDC2016E25 corpus was used to perform all experiments.

[8]Google Translate API was used due to the good results obtained in Machine Translation. Eventually, other MT systems could be used. Available at `https://cloud.google.com/translate/`.

[9]In this work, F measure is defined as the harmonic mean of BLEU and ROUGE scores.

[10]In this step, both the use of the mean plus one standard deviation and the 25% of the intersection were used as a threshold empirically defined.

these alignments were used to change the alignments (the numbers) in the AMR graph and to replace the English concepts by their respective BP concepts.

It is worth noting that not all concepts in the AMR graph were changed as some of them were not aligned in the corpus. Also, some concepts belonging to PropBank (PropBank framesets) were replaced by their corresponding framesets in BP using Verbo-Brasil (Duran and Aluísio, 2015). PropBank concepts (framesets) that could not be mapped to Verbo-Brasil framesets were kept in their English version. In general, 825 of 3,965 framesets were translated, representing 20.81% of the framesets. All other aligned English concepts were replaced by their corresponding BP ones in the sentence-alignments, excepting AMR-defined framesets, modal verbs, and AMR-defined entities. Besides, some rules were applied to change some concepts like ly-adverbs.

Concerning the alignment types, we note that there were some issues in "1-n" and "n-1" alignments. In the case of "n-1" alignments ("n" English tokens corresponding to 1 BP token), all "n" concepts were replaced by the same one concept, and in the case of "1-n" alignments, the one English concept was replaced by the concatenation of all "n" BP concepts. Figure 2 shows the pipeline of the AMR graph translation. Tokens and numbers in bold are the ones which were translated.

4.2 Experiments

Experiments were performed using the Statistical Machine Translation (SMT) and Neural Machine Translation (NMT) methods provided by Castro Ferreira et al. (2017) to compare how each method behaved in the evaluated context.

The SMT method used the same parameters proposed by Castro Ferreira et al. (2017) and a 5-gram language model trained on the BP corpus provided by Hartmann et al. (2017). Also, the AMR graph pre-processing comprised a compression and a pre-ordering step without delexicalization (described as -Delex+Compress+Preorder in the original paper) as this configuration got one of the best results.

The NMT method used similar parameters to Castro Ferreira et al. (2017). The encoder was bidirectional RNN with GRU, each with a 1024D hidden unit. Source and target word embeddings were 300D each and both were trained jointly with

the model. Also, the vocabulary was shared. All weights were initialized using a Xavier uniform, which draws samples from a uniform distribution within a range. The decoder RNN also used GRU with an attention and a copy mechanism (Bahdanau et al., 2015).

We applied dropout with a probability of 0.3. Models were trained using the Adadelta optimizer with a learning rate of 1.0 and a learning rate decay of 0.7 every 5 epochs, and mini-batches of size 64. We applied early stopping for model selection based on accuracy and perplexity scores so that if a model does not improve on the development set for more than 25 epochs, training is halted.

Besides, the AMR graph pre-processing was composed of a delexicalization and a pre-ordering step without compression (described as +Delex-Compress+Preorder in the original paper) as this configuration got one of the best results.

These methods were trained according to two configurations and evaluated using the automatically generated development set described in §4.1.1. The two configurations are described as follows:

- training on each cut described in §4.1.1 independently. It was expected that the performance decreases in each cut as the cut quality decreases as well.

- training on cut 1 plus each cut included progressively. At the beginning, the training set was composed by the cut 1. Then, a lower quality cut was added to the training set at each training phase until all the cuts were included. The goal of this experiment was to evaluate how the method performance varied when lower quality data was inserted into the training set.

It is worth noting that each configuration was performed using the cuts generated by F and METEOR to evaluate the quality measure in the corpus selection task. The test was performed on the automatically generated test set described in §4.1.1. In order to compare the results in a real context, the methods were also evaluated on the AMR-annotated BP dataset described in §3. Similar to Castro Ferreira et al. (2017), we used BLEU (Papineni et al., 2002), METEOR (Lavie and Agarwal, 2007) and TER (Snover et al., 2006) as metrics to evaluate fluency, adequacy and post-editing efforts of the models, respectively.

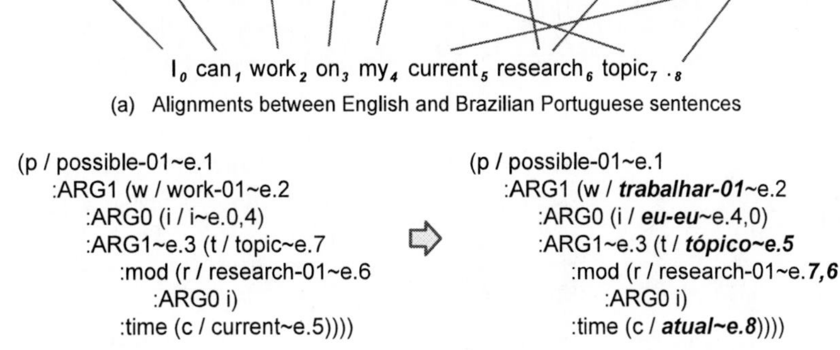

(a)   Alignments between English and Brazilian Portuguese sentences

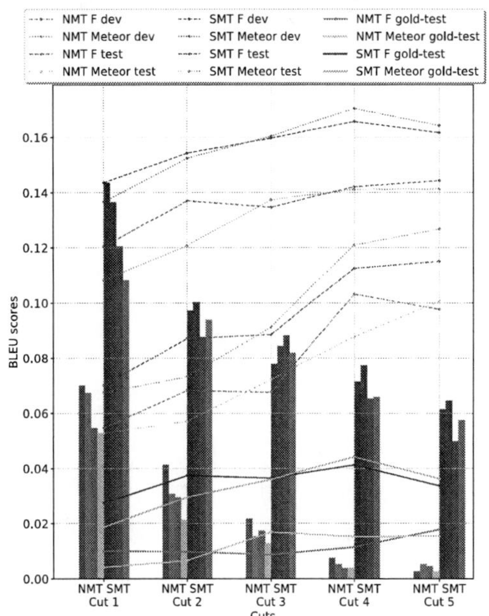

(b)   Conversion of AMR graph from English to Brazilian Portuguese according to alignments

Figure 2: Pipeline for the translation of the AMR corpus

5   Results and discussion

5.1   Overview

Figures 3, 4, and 5 show the results obtained by the NMT and SMT approaches using cuts generated by F and METEOR and evaluated on the development, test and gold test sets for each metric (BLEU, METEOR, and TER). Bars show the results of the first configuration (each cut independently) and lines represent the results of the second experiment (training on cut 1 plus each cut included progressively).

In general, results show that the performance on development and test sets increased while more data (no matter that was of lower quality) was incorporated (except on the last cut). On the other hand, the performance decreased when a lower quality cut was used as training data. Also, results on the curated test[11] (also called gold test) showed that there are many improvements to perform in order to achieve similar results to the development and test sets. In this set, BLEU and TER were the most affected metrics as values between 0.02 and 0.04 were obtained for BLEU (Figure 3), and 0.73 and 0.92 were obtained for TER (Figure 5).

5.2   Discussion

Quality or Quantity?   At first glance, quantity seemed to be more important than quality. Also, in the case of NMT, quantity seemed to be still more important than in the case of SMT. A detail to note is that the increase in the performance was lower when the latest cuts (with lower quality) were incorporated into the training set. Besides, the performance decreased when the latest

Figure 3: BLEU scores

cuts were incorporated in some cases (cut 5 in Figure 3). Thus, a different analysis is required to check if the quantity is more important than quality as the size of the training set could hide some problems caused by the lower quality cut.

In order to perform this analysis, four training sets were built. Each training set was composed by the cut 1 and another different cut (from highest to lowest quality cuts). Figures 6, 7, and 8 show the results of this experiment for each metric. Bars show the results on the development and test sets, and lines represent the results on the gold test set.

In this case, results on development set did not show a decrease in performance. However, results

---

[11]The curated test was composed by the manually-annotated 299 BP sentences.

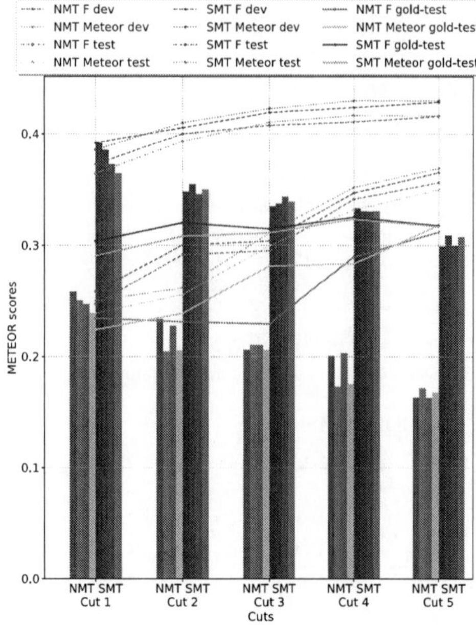

Figure 4: METEOR scores

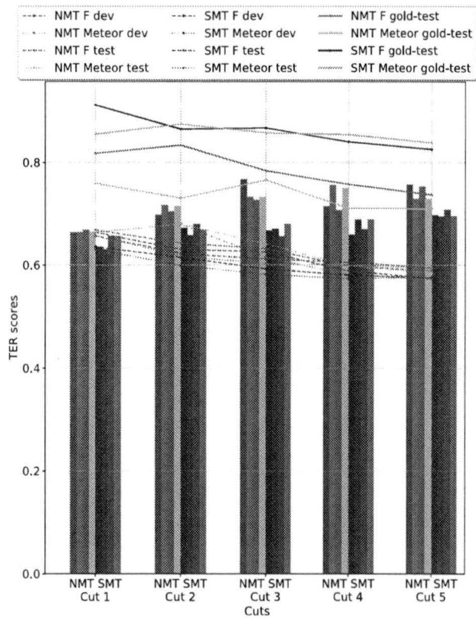

Figure 5: TER scores

increases and decreases in performance. A possible explanation to the slight (or no) variation in the results obtained was that Google Translate API usually produced good translations, and, although some translations could show low scores in terms of F or METEOR, they could be paraphrases or sentences with synonyms of some words of the original sentences. Thus, it is expected that in cases of languages where machine translation systems present worse performance, this analysis will show more useful information to select better cuts.

Finally, from a quality perspective, it is important to note that it would be useful considering cuts with higher quality to perform better corpus analysis. However, another problem emerges in the context of semantic representations. Alignments between English and BP sentences may not be "1-1" and this could make the correct generation of semantic representations for some sentences more difficult. Thus, an interesting research would consist in evaluating how alignments may affect the performance of the methods in this context.

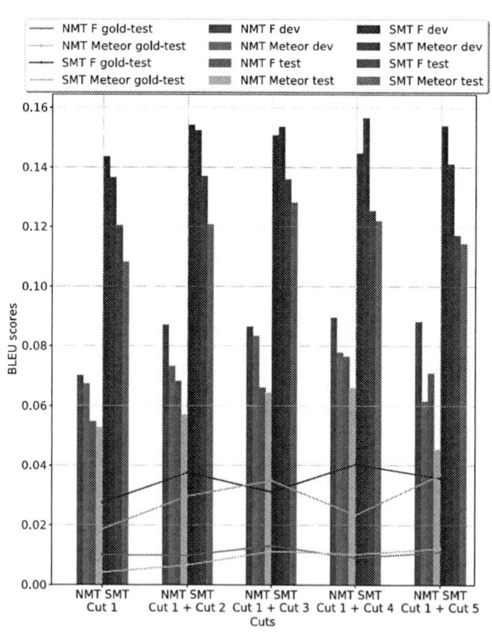

Figure 6: BLEU scores for the cut 1 plus the other cuts

What is the best quality measure? Following the idea that Google Translate API generates paraphrases or sentences with synonyms of some words of the original sentence, it would be expected that METEOR shows better results (due

on test set showed that the performance decreased when lower quality sets were incorporated (see cut 1 + cut 4 and cut 1 + cut 5 in Figures 6 and 7). In the case of the gold test set, results showed slight increases and decreases in performance, hindering the analysis. Similarly, TER results showed slight

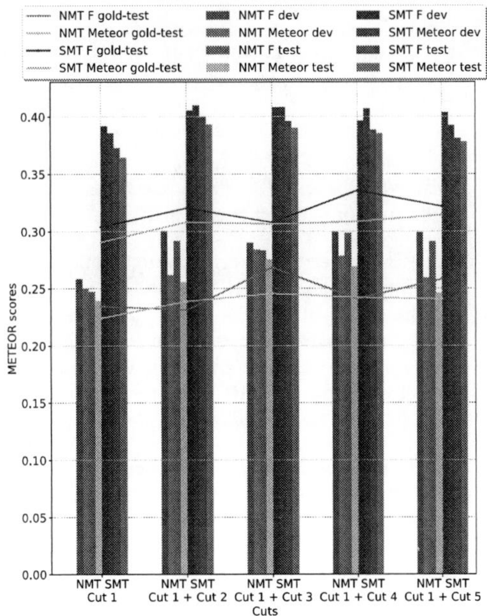

Figure 7: METEOR scores for the cut 1 plus the other cuts

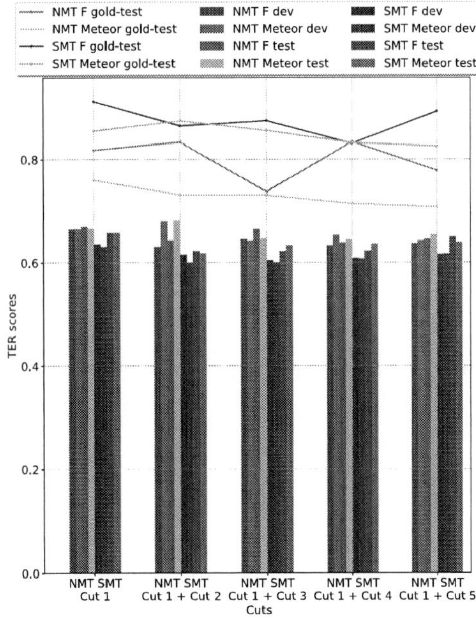

Figure 8: TER scores for the cut 1 plus the other cuts

to the fact that METEOR considers synonyms and stems). However, analysing the test set, it is possible to see that F produced stable and better results in BLEU and METEOR metrics (see Figure 6 and 7). In the case of TER, both F

and METEOR produced mixed results (Figure 8). Besides, in the gold test set, F also produced better results than METEOR, excepting in the TER metric (Figure 8).

How is each approach affected? As expected, SMT outperformed NMT on the three sets in most cases. In the case of TER, NMT outperformed SMT on the gold test set (Figure 5). In the case of development and test sets, the difference between results was small and decreased while more data was incorporated into the training set, regardless of their quality. Also, the tendency of TER values to vary was lower than for METEOR and BLEU. On the other hand, it is important to highlight the greater trend of NMT to increase when more data was incorporated.

Are the results comparable in curated datasets? In general, the results in the BP corpus (gold-test set) were quite worse than in the test and development sets for all metrics, excepting METEOR. Although the METEOR values were low, the difference between these values and the values obtained in the development and test sets was not as big (principally considering NMT) as the other metrics. Also, the values were close to the ones obtained with the NMT approach in the last cut (Figure 4).

There were two reasons that we hypothesize that could lead to these results. Firstly, the number of words in the gold test set that were not in the training vocabulary. Even though the BP AMR corpus and the original AMR corpus were focused on general domains, it is necessary to analyze the overlap between them. The other problem was related to alignment types. There were several translated sentences in the corpus that present alignments "1-n", "n-1", or "1-n and n-1" and the generation of their respective semantic representations presented some issues like the concatenation between two tokens (token "eu-eu" in Figure 2). This could generate more sparsity and decrease the performance of the methods.

6 Conclusions and Future Work

This paper presented an exploratory study that aimed to evaluate the usefulness of back-translation in NLG from semantic representations. The followed pipeline showed how to perform a simple back-translation process in an NLG context and this may be applied to any language. Results showed that quantity is important when Machine Translation systems are good enough. However, quality may be critical in the context of low-resource languages, when translations may be too poor.

It is worth noting that the selection of cuts to be included in the training set has to be performed carefully. In this study, we proposed to analyze the performance considering 5 cuts and the last cut did not contribute positively to the performance (due to the poor quality scores). However, a deep analysis of the use of cuts may be performed to better determine the number of cuts that allow for filtering out the worst instances in order to improve the performance of the models and provide a high-quality translated dataset.

On the other hand, there are several improvements to be made to achieve similar results in real (curated) datasets. It is necessary to analyze the alignments and out-of-vocabulary words. Thus, a research direction is to analyse how these issues affect the NLG task in non-English languages. Also, we plan to explore the text generation in a curated dataset as a domain adaptation problem.

Acknowledgments

The authors are grateful to CAPES and USP Research Office for supporting this work, and would like to thank NVIDIA for donating the GPU. This work is part of the OPINANDO project (more details can be found in `https://sites.google.com/icmc.usp.br/opinando/`), and has been partly supported by the European Commission in the framework of the H2020 Programme via contracts to UPF, with the numbers 779962-RIA, 700475-IA, 7000024-RIA, and 645012–RIA.

References

Rafael Anchiêta and Thiago Pardo. 2018. Towards AMR-BR: A SemBank for Brazilian Portuguese language. In *Proceedings of the Eleventh International Conference on Language Resources and Evaluation*, pages 974–979, Miyazaki, Japan. European Languages Resources Association.

Dzmitry Bahdanau, Kyunghyun Cho, and Yoshua Bengio. 2015. Neural machine translation by jointly learning to align and translate. In *Procceddings of the 3rd International Conference on Learning Representations*, San Diego, CA, USA.

Laura Banarescu, Claire Bonial, Shu Cai, Madalina Georgescu, Kira Griffitt, Ulf Hermjakob, Kevin Knight, Philipp Koehn, Martha Palmer, and Nathan Schneider. 2013. Abstract meaning representation for sembanking. In *Proceedings of the 7th Linguistic Annotation Workshop and Interoperability with Discourse*, pages 178–186, Sofia, Bulgaria. Association for Computational Linguistics.

Thiago Castro Ferreira, Iacer Calixto, Sander Wubben, and Emiel Krahmer. 2017. Linguistic realisation as machine translation: Comparing different mt models for amr-to-text generation. In *Proceedings of the 10th International Conference on Natural Language Generation*, pages 1–10, Santiago de Compostela, Spain. Association for Computational Linguistics.

Marco Damonte and Shay B. Cohen. 2018. Cross-lingual abstract meaning representation parsing. In *Proceedings of the 2018 Conference of the North American Chapter of the Association for Computational Linguistics: Human Language Technologies, Volume 1 (Long Papers)*, pages 1146–1155, New Orleans, Louisiana. Association for Computational Linguistics.

Magali Sanches Duran and Sandra Maria Aluísio. 2015. Automatic generation of a lexical resource to support semantic role labeling in Portuguese. In *Proceedings of the Fourth Joint Conference on Lexical and Computational Semantics*, pages 216–221, Denver, Colorado. Association for Computational Linguistics.

Chris Dyer, Victor Chahuneau, and Noah A. Smith. 2013. A simple, fast, and effective reparameterization of IBM model 2. In *Proceedings of the 2013 Conference of the North American Chapter of the Association for Computational Linguistics: Human Language Technologies*, pages 644–648, Atlanta, Georgia. Association for Computational Linguistics.

Sergey Edunov, Myle Ott, Michael Auli, and David Grangier. 2018. Understanding back-translation at scale. In *Proceedings of the 2018 Conference on Empirical Methods in Natural Language Processing*, pages 489–500, Brussels, Belgium. Association for Computational Linguistics.

Claire Gardent, Anastasia Shimorina, Shashi Narayan, and Laura Perez-Beltrachini. 2017. Creating training corpora for micro-planners. In *Proceedings of the 55th Annual Meeting of the Association for Computational Linguistics (Volume 1: Long Papers)*, pages 179–188, Vancouver, Canada. Association for Computational Linguistics.

Judith Gaspers, Penny Karanasou, and Rajen Chatterjee. 2018. Selecting machine-translated data for quick bootstrapping of a natural language understanding system. In *Proceedings of the 2018 Conference of the North American Chapter of the Association for Computational Linguistics: Human Language Technologies, Volume 3 (Industry Papers)*, pages 137–144, New Orleans - Louisiana. Association for Computational Linguistics.

Nathan Hartmann, Erick Fonseca, Christopher Shulby, Marcos Treviso, Jéssica Silva, and Sandra Aluísio. 2017. Portuguese word embeddings: Evaluating on word analogies and natural language tasks. In *Proceedings of the 11th Brazilian Symposium in Information and Human Language Technology*, pages 122–131, Uberlândia, Brazil. Sociedade Brasileira de Computação.

Roman Klinger and Philipp Cimiano. 2015. Instance selection improves cross-lingual model training for fine-grained sentiment analysis. In *Proceedings of the 19th Conference on Computational Natural Language Learning*, pages 153–163, Beijing, China. Association for Computational Linguistics.

Alon Lavie and Abhaya Agarwal. 2007. METEOR: An automatic metric for MT evaluation with high levels of correlation with human judgments. In *Proceedings of the 2nd Workshop on Statistical Machine Translation*, pages 228–231, Prague, Czech Republic. Association for Computational Linguistics.

Noelia Migueles-Abraira, Rodrigo Agerri, and Arantza Diaz de Ilarraza. 2018. Annotating abstract meaning representations for Spanish. In *Proceedings of the 11th International Conference on Language Resources and Evaluation*, pages 3074–3078, Miyazaki, Japan. European Languages Resources Association.

Simon Mille, Anja Belz, Bernd Bohnet, Yvette Graham, Emily Pitler, and Leo Wanner. 2018. The first multilingual surface realisation shared task (SR'18): Overview and evaluation results. In *Proceedings of the 1st Workshop on Multilingual Surface Realisation*, pages 1–12, Melbourne, Australia. Association for Computational Linguistics.

Teruhisa Misu, Etsuo Mizukami, Hideki Kashioka, Satoshi Nakamura, and Haizhou Li. 2012. A bootstrapping approach for SLU portability to a new language by inducting unannotated user queries. In *2012 IEEE International Conference on Acoustics, Speech and Signal Processing (ICASSP)*, pages 4961–4964. IEEE.

Fabricio Monsalve, Kervy Rivas Rojas, Marco Antonio Sobrevilla Cabezudo, and Arturo Oncevay. 2019. Assessing back-translation as a corpus generation strategy for non-English tasks: A study in reading comprehension and word sense disambiguation. In *Proceedings of the 13th Linguistic Annotation Workshop*, pages 81–89, Florence, Italy. Association for Computational Linguistics.

Jekaterina Novikova, Oliver Lemon, and Verena Rieser. 2016. Crowd-sourcing NLG data: Pictures elicit better data. In *Proceedings of the 9th International Natural Language Generation conference*, pages 265–273, Edinburgh, UK. Association for Computational Linguistics.

Martha Palmer, Daniel Gildea, and Paul Kingsbury. 2005. The proposition bank: An annotated corpus of semantic roles. *Computational Linguistics*, 31(1):71–106.

Kishore Papineni, Salim Roukos, Todd Ward, and Wei-Jing Zhu. 2002. Bleu: a method for automatic evaluation of machine translation. In *Proceedings of the 40th Annual Meeting of the Association for Computational Linguistics*, pages 311–318, Philadelphia, Pennsylvania, USA. Association for Computational Linguistics.

Shrimai Prabhumoye, Yulia Tsvetkov, Ruslan Salakhutdinov, and Alan W Black. 2018. Style transfer through back-translation. In *Proceedings of the 56th Annual Meeting of the Association for Computational Linguistics (Volume 1: Long Papers)*, pages 866–876, Melbourne, Australia. Association for Computational Linguistics.

Ehud Reiter and Robert Dale. 2000. *Building Natural Language Generation Systems*. Cambridge University Press, New York, NY, USA.

Rico Sennrich, Barry Haddow, and Alexandra Birch. 2016. Improving Neural Machine Translation models with monolingual data. In *Proceedings of the 54th Annual Meeting of the Association for Computational Linguistics (Volume 1: Long Papers)*, pages 86–96, Berlin, Germany. Association for Computational Linguistics.

Matthew Snover, Bonnie Dorr, Richard Schwartz, Linnea Micciulla, and John Makhoul. 2006. A study of translation edit rate with targeted human annotation. In *In Proceedings of Association for Machine Translation in the Americas*, pages 223–231. Association for Machine Translation in the Americas.

Marco Antonio Sobrevilla Cabezudo and Thiago Pardo. 2019. Towards a general abstract meaning representation corpus for Brazilian Portuguese. In *Proceedings of the 13th Linguistic Annotation Workshop*, pages 236–244, Florence, Italy. Association for Computational Linguistics.

Nianwen Xue, Ondřej Bojar, Jan Hajič, Martha Palmer, Zdeňka Urešová, and Xiuhong Zhang. 2014. Not an interlingua, but close: Comparison of English AMRs to Chinese and Czech. In *Proceedings of the 9th International Conference on Language Resources and Evaluation*, pages 1765–1772, Reykjavik, Iceland. European Languages Resources Association.

Author Index